PUBLIC RELATIONS AND THE PRESS

Medill School of Journalism
VISIONS *of the* AMERICAN PRESS

GENERAL EDITOR
David Abrahamson

Other titles in this series

HERBERT J. GANS
Deciding What's News: A Study of CBS Evening News, NBC Nightly
News, Newsweek, *and* Time

MAURINE H. BEASLEY
First Ladies and the Press: The Unfinished Partnership of the Media Age

PATRICIA BRADLEY
Women and the Press: The Struggle for Equality

DAVID A. COPELAND
The Idea of a Free Press: The Enlightenment and Its Unruly Legacy

MICHAEL SWEENEY
The Military and the Press: An Uneasy Truce

PATRICK S. WASHBURN
The African American Newspaper: Voice of Freedom

DAVID R. SPENCER
The Yellow Journalism: The Press and America's Emergence as World Power

TOM GOLDSTEIN
Journalism and Truth: Strange Bedfellows

PUBLIC RELATIONS AND
THE PRESS
THE TROUBLED EMBRACE

Karla K. Gower

Foreword by Kurt Andersen

MEDILL SCHOOL OF JOURNALISM

Northwestern University Press
Evanston, Illinois

Northwestern University Press
www.nupress.northwestern.edu

Copyright © 2007 by Karla K. Gower
Published 2007 by Northwestern University Press.
All rights reserved.

Printed in the United States of America

10 9 8 7 6 5 4 3 2 1

ISBN 978-0-8101-2434-9

Library of Congress Cataloging-in-Publication Data

Gower, Karla K.
    Public relations and the press : the troubled embrace / Karla K.
Gower ; foreword by Kurt Andersen.
        p. cm. — (Visions of the American press)
    Includes bibliographical references and index.
    ISBN-13: 978-0-8101-2434-9 (pbk. : alk. paper)
    ISBN-10: 0-8101-2434-3 (pbk. : alk. paper)
    1. Journalism and public relations—United States. 2. Public
relations—United States—History—20th century. 3. Journalism—
Objectivity—United States. 4. Mass media—Objectivity—United
States. I. Title. II. Series.
    HD59.6.U6G68 2007
    659.20973—dc22

                                        2007007892

    ∞ The paper used in this publication meets the minimum
requirements of the American National Standard for Information
Sciences—Permanence of Paper for Printed Library Materials,
ANSI Z39.48-1992.

In loving memory of my parents

CONTENTS

FOREWORD

Kurt Andersen

In New York a century ago, as Professor Karla Gower so ably tells us, a twenty-seven-year-old man named Ivy Lee established Parker and Lee, the first firm devoted exclusively to managing spin, and thereby became a founder of the new business of public relations. The term *public relations (PR)* hadn't been coined in 1904, but press agents were already familiar metropolitan figures—and automatically suspect, as they have remained. The muckraking New York reporter and photographer Jacob Riis, in an 1899 issue of the *Atlantic Monthly,* acidly referred to an employee of the corrupt local political machine as "Tammany's press agent."

Indeed, press agentry and ad hoc public relations—the shaping of newspaper and magazine coverage to benefit particular private interests—had been powerfully, increasingly in evidence for most of the nineteenth century. The mass media and mass merchandising were born in the 1830s and 1840s as cities boomed and high-speed printing presses made newspapers and magazines cheap and plentiful. And peddlers of every sort saw the burgeoning press as a prime new promotional venue. They could buy advertisements, but even better, they could wheedle and pressure writers and editors to promote their wares for free—clothes, furniture, gadgets, plays, books, ideas, politicians, whatever.

The embrace was troubling to some of those writers and editors from the get-go. "It is a pity," wrote one in the *New England Magazine* in 1835, "that some efficient method could not be adopted to do away with the present system of indiscriminate puffery. Little or no reliance can be placed on newspaper opinions about a new book; and we are sorry to add that contemporary periodicals . . . cannot be consulted with a better chance of finding out the truth. The editors of journals seem to conspire with . . . publishers of books to practice the grossest deceptions upon the reading community." Not coincidentally, the presidential election of 1840 was the first in which candidates were marketed in the modern sense: shrewd public relations spin—a campaign featuring miniature log cabins, raccoon mascots, and whiskey-jug trinkets—refashioned the rich Whig candidate William Henry Harrison as a rustic man of the people and helped win him the presidency. Newspapers at the time were unabashedly partisan, their news coverage extravagantly opinionated. The great journalist Horace Greeley, before he founded the *New York Tribune* in 1841, had been editor of an official Whig party organ. Moreover, the distinctions between the emerging forms of mass communication—between journalism and public relations—were blurry or nonexistent, and practitioners moved between the occupations freely.

Indeed, seventy years before Ivy Lee hung his public relations shingle, the first great PR visionary took up the trade—with the crucial insight that stirring up public attention could be the *basis* of a business. Phineas T. Barnum was a young newspaper publisher and editor—he'd founded a weekly in Connecticut at age nineteen—but at twenty-five, in 1834, he moved to New York City to become a new species of impresario: as a former newspaperman, he understood that getting the papers to write about his eclectic entertainments, flatteringly or not, would sell tickets. As long as his fabrications were interesting—such as the very elderly black woman he put on display, claiming she had been George Washington's nursemaid a century earlier—the public debate over their veracity became part of the show business. When Barnum was promoting the first American concert tour of the celebrated Swedish soprano Jenny Lind, he used the newspapers to generate such excitement that as her transatlantic ship arrived in New York, fully a tenth of the city's population thronged the docks to get a glimpse or anyway to join in the PR-induced hysteria.

The propagation of the romantic, archetypal vision of the wild and free American West was the great American public relations project of the nineteenth century. One man, Edward Z. C. Judson, a journalist turned impresario and New York contemporary of Barnum's, was its visionary mastermind. Under the pseudonym Ned Buntline, Judson produced magazines *(Western Literary Journal, Ned Buntline's Own, Ned)*, plays *(Scouts of the Prairie)*, and innumerable pulp novels that essentially invented the mythic popular conception of the Wild West—and did so in real time, from the 1840s through the 1880s, by recruiting and promoting real, emblematic figures such as the twenty-six-year-old hunter and army scout Buffalo Bill Cody to star in literary and theatrical versions of their exploits.

Some of those emblematic figures, such as the lawman Wyatt Earp, did extravagant and highly effective public relations work on behalf of their own careers. Bat Masterson, Earp's lifelong friend and fellow iconic gunslinger, was reputed to have shot and killed dozens of people; in fact, he may have killed no more than one man in a gunfight. After leaving law enforcement, he became a boxing promoter and then a celebrated newspaperman. At age fifty, he moved east and spent the last fourteen years of his life as a columnist, editor, and executive for the *New York Morning Telegraph*.

Meanwhile, the West was being settled once and for all, and corporate public relations was used to tidy up the collateral damage. In the course of a long, violent strike by workers at Rockefeller-owned coal mines in Colorado in 1914, the local militia killed several miners and their families, and a New York public relations counselor was engaged to deal with the bad press attending "the Ludlow massacre." He spun wildly, putting out the story that the deaths of women and children in Ludlow had been caused by an accidentally overturned stove—the kind of claim that prompted the poet Carl Sandburg to declare him "below the level of the hired gunman." The Rockefellers' PR man was Ivy Lee.

Not all journalists are honest, disinterested searchers for the truth, and not all public relations people are fabulists and liars. Some of my best friends work in PR. While I never expect them to tell me the whole truth about the people or products they represent, as far as I know they've never lied to me, either. And as schedulers and evangelists, they can be useful. But the basic tension is there: their jobs are to provide positive information about clients (and negative information about those clients' rivals and enemies), and if that requires dissembling, they dissemble. They are interested in the truth to the extent it reflects well (or not badly) on the people paying them.

They use journalists, but journalists use them, too. When I was editor in chief of *New York* magazine in the 1990s, I got a call one day from a big-time PR man who represented the defendant in an infamous multimillion-dollar lawsuit involving various well-known New Yorkers. He said he wanted to send over some information he thought I'd be interested in. That afternoon, I received a thick loose-leaf notebook filled with theretofore confidential documents, neatly tabbed and organized, that portrayed the plaintiff in a negative light. And one of my writers proceeded to report and write a story based partly on those documents. In the years since, I've occasionally run into the PR guy, who's now a publisher and philanthropist. Each time, I think about our slightly skevey professional history, and I wonder how many scores of such transactions he brokered over the years. I also sometimes run into the man he used me to besmirch and always feel a frisson of guilt. A troubled embrace indeed.

As ever, public relations people do wield real power over media coverage and, thus, the rise and fall of reputations. At the relatively inconsequential end of the spectrum are handlers of Hollywood stars who permit or withhold their clients' cooperation with the celebrity-hungry media. And then there are the PR people who are the gatekeepers to important figures of legitimate public interest—corporate leaders, powerful government bureaucrats, elected officials.

Of course, much or most public relations power is granted by reporters and editors who accede to their demands and interference—by letting PR people veto a particular journalist whom they deem insufficiently friendly, or agreeing not to broach certain subjects in interviews, or simply not pushing hard enough toward the truth. Publicists, like police, often exercise power over reporters simply because they can. And sometimes in this game of cat and mouse, journalists find it hard not to do the same. For instance, I'm surprised how often PR people, when they are negotiating access to their principals (as opposed to acting explicitly as spokespeople), make stupid or impolitic remarks, as if such behind-the-scenes conversations are inherently off the record; quoting them can be an irresistible bit of comeuppance.

A couple of years ago, after I wrote an article about the top executives of a large corporation, the chairman phoned me and left a hurt and angry voice mail: "What did I ever do to you," he asked, "to deserve *this*?" It was odd and pathetic, not the way the game is supposed to be played. I let one of his underlings know about the message, and within an hour, the company's PR chief was on the phone, her anxiety audible. She wanted to know if I was going to write about her boss's unfortunate voice mail. *No plan to do so,* I told her, maybe or maybe not suppressing a small, evil smile, *at least no time soon.*

I don't think any single PR person today has a dangerous amount of influence. But as this insightful volume by Professor Gower demonstrates, as a collective force, American public relations is staggeringly powerful. It's probably fair to say that most major stories in the press, in every publication, and on every TV news program were placed or impeded or significantly shaped by public relations professionals. When I was a magazine editor—of *Spy* as well as *New York*—I tried repeatedly to assign an epic piece of investigative journalism that would illustrate and deconstruct this tentacular, ubiquitous influence. My idea was to take one day's *New York Times* and try to detect the various PR fingerprints on every story in the paper. For whatever reason—the daunting scale of the project or reporters' fears of alienating in one fell swoop the entire public relations apparatus—I never managed to persuade anyone to do the piece.

PREFACE

I grew up in a household full of news. My parents read two daily newspapers plus a weekly. They watched the evening and nightly local and national newscasts, as well as one or two weekly news-magazine programs. My father was a professional photographer who also freelanced for the daily newspaper in a nearby city. Later, my mother became a reporter for the same paper. But my father was the creative one and unwittingly became involved in public relations. During World War II, he painted signs and billboards promoting the war effort at home.

I learned early the power of the press to move public opinion and how important perceptions of events can be. On one occasion, I went with my father outside our town to take a picture of a tree at the side of the road. The county was widening the road and intended to remove the tree. A local environmental group was protesting the removal, and my father wanted to get a picture of the tree to accompany my mother's story on the protest. Expecting to find a stately old oak tree, we were both a little disappointed to come upon a rather slender young tree. "Oh, this will never do," my father said. He walked slowly around the tree, sizing it up with his photographer's eye. Finally, he settled on a shot. He framed that young tree against a backdrop of the grand old oaks that lined the driveway of a farmhouse. When the picture appeared in the paper the next day, it was obvious that this now beautiful and bountiful tree was indeed worth saving. And saved it was—because people perceived it to be a tree worth saving.

Not surprisingly, given my background, I grew up to be a news junkie. I have a great deal of respect for journalists and believe they serve a vital role in a democracy. It is through the press that we learn about our world. Moreover, reporters are responsible for informing us so that we can make reasoned decisions about our governance. But instead of becoming a journalist myself, I opted first for a legal career and then went into public relations (PR), another profession that I believe plays a critical role in democracy. PR gives organizations a voice and the ability to participate in the democratic process. It also helps organizations respond to public opinion. Public relations and journalism work together in a symbiotic, albeit troubled, relationship.

Journalists, of course, have always been dependent on their sources. Without a source of information, the journalist has little to report. What the development of public relations brought to the table was, in effect, the professional source. PR practitioners arrange sources for journalists and serve as sources themselves by providing journalists with information. But PR practitioners are not neutral providers of sources or information; they are advocates for their clients and work to tell their clients' stories. Thus, journalists seek sources and information for news, and PR practitioners seek to influence the news by controlling access to those sources and information.

What is troubling today is the blurring and shifting of the roles. Sometimes, it is hard to tell the journalists from the public relations practitioners. Journalists are not asking the tough questions of politicians or corporate spokespersons. Interviewees are let off the hook. They evade questions; they change topics. Everyone stays on message and on point, no matter what is asked. There is nothing wrong with staying on message, but when taken to the extreme, the tactic can hinder rather than contribute to the public discourse. Another troubling feature today is the seeming lack of accountability for one's words and actions. That culture has permeated not just Washington and corporate boardrooms but also newsrooms and public relations agencies. Numerous instances of plagiarism and fabrication by journalists have surfaced in recent years, as have stories about PR practitioners being involved in distributing "fake news" releases and using fake sources.

A corporate mentality is influencing newsrooms and agencies through cuts in resources and an increased push to contribute to the bottom line. Corporate media owners have their network news shows busy promoting their entertainment programs. But time spent on promotional pieces means less time for real news, news that is actually beneficial to viewers.

And as the mainstream news media lose credibility, young people are either tuning out or deciding they have no reason to tune in, becoming more interested in news as satire (as presented by *The Daily Show* with Jon Stewart) or in interacting with each other. Information has become increasingly democratized, to the point that even traditional media outlets such as Cable News Network (CNN) are turning to consumer-generated news in an attempt to remain relevant to viewers. Part of the reason the media seem less relevant is that our political discourse has been reduced to talk of "values" rather than meaningful debate about policy issues. In fact, there is precious little meaningful debate in society today. How did we ever get to this point?

Attempting to answer that question requires an examination of journalism and public relations, two professions about which I care deeply. Thus, I was honored when David Abrahamson approached me about writing this book for the Medill School of Journalism series entitled Visions of the American Press. I owe a debt of gratitude to him for the opportunity.

This book explores the relationship of journalists and public relations practitioners from World War II until 2006. It focuses on how people in the public and private sectors have interacted with journalists over the course of sixty years and the developments that led us to the divisive and hyperpromotional state in which we live. Much has been written on the relationship between the media and the various presidents in this period, and I rely heavily on that scholarship here. Less has been done on the media's relationship with public relations practitioners from corporations and nonprofit groups. Thus, I have fleshed out the information from secondary sources by examining such primary sources as trade publication articles, magazine articles, and speeches.

The book is not meant to be a history of the latter half of the twentieth century and opening years of the twenty-first. Readers will not find every event or situation involving journalists and PR practitioners detailed here. But they will find coverage of events that illustrate trends and shifts in practices and concepts. My central thesis is that the interaction between public relations practitioners and journalists has resulted in a shift in power, which raises questions about both the purposes of media in a democratic society and the future of journalism. But it is not really the public relations industry that is the cause for concern, although it tends to take the blame. It is the development of a marketing mind-set that has developed into a potent force in government, corporations, and nonprofit groups at the same time that journalism has been weakened by budget cuts and increased competition. Television has reduced our political discourse to sound bites and slogans, and market research on segmentation has made us all markets of one. We are told what politicians and corporate and nonprofit spokespersons think we want to hear, rather than what we need to hear. And they no longer need the news media to communicate with us. They reach us directly through the Internet or direct mail, further weakening the news media's ability to serve as a watchdog of our institutions and provide information for meaningful debate. I hope this book, while not providing answers to the question of where we go from this point forward, at least provides an answer as to how we got here.

In addition to thanking David Abrahamson and Northwestern University Press, I want to thank my life partner, who has been by my side from the moment I began this volume—ready to listen, discuss ideas, make suggestions, and help in any way I needed him to. He has not simply endured the whole process of writing this book, he has also shared my passion for it, and I am deeply grateful to him for that.

KARLA K. GOWER

ONE

INTRODUCTION

We are living in, as one author described it, highly "promotional times."[1] Governments, corporations, nonprofit organizations, and special interest groups all seek to get their messages across to the public via the media. Spin doctors and the discussion of the use of spin are everywhere. Journalism and public relations have become so blurred it is hard to determine where the one stops and the other starts. Understanding how we arrived at this point of hyper-spin is important for understanding the current state of journalism and the future of democracy.

Sources today bypass traditional news outlets in favor of entertainment outlets and the Internet; for example, political candidates announce their intentions to run for office on late-night talk shows instead of calling news conferences. More insidious are the "secret" efforts to control the information we receive, such as the practice of paying columnists to tout a particular stance on a policy issue or the government's distribution of video news releases (VNRs) as objective news stories. Such techniques raise serious questions about the quality of the information we receive, for we cannot develop an informed opinion about an issue if the information we receive is based on deception. Although vigilant news outlets disclosed the deception in these cases, the damage had been done: many people did not see or pay attention to the subsequent stories. Even more troubling is the sense that deceiving the public and being caught at it is not a big deal. Everyone quickly moves

1

on to something else, and there is no accountability for those involved. While public relations practitioners and journalists are not necessarily responsible for the deception, the role they play in enabling such deception needs to be explored because it directly impacts the state of our democracy.

Journalists have always depended on sources. Without a source of information, the journalist has little to report. What the development of public relations brought to the table was, in effect, the professional source. PR practitioners arranged sources for journalists and they themselves served as sources by providing journalists with information. But PR practitioners are not neutral providers of sources or information; they are advocates. Thus, journalists seek sources and information for news, and PR practitioners seek to use the media to get their clients' messages to their various publics.

This dependent relationship has always been an uneasy one. Although journalists and public relations practitioners need each other, the idea that news can be managed threatens the journalistic ideals of objectivity, truth, and balance. But the symbiotic relationship worked so long as the traditional hierarchy between media and source existed—that is, so long as journalists maintained editorial autonomy and public relations remained relatively underdeveloped and underresourced. Today, the practice of public relations has expanded and become more sophisticated at the same time that editorial resources have declined. The news media in the United States are increasingly subject to competition from new media, concentrated ownership, and deregulation. Journalists are being asked to do more with less resources in a 24-7 world, forcing them to rely more and more on information from public relations practitioners. Although they retain their editorial autonomy over what does get covered and how it is covered, they are being forced increasingly into reactive, passive positions rather than pursuing their own investigations. At the same time, competition for audience share has grown with the expansion of media sources, such as cable, satellite, and the World Wide Web. Media outlets have turned to advertorials, celebrity news, crime reporting, and human interest stories to entice people to tune in, rather than reporting news that affects the community's governance.

The result has been a shift in power that affects the journalist–news source relationship and the provision of information. It also raises questions about the purpose of the mass media in a mediated society. If democracy is based on the premise that individuals can make rational decisions when given the information to do so and if, in a complex society, that information must come through the mass media, then what is the media's role? What obligation do the mass media have to provide the people in a democracy with the information they need? The U.S. media have long prided themselves on being free—on being independent of government control. But what is the nature of media independence in today's society? Can journalists within a corporately owned news outlet be truly independent? And if the concept of objectivity requires journalists to rely on official sources, are journalists even independent of the government? Some argue that the power elites, such as government and corporations, have extended their control and influence over the media and, by extension, over society. Others suggest that the development of public relations has allowed special interest groups the opportunity to participate, through their access to the media, in the public discourse in ways that were closed to them previously. Regardless of which view is correct, the journalistic ideals of objectivity and balance have been threatened.

The purpose of this work is to examine how the shift in power came to be. Although others have decried the impact of commercialization on American culture and the way in which corporate ownership of media outlets has caused the blurring of news and entertainment, this book will focus on the relationship between public relations and the press. Public relations can, of course, be considered part of the whole commercialization package, but while advertising and marketing sell products and services, public relations promotes images and concepts. All deal with persuasion, but public relations involves issues that affect democracy itself.

A democracy works when individuals have access to quality information, that is, when they have access to various arguments and facts from which to form opinions and make decisions. In a mediated society, that information comes from the mass media. The watchdog role and the value of objectivity posit that journalists serve, in a sense, as stand-ins for, or representatives of, the people. Journalists are to seek out various sources of information and provide the people with an objective and balanced view of what is going on so that the people can formulate opinions from that information. But as the power has shifted from the journalist to the source, the media have become not a stand-in for the people but a stand-in for the source. Thus, the source effectively controls the information the people receive. If the people do not have access to quality information on which to make valid decisions or if they do not actively engage with such information, then they are not exercising sovereignty—they are merely doing what they are told to do. The democracy is a facade and illusory.

This book examines the development of public relations in the business, government, and activist group sectors after World War II and how that development affected the media. It also examines the factors affecting journalists' ability to interact with their sources and provide newsworthy information. The focus is on the interaction between journalists and public relations practitioners on three different levels: the physical (the process of gathering and collecting the news), the social (the social relationships between journalists and PR practitioners), and the cultural (the professional or societal beliefs, values, and expectations held by journalists and PR practitioners). I argue that passive journalistic practices brought on by economic and competitive pressures have contributed, in part, to the shift in power and have given public relations practitioners a greater ability to manage the news. The book does not—and is not meant to—suggest that the growing power of PR is necessarily a dangerous or bad thing. PR practitioners provide information and story ideas to journalists and, by extension, the public to which they would not otherwise have access. The real problem with the power shift is that the news media are losing credibility, and that is dangerous for everyone—journalists, PR practitioners, and the public. It should be noted, however, that the book investigates just one aspect of public relations—media relations, or the use by PR practitioners of the mass media to get their clients' messages to their publics. It should also be noted that the examination is restricted to the federal government, especially the presidency, because presidents are inherently newsworthy and, for obvious reasons, vital to a democracy. World War II is the starting point because public relations as a profession really developed in the aftermath of the war.

Most scholars agree that modern public relations arose at the end of the nineteenth century in response to social and cultural changes such as industrialization, urbanization, growing literacy rates, and the rise of newspapers as a mass medium. PR scholars

Melvin Sharpe and Betty Pritchard argued that public relations emerged as a profession in response to the empowerment of public opinion as a result of three converging factors: democracy, social interdependence, and instantaneous communication abilities.[2] Thus, it is no surprise that a need for public relations arose as newspapers became more professional and their reach broadened. Journalists came to see themselves and their product as supporting the public good. They were the watchdogs of government, the defenders of democracy, and the champions of the people. The traits of objectivity—"fairness, detachment, nonpartisanship, and balance"—were in place and were held up as the ideal.[3] And the techniques of objective reporting were established: relying on official sources, giving both sides of an issue, and providing some context for the event being covered.[4]

The combination of the watchdog role and objectivity led to an increase in what was called publicity but was essentially reporting on local events. Publicity expanded the definition of news, encroaching on what had previously been considered private information: what had once been seen as private (how a business was run, for instance) was now deemed public. And the evils of corporate monopolies became a favorite target of publicity. Because of this change in public sentiment toward corporate expansion, fueled by a burgeoning newspaper industry that blurred the traditional public-private boundary, corporate public relations became a necessity. The magazine *Century* claimed in 1903 that "modern publicity is, indeed, playing so large a part in the psychology of our day that its effects are believed by thoughtful minds to be deep and pervasive."[5] Companies slowly came to the realization that silence in the face of attack was an erroneous policy—and that they were, in fact, public institutions, whether they liked it or not. Standard Oil released a public statement for the first time in 1904, and

John D. Rockefeller hired publicist Ivy Lee in 1914 to help him with his public image. Public opinion was beginning to be a force to be reckoned with at that time. In a 1908 article titled "The Passing of Corporate Secrecy," the magazine *World's Work* noted that "there is an inevitable prying quality in public opinion, which has no doubt been made very acute by the prying quality of our newspapers for a generation—an illegitimate curiosity that goes beyond the public's rights. But whether this curiosity be legitimate or not, it is wise to heed it. It is necessary in fact."[6]

Corporations and governments did come to heed public opinion, but the degree to which they did so varied throughout the first half of the twentieth century. It was not until after World War II that the three factors Sharpe and Pritchard identified as necessary for the empowerment of public opinion really came together and forced organizations and governments to consistently consider public opinion in their decision making.

Therefore, this book begins with an examination of the rise of the professional source after World War II. The field of public relations experienced unprecedented growth in that period. Part of the expansion was attributable to the returning men and women who had served as government public information officers during the war and now sought to use their newly acquired skills in the private sector. The other part was attributable to the booming economy, which opened up new consumer markets for businesses. Public relations practitioners who had entered the field before the war complained that the influx of new practitioners would bring down the reputation of the field. Thus, they called for a greater emphasis on professionalism and ethical standards.

Practitioners themselves were not the only ones critical of the expanding profession. Social critics lamented the growing commercialization of the American culture. Vance Packard in *The*

Hidden Persuaders and Irwin Ross in *The Image Merchants* attempted to expose what they perceived as the insidiousness of public relations. Unlike advertisers, PR practitioners operated behind the scenes to "sell" images, not products, and shape beliefs. At the same time, television was beginning to impact politics and journalism, as people working in those fields experimented with the new medium. Some journalists also came to question whether their devotion to objectivity had provided Senator Joseph McCarthy with a bully pulpit. Chapter 2, then, discusses the development of public relations following World War II, especially in terms of its growth and professionalism. It also considers how the media reacted to the expansion of public relations and examines the rise of television and its impact on politics.

Chapter 3 examines the 1960s, a decade of great social unrest. Activists in the civil rights movement at first found it difficult to achieve meaningful social change. But soon, they realized they could harness the power of the press to achieve their goals of social change by organizing planned events. Those events, such as lunch counter sit-ins and the march on Selma, are etched into the American collective consciousness thanks to the television coverage they received. The media did not always take the activists and their demands seriously, but they did cover them, and people did take notice. Much as television recorded the events of the civil rights movement, it also recorded presidential debates and battles in Vietnam. Journalists and politicians were learning about the power of television and the visual. Meanwhile, corporations, fearing change they were not controlling, responded to the civil rights movement by developing the process of issues management, a means of monitoring the environment for emerging issues and determining appropriate ways of dealing with those issues in advance.

The civil rights movement of the 1960s led to the consumer movement of the 1970s, which is examined in chapter 4. As the economy took a downturn, people laid the blame on businesses and anticorporate sentiment grew. Corporations were seen as arrogant, uncaring, and "soulless" entities. In response, corporations turned to advocacy ads to tell their side of the story. Advocacy ads put a "face" on corporations by setting out corporate positions on important issues of the day. Businesses also sought to improve the way their executives interacted with journalists. Media-training consultants sprang up to meet the corporate demand, offering guidance to company officials on what to wear, how to look, how to speak in sound bites—how to, in other words, manage an interview.

Chapter 5 moves on to President Richard Nixon. Presidents and the media have always had an adversarial relationship, but Nixon took that antagonism to a new high. He tried to strong-arm the press through intimidation. In return, the media began investigating the government more actively, especially in light of the Vietnam War and the Watergate political scandal. This chapter looks at the media's investigative reporting and its effect on politics in the 1970s. It also examines the impact of television on politics and how the government began to take a more active role in managing the news.

The fallout from the Nixon years is explored in chapter 6. Despite investigative reporting by the media in the previous decade, the public's confidence in the press declined in the 1980s. Believing the public blamed them for President Jimmy Carter's demise, the media softened their approach to the presidency. Corporations, also the target of the media's investigative reporting in the 1970s, returned fire with public relations campaigns that refuted the media coverage. At the same time, the media experienced corporate buyouts and shrinking newsroom resources. The result was an increasingly malleable press that was susceptible to the Reagan administration's efforts to control the message. President Ronald Reagan's advisers were well versed in the media's routines and values. They actively sought to provide members of the press with what they wanted: great visuals. They also tried to keep Reagan away from the media whenever necessary. Thus, they used staged events to make the president appear accessible while simultaneously shielding him from journalists.

While chapter 6 examines relations between the presidency and the press, chapter 7 moves into the corporate realm. The reaction of corporations to the anticorporate sentiment of the preceding decade led this sector to work more vigorously in the 1980s to control the information flow through the media and hence the message. PR practitioners emphasized strategic planning and the integration of advertising, public relations, and marketing. Meanwhile, activist groups changed their tactics and became legitimate sources of news. Unions, which had seen declining public support since the 1960s, were the first of the activist groups to recognize that a change in tactics could be beneficial. The initial step was the hiring of PR practitioners. These practitioners used traditional public relations strategies and tactics for dealing with the media. They developed relationships with media contacts, served as reliable and professional sources for the media, and fed the media story lines.

Chapter 8 brings the discussion to the present. By the end of the twentieth century, the power shift from journalist to source was virtually complete. And today, it is difficult to know where public relations stops and journalism begins. For example, corporations, activist groups, and the government/politicians still send out news releases to the media, but those releases are posted on their own Web sites at the same time. The public can access information directly from those private sites, unfiltered. Media outlets have assisted in the blurring of the lines by running video news releases produced by the government without indicating the source. In effect, the government has become both source and journalist. And some columnists have admitted they have been paid by the government to advocate a particular point of view. This chapter explores the blurring of news and persuasion and the rise of the Internet and other new technologies from the 1990s to the present.

TWO

THE RISE OF THE
PROFESSIONAL SOURCE

Public relations, in a formal sense, developed at the end of the nineteenth century as a result of a combination of factors.[7] Industrialization and mechanization had created huge corporations. There was a sense that the economic doctrine of laissez-faire, which depended on market forces to regulate business, was no longer viable. As a result, reformers called for governmental regulation of industries. The reformers were successful in part because journalism had become more professional. Objectivity became a journalistic standard, and journalists sought to shine the light of publicity on corporate behavior. Meanwhile, literacy rates improved, which meant it was now possible to reach the masses.

Confronted with negative public opinion and the possibility of governmental regulation, corporations turned to "press agents" to get their stories out.[8] Press agents were generally former journalists who used their knowledge of the media to get factual information about their clients or employers into newspapers and magazines. Ivy Lee is the best known of the press agents. A former journalist, he opened a press agency, Parker and Lee, in 1904 in New York City and issued a declaration of principles shortly thereafter. The declaration promised the media that, as a press agent, he would deal fairly with them and provide them with accurate, truthful information about his clients.[9] Although he did not always live up to the strict letter of his promises, Lee did garner favorable media attention for such clients as the Rocke-fellers. The focus for Lee and for most of the others who opened press agencies at the time was on getting factual information about corporations to the public through newspapers in an effort to legitimize the actions of those businesses. The belief was that if only people understood why the railroads had to raise their fares, for example, they would not object to the increase.

While the early press agentry work involved getting out factual information, World War I and the Committee on Public Information (CPI), also known as the Creel Committee after its chair-man, George Creel, revealed how images and symbols could be used effectively to influence the public. The CPI's purpose was to engender public support for U.S. involvement in the war. Al-though the CPI started out distributing factual information, it soon moved into the realm of propaganda, making heavy use of fear and emotional appeals. Germans were demonized as the personifica-tion of evil in movies, pamphlets, and illustrations. The result was an anti-German hysteria that permeated the country. The power of communication to create such an atmosphere was not lost on many who worked for the committee, several of whom became public relations practitioners. Edward Bernays, for example, who coined the term *public relations counsel,* took away from his experi-ences the idea that consent could be engineered and used his skills to promote products in the 1920s. The economy was booming, and corporations no longer needed the legitimizing tactics of the earlier era.[10]

But the good times in the decade after the war did not last. When the Great Depression hit, people blamed big business and turned to the federal government for a solution to their economic woes. President Franklin D. Roosevelt successfully sold his New Deal measures to the American people as the answer. And Roosevelt's policies did appear to help. But as the economy turned around in the 1930s, the president gave no sign that he intended to dismantle the social protections he had instituted. In fact, business-people became concerned that the government was increasingly controlling the economy, rather than returning to the pre-Depression system of market controls. As a consequence, business leaders began looking more frequently to public relations strategies to promote the idea of free enterprise and "restore the public's faith in business."[11] The idea was that if the public again believed in the marketplace and its ability to regulate the economy, Roosevelt would be pressured to remove the regulatory controls.

World War II, of course, brought an abrupt end to any such campaign. At first, businesses continued to advertise their products and boast about their profits, but the American people, who had rallied behind the war effort, were turned off by such self-interested pronouncements. Businesses learned quickly that to not promote the war was to suffer the public's approbation.

But the end of the war meant returning soldiers, and business leaders were concerned about how to accommodate them.[12] Public relations practitioners were particularly concerned about the potential influx of soldiers into their industry.[13] The Office of War Information had taken a decentralized approach to communications during the war. Therefore, each military sector had its own communications division to deal with reporters and to keep their troops informed of military matters. Reportedly, as many as seventy-five thousand men and women were trained as public information officers or communication specialists during the war.[14] Public relations practitioners feared that many of them would want to continue in communications on their return to the private sector.[15] A market for PR practitioners certainly existed. A 1946 survey of companies found an increased interest in public relations that year. Nine out of ten companies surveyed reported that they had augmented their expenditures for PR activities.[16]

Several factors accounted for the greater emphasis on public relations. People had a pent-up desire to make those purchases they had put off during the war, and they had the money to buy things.[17] In addition, technological advancements had resulted in new products (such as electric refrigerators and televisions) that were ready to come to market.[18] Thus, the business sector was excited about the possibility of economic growth, although business leaders were also aware that consumers might be cautious about spending because the Depression was still fresh in people's minds. Yet there was also reason for pessimism. Of some concern to business, for instance, was the degree to which President Harry Truman might keep and even extend Roosevelt's New Deal provisions, especially given the growing successes of communism and socialism abroad.[19] If those ideologies caught on in the United States—and the strength of organized labor after the war suggested that they might—the capitalist system would be destroyed.[20] In fact, some considered labor to be business's number one problem.[21] Corporations then sought, with a renewed vigor, to promote free enterprise and sell the American way of life to the public.[22] It was only by making Americans see the advantage of the capitalist system that businesses could prevent further regulations on the economy. For that selling job, they needed public relations practitioners and the press.

Although business leaders knew what they wanted to do, they were not always astute at using public relations or the media to achieve their goals. They failed to realize that they needed to tell the good and the bad about themselves to the public through the press and to do it in a timely fashion. As PR practitioner James Irwin put it in 1948, "For years industrialists have let bureaucrats and labor unions outsmart them when it comes to public rela-tions."[23] Bureaucrats and labor unions communicated often with the press, telling their side of a given story. But industries were slow to respond with statements of their own, leaving reporters to print the news as they had it. Business executives compounded the problem by neglecting to take PR practitioners into their confi-dence or provide them with the authority to discuss a matter with the press. The result was often a negative story or one that failed to include the company perspective.[24]

News coverage that appeared to be antibusiness at worst and one-sided at best was not just the fault of business leaders: public relations practitioners and reporters shared some of the blame. Thus, one practitioner acknowledged that the field itself was at fault for giving in to clients or employers who saw PR simply as "free" publicity and sending out releases that contained no real news.[25] But in covering business stories, the press also had a re-sponsibility to send reporters who knew something about business and who were not openly antibusiness themselves.[26] Furthermore, labor unions and politicians who were critical of big business got onto the front pages of the newspapers, whereas corporate re-sponses and general economic news were presented on the finan-cial pages, which few but the elite read. The result, in the eyes of one PR practitioner, was that the "press, inadvertently, has given those who attack the capitalistic system and industry access to the public mind that is largely denied proponents of the system."[27] Still others criticized the press for its lack of professionalism. Al-though editors were quick to malign public relations practitioners, it was clear they needed their help because newsrooms were too short-staffed to gather all the news that was wanted.[28] And yet, one PR practitioner confessed that "the inaccuracies, the short-comings of reporting today by staff men, make me raise a question on the value of granting an interview, unless a crisis requires it."[29] She called for her fellow practitioners to help editors see "the need for imagination, accuracy in reporting, timeliness, and fairness to story sources."[30]

Professionalism was an important issue to PR practitioners in the immediate postwar period. A 1944 survey of 123 practitioners revealed that 60 percent had been in public relations for five or more years and that more than half were college graduates, despite the fact there were no degrees and only a few university courses in public relations as of the survey year. None of the respondents had gone directly into PR from college. Most had worked in two or more occupations before settling in the field, most commonly in journalism or some other form of writing career.[31] Given their relatively high education levels for the time, it was not surprising that some practitioners feared the growing demand for their services might encourage people with no experience or even unethical individuals to call themselves PR practitioners and thus bring down the field. They were also concerned that the returning soldiers who had been involved in communication during the war would attempt simply to transfer their military PR expertise into the private sector without realizing the two arenas were quite different.[32] These perceived threats were particularly troubling because they were coming at a time when those in the PR field were trying to make the practice more professional, with some level of standardization.[33]

One step toward professionalization was the creation of the Public Relations Society of America (PRSA) in 1947 through the amalgamation of two previous organizations. The goal was to establish a national association and elevate the status of the field.[34] Courses in public relations also appeared. As of 1946, thirty colleges and universities were offering forty-seven PR courses.[35] One year later, the first school of public relations was started, at Boston University; in 1948, more than one hundred colleges and universities offered courses in public relations.[36] The hope was that such courses would give PR some standardization, as reporting courses had done for journalism.

The first school of journalism was established in 1908 at the University of Missouri. Developing a journalism curriculum was part of a movement among editors to professionalize the field and propagate journalistic values and conventions, including objectivity.[37] The concept of objectivity has changed over the years, but at the end of World War II, it meant "straight reporting."[38] Journalists were expected to report what sources said and what witnesses saw, while ignoring their own sense of events. With the focus on an objective reality, they also tended not to report on things that did not occur in public because that would require them to interpret what they saw or heard.[39] As Arthur Hays Sulzberger, publisher of the *New York Times,* told a group of New York City teachers in 1945, "Our chief responsibility lies in reporting accurately that which happens. Whichever way the cat may jump, we should record it, and we should not allow our excitement about the direction which it takes, or plans to take, to interfere with our primary mission."[40] Opinions, judgments, and criticism from the editorial staff were strictly confined to the editorial page in the form of editorials and columns and kept apart from the news.[41] Although the 1947 report on press freedom, entitled "A Free and Responsible Press," criticized the notion of straight reporting, it was the junior senator from Wisconsin, Joseph McCarthy, who really revealed its shortcomings.[42]

In February 1950, McCarthy appeared before a group of Republican women in Wheeling, West Virgina, and held up a sheet of paper that he said contained the names of 205 known

Communists in government. In doing so, he was capitalizing on the public's existing fear of communism and his own understanding of the press's practices.[43] He knew the topic—Communists in government—would garner media attention, but he also knew news cycles and how to get the most out of that attention. At the time, the three wire services, the Associated Press (AP), the United Press International (UPI), and the International News Service, were engaged in stiff competition. McCarthy realized that their reporters were under pressure to find new leads every few hours in order to meet the demands of the morning and afternoon newspapers. Thus, knowing that the afternoon papers went to press about noon, McCarthy would hold a morning press conference to announce an afternoon press conference, thereby generating two sets of headlines.[44] Similarly, if an official tried to deny his allegations, McCarthy would provide a quote that would become the new lead for the next papers, effectively burying the official's denials. As political reporter Edwin Bayley put it, "A new lead, for most papers, took precedence over yesterday's real news," and McCarthy seemed to have his timing down so that he knew when reporters would have no choice but to print what he said.[45] Rebuttals and denials rarely managed to catch up with McCarthy.[46]

Headline writers also helped Senator McCarthy by exaggerating and sensationalizing his charges. Of course, the more outrageous his claims were, the more outrageous the headlines became. And the accompanying stories often lacked context or background, leaving the reader with false impressions. Editorials should have been the place to remedy those misimpressions, but some editors hesitated to criticize McCarthy. Bayley suggested it was because they could not believe someone would actually make up such allegations, but with communism a real fear in the country, it may have been that some were hesitant to go against public sentiment.[47]

Some newspapers, most notably the *New York Times,* did investigate McCarthy's allegations, but it was not always easy to do. McCarthy himself stonewalled reporters by not giving them documented evidence to prove his accusations; the original list of names he said he had, for example, was never produced. He also attempted to intimidate the press by labeling newspapers that were critical of him, such as the *New York Times, Washington Post,* and *St. Louis Post-Dispatch,* as left-wing organs, openly attacking them in his speeches. He apparently once said that "if you can show a paper as unfriendly and having a reason for being antagonistic, you take the sting out of what it says about you," a strategy still used by politicians today.[48]

McCarthy did not rely entirely on the print media; he also used radio and later television to get out his message. At the beginning of the 1950s, radio was the dominant form of broadcasting, with 94 percent of American families having at least one radio set in the home.[49] Each week, McCarthy would send out phonograph records to radio stations in his home state of Wisconsin. The records involved a staged interview with McCarthy in which the interviewer would pretend to be a reporter. Such recordings were used regularly by radio stations and allowed McCarthy to take his message directly to the people without the risk of having reporters question him or probe his allegations. Therefore, he could come across as legitimate.[50]

Many of McCarthy's accusations were unsubstantiated, but their effect was devastating to those he named. Richard L. Strout was one of the first journalists to write about how straight reporting, or objectivity, was assisting McCarthy. He wrote in the *Christian Science Monitor* on May 27, 1950, that objectivity was allowing elected officials to use the press for their own ends.[51] Murray Marder of the *Washington Post,* in reflecting on the times, said reporters were "caught in an illusory concept of objectivity, a narrow definition of journalism—don't intrude on the story—that served as a vehicle for McCarthy's multiplying accusations."[52] The effect of the reporters' insistence on objectivity as straight reporting was that McCarthy's subjectivity became the reality. News stories on him did not contain interpretation, context, or quotes from anyone else, leaving his allegations to stand on their own, unchallenged.

McCarthy produced a debate in journalism circles over objectivity versus interpretation.[53] At an Associated Press Managing Editors Association meeting in 1953, the members discussed what to do about McCarthy and his allegations. Those in favor of maintaining the traditional objectivity argued that they had to report what he said because he was a senator, an authoritative source of news. Those on the other side, who were in favor of moving toward a more interpretative reporting style, argued that if they reported only what McCarthy said, the American people would come to trust no one. Edwin Bayley suggested that editors who were fundamentalists on objectivity tended to support McCarthy and editors who called for interpretation tended to be critical of him. Eventually, McCarthy's exploitation of the straight reporting convention did result in a move toward interpretative reporting, a move Bayley said was accelerated because television became the principal source of spot news. Newspapers shifted to more interpretative reporting in an effort to remain competitive.[54] By 1954, the shift was complete, but by then, McCarthy had moved into television.[55]

In February 1950 when he made his Wheeling speech, 98 television stations were operating and 3.7 million sets were in existence. By the end of that year, there were 106 television stations in 65 cities and 10 million sets. And just four years later, there were

35 million television sets and 413 stations operating in 273 cities.[56] By controlling the coverage at first, McCarthy moved easily into the television realm.

Chairing public hearings into allegations of subversion at the Voice of America in February 1953, McCarthy first heard witnesses in closed sessions. Then he arranged for those witnesses he wanted the public to see to give testimony again in open sessions during the two hours a day the hearings were televised. If a witness tried to deny being a Communist or having ties to communism, McCarthy would look away and talk with his aide, giving the impression he did not believe the witness. It was, as Bayley noted, show business; it was McCarthy as television director and producer.[57]

But McCarthy's ever-escalating accusations began to catch up with him as he targeted more-powerful opponents.[58] In November 1953, he had demanded free airtime to respond to a press conference held by former president Truman, defending himself and one of his aides against attacks from the Eisenhower administration. All three networks—ABC, CBS, and NBC—granted the request, giving McCarthy thirty minutes. But then, the senator started attacking Republicans. Eisenhower, who had not spoken publicly on the McCarthy issue, could remain silent no longer. He decided to hold a press conference in which he intended to denounce McCarthy. But when McCarthy appeared conciliatory in the time leading up to the conference, Eisenhower backed down and opted not to mention his name. Two hours later, however, McCarthy called his own press conference and read a prepared statement. The two conferences came close enough together that they were aired together on the news, as McCarthy knew they would be. But the next time he asked for time, which was to respond to a speech by presidential candidate Adlai Stevenson on

March 7, the networks refused him access to the airwaves. Public sentiment had begun to turn against him.[59]

The 1954 hearings into communism in the army gave the American people a chance to see McCarthy in action, as did Edward R. Murrow's broadcast on the senator.[60] In the army-McCarthy hearings, viewers saw the senator browbeating generals and by and large being rude and disrespectful. Murrow, who had been a well-known radio personality, had successfully made the transition to television with his *See It Now* public affairs show. In March 1954, he aired a segment on McCarthy. Murrow's technique was to splice footage of the senator such that his contradictions and lack of evidence became clear.[61] Thus, the same medium McCarthy exploited to gain fame also led to his downfall.

McCarthy was ultimately unsuccessful in his bid to use television for his own ends, but he was not the only politician to recognize the medium's potential. Dwight Eisenhower, who came to power in 1952, was the first president to consciously use television to promote his candidacy and later his presidency.[62] In fact, he told his advisers that they needed to sell the presidency as if it were a product.[63]

Eisenhower's understanding of promotion came from his younger brother, Milton, who had served as director of public information for the Department of Agriculture during the Depression. In that role, Milton supervised one of the largest press services in the federal government and was one of the first to use national radio broadcasts to issue agency statements. He also quickly learned how to court Washington reporters. He maintained a position of openness with journalists but also got to know them on a personal level by entertaining them at cookouts and informal parties, which his brother Dwight often attended. Milton's expertise in media relations led President Roosevelt to give him the responsibility of conducting a study into wartime public information. Out of that study came the Office of War Information. Milton believed that information on the war effort should come from commanders at the battlefield rather than from officials in Washington, as was the case with the Creel Committee in World War I.[64] His understanding of press relations had a direct impact on his brother, who served as supreme commander of the Allied forces for the D day invasion on June 6, 1944.

Dwight Eisenhower took Milton's lessons to heart and chose as his campaign press adviser Harry Butcher. Butcher was a personal friend and had been a vice president at CBS before the war. As broadcast historian Craig Allen demonstrated, Butcher's goal was to facilitate the appearance of complete frankness and trust with the press.[65] But soon after becoming president, Eisenhower realized that his press efforts to that point had not been enough. During the war, he had interacted with a small group of reporters in his role as military commander. He knew them personally. But the Washington press corps, composed of more than three hundred reporters, was too large for him to know in similar fashion.[66] Eisenhower was also having trouble with his own party, which impacted media coverage of his presidency. He was a moderate Republican; in fact, the Democratic Party had tried to get him to run on their ticket. Republicans controlled Congress, but conservative Republicans sought to pressure him to do what they wanted. When he tried to compromise with them, the press labeled him too soft.[67]

Eisenhower decided that he needed to be more visible, to sell his administration to the American people. Such an approach was actually what his advisers had been suggesting all along. Prior to his inauguration in 1953, one of his advisers proposed that Eisenhower hold a monthly series of telecasts from the White House, similar to Roosevelt's radio fireside chats. The idea was that the telecasts would allow the president, who was very charismatic, to go directly to the people. He agreed to a 1953 Christmas Eve telecast.[68]

The telecast, to be carried live by the three networks and simultaneously by the radio networks, was different from previous White House broadcasts. The president did not need to address the people of the nation: he simply wanted to. The event itself, as his advisers understood, was the news, a "new living-room experience for the American public: a person-to-person style program hosted by the nation's chief executive."[69] To ensure the telecast went off without a hitch and was an exciting TV moment, Eisenhower brought in Robert Montgomery, a Hollywood actor, to produce it. The telecast was a success, and Montgomery stayed on after the broadcast, becoming the president's personal style manager and handling all of his on-camera appearances.[70]

Eisenhower was particularly open to having his image "managed" because of his brother Milton's influence and his own experiences as a military commander. He understood that dealing with the mass media required trained professionals, not bureaucrats. In fact, he saw the presidency in business terms. The president was the chief executive officer of the United States, and he wanted his administration's public relations to be comparable to that of a corporation—thus his emphasis on selling and promoting the presidency. To that end, he sought to pattern his administration's operations on a corporate model. Among other things, he wanted to create a board of strategy, whose mission would be to reduce the goals of the administration to simple concepts that could be easily communicated through the media. He also wanted to create a director of communications position to reflect the trend in many large businesses. The board of strategy did not materialize, although the idea resurfaced during the Nixon administration and finally came to be realized in the Reagan years.[71]

Ironically, despite his apparent understanding of the importance of public image—and of the mass media's role in the creation of that image—and despite his brother's influence on him, Eisenhower did not understand reporters. He grasped their need for conflict, for news, but did not grasp why they tended to base their reporting on their questions, rather than his answers to those questions. For instance, in 1953, the Justice Department announced it was investigating Harry Dexter White, an assistant secretary of the treasury in the Truman administration. White was deceased by that time and could no longer defend himself. Instead, Truman gave a televised speech in which he defended White and blamed Eisenhower for supporting McCarthy. Eisenhower believed that the Justice Department had valid reasons for investigating White and tried to explain those reasons at a press conference. But reporters were only interested in Eisenhower's reaction to Truman's personal attacks, which the president did not want to address.[72] As a result of such experiences, Eisenhower tended to consider reporters as workers with no talent. He did maintain personal friendships with publishers such as Henry Luce of *Time* magazine, but he essentially ignored individual reporters.[73]

Eisenhower realized that, ultimately, it was not what the reporters themselves thought that mattered but what the American public thought. As a result, his advisers began tracking people's attitudes toward their president. Tracking was a procedure developed by Batten, Barton, Durstine, and Osborn (BBDO), an advertising agency, to test and market products. The Republican National Committee (RNC) hired BBDO to develop ads for Eisenhower's 1952 presidential campaign, and the agency was kept on after the campaign to track public opinion. Every Sunday,

BBDO would conduct a telephone survey of between fifty and one hundred people to determine attitudes toward a variety of issues, and then it would report those results to the White House by Monday afternoon.[74]

Although the Eisenhower administration was using the technologies available to it at the time to determine public sentiment and although Eisenhower himself was less than thrilled with the capacities of individual reporters, he still had to deal with the presidential press conference. Upset by the reporters' treatment during the White investigation, he decided to read a prepared statement at his December 2, 1953, conference. It was not the first time such a statement had been read by a president at a press conference, but it set a precedent. Traditionally, presidential conferences had been "for background" only. Woodrow Wilson instituted the press conference in 1913 with the idea that they would be used to provide background information for reporters, and it was understood by all involved that statements made at the conferences would not be attributed to the president. These sessions were a way for presidents to test the waters and get ideas before the American people without having to publicly endorse them.[75]

But now, Eisenhower sought to put his statements on the record and therefore before the public without the reporters' filter. Although this change may not seem significant, it was a major departure for the White House press corps. By not making the announcement ahead of time, Eisenhower and his staff headed off any criticism by the press and also established that the administration was in control of information flow. In addition to putting comments on the record, Eisenhower also released transcripts for print media and audio recordings for radio media.[76] It was not until January 19, 1955, however, that the first press conference was taped, edited by the White House, and released for television.[77]

The use of television became even more important for the president after his heart attack in September 1955. His advisers were concerned that he would not be well enough to make the usual exhausting campaign stops for the 1956 election. Television offered a way for Eisenhower to campaign while essentially staying put in Washington and protecting his health.[78] Of course, the fact that the number of households with televisions had more than doubled between 1952 and 1956 (from sixteen million to thirty-five million) made the televised campaign a practical one. Survey results from the Survey Research Center at the University of Michigan showed that in 1952, some 31 percent of respondents received their political news from television, 28 percent from radio, and 22 percent from newspapers. But just four years later, 49 percent of respondents received their political news from television, 24 percent from newspapers, and just 10 percent from radio.[79]

Although the election of 1960 is usually considered the television election, Craig Allen called 1956 "a defining moment in 20th century electioneering, marking the point at which television was fully injected into the process and a major showdown between the video campaign and the system it replaced."[80] During their convention, the Republicans played to the television cameras and the audience at home. The convention was held in San Francisco, but the daily events started at 4:00 P.M. so that viewers on the East Coast could see them at 7:00 P.M. The speakers were kept on a strict time schedule so that the largest number of viewers would see the highlights of the day. Even the speeches were written with television in mind. While the Republican National Committee used the services of BBDO to script the convention, Eisenhower himself hired David Levy of the television department of the Young & Rubicam advertising agency. Levy placed emphasis on "informality, feeling, and emotion" instead of the hard-sell tactics that had been used in the 1952 campaign. He recognized that television was a more emotional medium than print or radio, and he inserted catchwords, such as *integrity* and *honesty,* in Eisenhower's speeches. He also de-emphasized speeches, once the staple of conventions, because they lacked visual appeal.[81]

The Democrats, by contrast, failed to take such details as time zones into consideration at their own convention. Their speeches ran long, often finishing after midnight on the East Coast. They essentially ran the convention the way they always had. The party regulars did their work in the back rooms, and the people at home were not considered part of the process.[82]

The difference in style between the two conventions was not lost on media analysts. In reporting on the events, they focused on the staging and the changed role of the news media in the convention process. As Craig Allen noted, "Instead of covering the conventions, it appeared the media now participated in them."[83] And it was the Republicans, not the Democrats, who were the masters of the new medium and the manipulation of the press. In fact, by 1960, Eisenhower's press secretary, Jim Haggerty, was so confident in his powers that he was able to tell the president he could trust his press office to "keep our news media informed . . . so that they will write what we want."[84]

While politicians were viewing television as a potent political force, however, intellectuals and liberals were blaming it for the conformity and baseness of American life. Some political commentators, such as James Reston, Dorothy Thompson, and Doris Fleeson, criticized what they viewed as the growing role of personality in politics. Sociologist David Riesman thought the phenomenon was part of the trend toward what he termed the "other-directedness" of American life. Americans, he argued, were becoming absorbed with consumption, and as a result, candidates were being sold like products.[85] The 1950s were certainly a decade of conformity and consensus, at least on the surface. Americans yearned for a period of stability and safety after the turmoil of World War II, and the economy cooperated by easing financial pressures for many citizens. As historian William Chafe wrote, "Rarely has a society experienced such rapid or dramatic change as that which occurred in America after 1945."[86]

By the mid-1950s, 60 percent of Americans had achieved middle-class status, compared to only 31 percent before the Great Depression. By the end of the decade, 60 percent of families owned their own homes, 75 percent their own cars, and 87 percent their own television sets. Productivity had increased 210 percent per capita between 1947 and 1956, thanks to technological advances. Those advances also changed the nature of jobs, with the number of factory workers falling 4 percent and the number of clerical workers increasing 23 percent between 1947 and 1957. As Chafe noted, the economy crossed the line from an industrial to a postindustrial state in 1956 when white-collar workers outnumbered blue-collar workers for the first time. Those white-collar workers comprised a new managerial class, as "to an ever-increasing extent, the economy was dominated by a few gigantic enterprises that depended for their efficiency on the particularized knowledge of skilled experts."[87] After work, the new "organization man" of the 1950s went home to his family in the suburbs. Those suburbs grew six times faster than cities, to the point that by 1960, they were home to one-quarter of the American population.[88]

Despite the relative prosperity, the period was also marked by fear. People were afraid of Communists, atomic bombs, propaganda, and juvenile delinquency, among other things.[89] McCarthy took advantage of the fear of communism and the desire for stability to fuel apprehensions about nonconformity. At the same time, writers and artists seemed to seek a sense of belonging. Books and movies of the period tended to have themes of "alienation, affluence, and youth neglect," according to historian Gary Donaldson.[90] Such works included *The Lonely Crowd,* published in 1950; *The Organization Man,* which came out in 1956; and *The Man in the Gray Flannel Suit,* a 1955 novel in which the hero was a public relations practitioner. And James Dean portrayed the angst of teen life in *Rebel without a Cause* in 1955.

Intellectuals and liberals lamented the conformity and what they saw as a lack of passion. According to historian William O'Neill, their dismay peaked in 1957. President A. Whitney Griswold of Yale said in his baccalaureate address that year that America had more to fear from "cultural submersion" than from "political subversion." For Griswold, the threat of a mass culture was greater than the threat of a Communist takeover. "Conferences had taken the place of individual invention, public opinion polls and public relations experts were robbing us both of our courage and our convictions," he said.[91] Griswold was not alone in putting the blame on PR practitioners. Journalist Irwin Ross sought to warn Americans about how they were being manipulated by exposing the techniques of public relations consultants in his 1959 book, *The Image Merchants.*

Ross's book revealed a profession that operated behind the scenes and used the media to influence public attitudes. It was the failure of PR practitioners to identify themselves as the source of information disseminated to reporters that seemed the most insidious and raised ethical issues for Ross. To cite one example, during the 1936 LaFollette hearings into the steel industry's record with labor, it was revealed that the public relations agency Hill &

Knowlton had paid columnist George Sokolsky to write stories promoting free enterprise and antiunionism. In the 1950s, the agency worked for the Tobacco Research Institute, which was secretly funded by the tobacco industry. Ostensibly independent groups such as the Tobacco Research Institute were used by public relations practitioners because they were perceived as more credible sources of information than the obviously self-interested client.[92]

Carl Byoir and Associates, another PR firm, used such groups (known in the trade as front groups) extensively in its campaign in behalf of the Pennsylvania railroads to encourage state regulations on the trucking industry. Railroads had been facing increasing competition from trucks for the long-distance freight business since the 1930s, but things had gotten even tougher after the war. The Byoir agency used freelance writers to generate numerous articles on the damage done to highways by overweight trucks and created letter-writing citizens' groups to put pressure on legislators. The agency's public relations tactics became news in their own right when the Pennsylvania Motor Truck Association sued Byoir's client, the Eastern Railroad Presidents' Council, for violating the Sherman Anti-trust Act by trying to force the truckers out of business. Episodes of this type caused the Public Relations Society of America to adopt a brief code of ethics in 1954; they also caused members of the association to spend the rest of the decade questioning themselves and the practice of public relations.[93]

PR practitioners only had themselves to blame for their growing reputation as manipulators of the mind. Speeches such as the one delivered by Ralph B. Wagner, professor of speech and applied psychology, to the St. Louis Paint, Varnish and Lacquer Association in 1945 reflected a belief in the ability and the desire to control consumers' minds. In his speech, titled "Don't Neglect Your Relations! Molding the Mass Mind," Wagner told his audience that businesses in the postwar era had to include a "definite and concerted program of enlightened publicity, propaganda, and promotion" if they hoped to succeed. He granted that there was no sure way to control public opinion but asserted that certain psychological principles could lead to "fairly successful control." Those principles were "based on scientific research findings that are sufficiently representative to enable us to accomplish rather startling results in molding mass mind."[94]

Although the early talk of mind control was just that, talk, it fit within the larger societal interest at the time in the workings of the human mind. Thanks to the growing field of psychology, individuals were now seen as socially constructed beings rather than creatures born with fixed natures. The logical result of that kind of thinking was the belief that individuals could therefore be socially engineered or conditioned to behave in certain ways. B. F. Skinner's 1948 novel, *Walden Two,* explored the possibility of behaviorally modifying individuals so that they could learn to live together in harmony.[95] Of course, European totalitarianism was a real-life example of social engineering as part of a political plan. In the hands of advertisers and marketers, such ideas were used to create a consumer mind-set, a thought no less frightening for intellectuals of the day than Skinner's ideal community.

In his 1957 book, *The Hidden Persuaders,* Vance Packard sought to expose the advertising industry's efforts in the area of motivation analysis or motivation research. Advertisers, he pointed out, wanted to know what motivated people to make choices, to buy one product over another. Packard argued that a fundamental shift in thinking had occurred among businesspeople in the early 1950s: they moved from a production mind-set to a market mind-set.

They had the goods to sell; now, they needed to ensure a market for those goods. After the war, new products such as televisions and electric refrigerators had come on the market, but there was no brand loyalty for those products. Thus, there was intense competition to get that first sale. At the same time, brands became increasingly similar. When brand X and its competitor, brand Y, were virtually the same in quality and price, selling brand X using a straight logical appeal or reason was difficult. And yet, consumers still preferred one of the brands over the other. Advertising agencies, therefore, wanted to find out why people did things at the subconscious level. What were their prejudices, fears, and assumptions, and how could those be used to get them to buy brand X?[96]

According to Packard, motivational research slowly entered the business world in the early 1950s, with *BusinessWeek* running a three-part series on the topic in August 1954 and *Fortune* devoting its June 1956 cover story to the trend. Part of the purpose of motivational research was to identify and then create a distinctive personality for a brand, to mold an image. The "image builders," as Packard called them, built into their products "the same traits that we recognize in ourselves—self-images."[97]

The media helped in creating the consumer mind-set, even as editors criticized public relations practitioners for trying to buy their attention with the use of gimmicks. In 1955, a hobby-kit maker launched a $100,000 campaign to promote a $4.95 hobby kit with the slogan "Give Dad a Hobby on Father's Day." NBC stars promoted the kit because there was a publicity value in it for an NBC show, *Victory at Sea*—the kit contained plastic toy battleships. Even the U.S. Navy got into the act by providing photographs and posters to be used as background material for window displays of the kit in Macy's department store. In another instance, men's clothing manufacturers decided to promote the idea of men's style to increase sales. "Dress Well—You Can't Afford Not To" became the industry association's slogan. Pitches to the fashion editors of newspapers paid off, as they began announcing in 1956 that "gabardine, knickers, and loud sports shirts were enjoying a revival and that men were mad about India madras."[98]

While Packard focused his attention on the advertising industry, other intellectuals of the day placed equal blame on the mass media for pandering to the public's lowest common denominator.[99] Henry Luce, the owner and publisher of *Time* magazine, noted in 1953 that newspapers were only about 15 to 20 percent news, with the rest of their pages being devoted to entertainment and features. What explains the trend to entertainment and away from serious news? According to Luce, it was because that was where the profitability lay, and "American newspapers have become, almost all of them, serious business propositions."[100] Public opinion analyst George Gallup called the movement toward "mass entertainment" a real threat to the nation's future place in the world. A study revealed that the average amount of time a reader spent daily on important news was less than four minutes, whereas ten times that amount was spent on sports, gossip, and entertainment stories.[101] In terms of television, "the total number of hours devoted by the American public to just *two* shows, 'I Love Lucy' and the 'Show of Shows,' is greater than the total number of hours spent on all information or educational shows put together," Gallup noted.[102]

Critics soon had more to lament about television than just the creation of a standardized mass culture. Millions had tuned in each week to watch ordinary people pitted against each other to answer trivia questions on the quiz show *Twenty-One*. Contestant Charles Van Doren became a hero as he foiled one opponent after another.

But the luster wore off when it was revealed that the show was rigged: Van Duren had been given the answers. The producers blamed the show's advertiser, Revlon, for pressuring them to make the quiz program more exciting for viewers. Revlon, in turn, blamed the producers for sullying the company's name.[103]

The scandal did more than affect Revlon's reputation; it showed that television could not be trusted. "By implication, then," it was asked, "might the networks' news broadcasts be fabricated or inaccurate?"[104] At the time, television nightly newscasts were fifteen minutes in length, and networks carried no more than about two hours of news and public affairs programming per week.[105] The quiz show scandal and the ensuing public attention on television forced networks to change their policies. The Federal Communications Commission (FCC) ordered the networks to produce at least one public affairs show per week and to put an end to their advertisers' manipulation of content. In addition, the networks began to emphasize news, and they attempted to rebuild their credibility by using their cameras to show viewers the stories.[106]

As television increasingly focused on spot news reporting, newspapers moved to more investigative pieces in an effort to compete.[107] But the continued effect of monopolization in the newspaper field and the greater focus on business meant shrinking newsroom staffs, which in turn meant an increasing reliance on public relations practitioners.[108] One public information officer for a federal laboratory noted that editors needed his services but that he was "getting a little tired of 'spoon-feeding' newspaper people, doing all their work for them." "More editors should insist that their men get out on the street and 'dig,'" he argued.[109] But at the same time, he recognized that journalists had a more difficult time of digging than they had in the past, given the size of the government and its ability to hide information.

Clark Mollenhoff, a Washington journalist for Cowles Publications, also lamented how the size of government had affected the press, but he was most concerned with governmental encroachments on the right of access to information. He cited a number of ways that public officials controlled information flow, including the use of "smooth public relations operators" who were so helpful that reporters came to rely on them rather than doing their own digging. The misuse of security classifications to withhold otherwise reportable information was another method, as was the practice of officials being unavailable for reporters known to be critical of the administration in power. But for Mollenhoff, the most important method was the arbitrary hiding of the records of executive agencies on the basis that they involved "some vague 'national interest.'"[110] This arbitrary refusal by the executive branch to produce records was apparently a new device used to "manage the news."[111] According to Mollenhoff, the Eisenhower administration had expanded the executive privilege doctrine by labeling all communications containing advice or recommendations "confidential executive business" and claiming an inherent executive privilege to hide such communications from the press, the public, and Congress.

The new doctrine had been made public on May 17, 1954, during the army-McCarthy hearings. President Eisenhower, in a letter, had authorized army counsel John Adams to refuse to testify at the hearings about conversations with presidential assistants. He had indicated that "in his view members of the executive branch should not be required to testify on conversations and communications with other members of the executive branch where recommendations and advice were involved."[112] Many newspapers apparently saw this letter as a blow to McCarthy only and praised Eisenhower for not giving in to him. It was not until several months later that they realized the administration intended to apply the doctrine in other situations. Although the policy did not ultimately affect much in the Eisenhower administration, Mollenhoff concluded with an important question: "What could such a precedent of arbitrary executive secrecy do under some later administration that may be less kindly in its basic outlook?"[113]

THREE

MANAGING SOCIAL CHANGE

"Ask not what your country can do for you; ask what you can do for your country."[114] With those words, delivered at his inauguration in January 1961, President John F. Kennedy heralded a new beginning for the United States. For some, the words promised a renewed sense of confidence in the abilities of Americans to rule the world. The launch of *Sputnik* by the USSR on October 4, 1957, had stunned Americans. The United States, not Russia, was the most technologically advanced country in the world, and yet, here was a Communist country beating the morally superior United States at its own game. Kennedy's call to action, then, was seen as a rallying cry designed to restore optimism and confidence in the nation.[115]

Kennedy's inauguration marked the end of a long campaign that pitted the young, Catholic northeasterner first against more established Democrats and ultimately against the seasoned vice president under Eisenhower, Richard Nixon. The 1960 presidential election has been called a turning point in American presidential political history. It was the point at which television solidified its position as the dominant mass medium and the point where the president became a created image.[116] Although Eisenhower had recognized the importance of image and, to a certain extent, had crafted his own image as president, it was Kennedy who took the image building to an entirely new level.

As a junior senator from Massachusetts, Kennedy's record was undistinguished, but he began to make a name for himself at the 1956 Democratic Convention. His supporters showed up with materials on him, such as reprints of favorable editorials, summaries of his senatorial record, and biographical data, to distribute to delegates.[117] Knowing he needed to have a national presence if he hoped to become a legitimate candidate for the Democratic nomination in 1960, Kennedy spent the next four years touring the country and meeting voters and reporters. These forays into the countryside allowed him to make himself more of a known commodity; they also allowed him to hone his media skills. In 1959, he ramped up his exposure by serving as a source for journalists and having his byline appear on several articles on a variety of subjects.[118]

By October 1959, Kennedy was putting his strategy team together for his candidacy. Among that team was Theodore Sorensen, who would later become one of his speechwriters. In his book on Kennedy, Sorensen wrote that no public relations experts were hired for the 1960 campaign, despite rumors to the contrary.[119] While that may be true, the Kennedy camp was not without a clear understanding of the mass media and the importance of image in a presidential campaign. According to Theodore White, in his *Making of the President, 1960,* one member of Kennedy's team was Louis Harris, a thirty-eight-year-old public opinion analyst who would poll in the next year more people than had ever been polled in American history. Kennedy came to base many of his decisions on the results of those polls.[120]

When Kennedy announced he was running for president at a press conference on January 2, 1960, columnists and press pundits presumed he was really running for vice president. Inside the Washington Beltway, it was believed that he did not stand a chance at becoming the Democratic nominee for president. But Kennedy was building his base from the bottom up.[121] He and his team were proponents of a new style of political organization in which the idea was to provide as many people as possible an opportunity to participate in the campaign because participation would give them a sense of belonging and a stake in the outcome. To build the working base, Kennedy's advisers discovered who the real leaders in a community were and then cultivated those leaders.[122] By the time of the Democratic Convention in Los Angeles, Kennedy and his advisers had a well-oiled machine in place.

The Democratic National Committee (DNC) had been slow to adopt the Republican practice of using public relations practitioners in planning their campaigns and conventions. The DNC did use PR practitioners in 1956, but they tended to come from nonprofit organizations, government, and the media. Even the advertising agency the DNC hired served in a technical role and provided no advice on policy or strategy. By contrast, the Republican National Committee used public relations practitioners from the corporate world or from PR agencies. The RNC also tended to involve their public relations people in the policy-making process. The result in 1956 was a new style of convention, aimed for television and maximum coverage.[123] By 1960, the DNC had learned its lesson, and it planned the convention with television in mind. When it was over, Kennedy was the Democratic nominee for president and Lyndon B. Johnson his running mate.

On the Republican side, Vice President Richard Nixon was the obvious choice for the presidential nominee. Nixon had recruited Herbert Klein, a public relations practitioner from southern California, early in 1959 to join his team.[124] But neither Nixon nor Klein seemed particularly adept at dealing with the media. Nixon believed the media were out to get him, and he treated reporters on the campaign trail with suspicion, although studies would later show that he actually had the support of the nation's newspaper editors and publishers. His suspicions about reporters were warranted, however: they did *not* seem to like him particularly. Certainly, the fact that most reporters were Democrats probably played a part, but so did Nixon's treatment of them. One of his aides supposedly said to Theodore White, "Stuff the bastards. They're all against Dick anyway. Make them work—we aren't going to hand out prepared remarks; let them get their pencils out and listen and take notes."[125] The reporters had to make their own travel arrangements to follow Nixon, in addition to listening to and reporting on his speeches. Rarely was Nixon or his staff available to answer questions.[126] Given his attitude toward reporters, it was natural that Nixon would attempt to bypass them and go directly to the American people with his message whenever he could.

Unlike his opponent, Kennedy had a genuine liking for reporters. The result was that his whole camp worked to cultivate relations with the press. His aides made arrangements for reporters' transportation and accommodation and would ride the press bus to ensure the journalists always had a source around them. Kennedy himself was accessible to reporters, even socializing with some of them. With his formal speeches, his aides made a transcript available to reporters within about an hour. Thus, the reporters were able to relax and listen to the speeches rather than having to take copious notes as they did when covering Nixon. All of these things led to a feeling of conviviality in the Kennedy camp, such that reporters felt they, too, were part of building Kennedy's New Frontier.[127]

Both Kennedy and Nixon were using television to reach the voters directly. Television was expensive, and audiences for half-hour shows by politicians tended to be small and made up of supporters. When candidates did use such shows, they timed them carefully in terms of what other programs they were displacing, for no one wanted to anger potential voters by preempting their favorite shows. During the 1960 campaign, the practice of buying two-minute to five-minute spots at the beginning or end of successful shows began. Such spots were more effective at reaching uncommitted or overtly hostile voters because audiences tended to sit through them while waiting for the regular programs to begin.[128]

By 1960, television was an established part of American life, with 88 percent of families owning a set. But a year earlier, the television industry had suffered two public scandals that threatened its ability to produce programming. Congressional hearings in 1959 into allegations that quiz shows had been fixed also revealed that recording companies had been paying the shows' producers to play the records of particular artists during the programs. That finding led to further congressional hearings into the practice of payola (making illegal payments in return for airplay) between recording companies and radio and television stations. The combined quiz show and payola scandals resulted in public outrage. The three networks were very concerned that that outrage would cause the Federal Communications Commission to regulate them even further. Serving the public interest by televising presidential debates was an appealing idea to them.[129]

Kennedy's aides were clearly in favor of a debate between the candidates. Shortly after his nomination, Kennedy had retained the services of J. Leonard Reinsch, a man who had provided Roosevelt and Truman with broadcasting advice. When Reinsch and Kennedy first met to discuss strategy, Reinsch is supposed to have said, "All I want is a picture of you and Nixon on the same television tube. We'll take it from there."[130] A debate would give

Reinsch his wish. In fact, Kennedy's people wanted five debates. Kennedy was still fighting the perception that he was too young and inexperienced, and his aides believed that any time the two candidates could be seen together, Kennedy's stock would rise because he would look as capable and as presidential as Nixon. Precisely because of that danger, Nixon's consultants originally did not want him to debate Kennedy, but Nixon, who had been a debater in college, thought he would crush the younger man. So the Nixon camp conceded to one debate. They ended up with four.[131]

The format for the debates was a panel of four reporters who would ask questions. The candidates could not use notes, but they were allowed eight-minute opening statements in the first and last debates. In addition, they had two and one-half minutes to respond to questions. The four debates were held between September 26 and October 21, 1960, and drew an average of between 65 and 70 million viewers.[132]

The first debate has been the subject of much study. Research has shown that those who watched the debate on television believed Kennedy won, while those who listened to it on the radio believed Nixon won. This result has been used to substantiate the argument that television has changed the focus of politics from issues to images. Without doubt, televised debates give voters a chance to participate in the democratic process in a way they were not able to before. Rarely in modern times would a voter have had an opportunity to see and hear and ultimately evaluate both candidates together. To that extent, debates serve a valuable purpose. But as PR practitioner Melvyn Bloom stated, their value is eroded by "the extent to which such voter choices are made on the basis of visual images, as opposed to political judgments based on reality."[133] The 1960 debates revealed differences between Kennedy and Nixon in terms of ideas and policies, "yet rarely in American history has there been a political campaign that discussed issues less or clarified them less."[134] For one thing, the broadcast media were not conducive to an in-depth discussion of issues or thoughtful responses, nor, for that matter, did the two and one-half minute response time allow for the development of a position.[135] The debates were all show business; unfortunately for Nixon, he did not realize that until it was too late.

Kennedy and Reinsch, his television adviser, met with the CBS director of the first debate the day before the broadcast to discuss the set design and shooting patterns.[136] Kennedy then spent the rest of the day going over facts with his advisers and making flash cards. The next day, he arrived at the studio in a dark-blue suit, looking trim, tanned, and in control. Nixon, by contrast, looked weak and perhaps a little out of control. He had arrived in Chicago for the debate late on Sunday evening without having been briefed. His television advisers had wanted him there on Saturday so he could relax and they could prepare him, but apparently, they were unable to reach either Nixon or his press secretary, Herbert Klein. He gave a speech in the morning and then spent the afternoon in his hotel room, incommunicado. One of his advisers did manage to ride with him on the ten-minute taxi drive to the studio, but the two men did not have much time to go over details.[137]

Nixon had been hospitalized for two weeks with a knee injury shortly before the debate, and he still looked rather pale. His gray suit made him fade into the gray background of the set, and the face powder used to hide his five-o'clock shadow made him look even paler than he was. Had he listened to his advisers, such problems could have been corrected beforehand, as they were by the second debate, but Nixon was a loner who did not take advice well. Also, he believed he knew television. He had, after all, saved his political career with his 1952 Checkers speech. But instead of doing what he did in that speech—play to the television audience—he treated the debate as just that, a debate. Theodore White said that in reading the transcript of the event, it became clear Nixon was debating Kennedy as if judges were scoring points. He answered each question directly, rebutting and refuting his challenger's statements.[138]

Kennedy had no illusions about this being a real debate: it was an opportunity to score points with the audience at home, and that is what he did. He ignored questions when it suited him and used others as a bridge to his main message, which was aimed at the hearts and minds of people across the country. The prestige of the United States, Kennedy argued, had declined in recent years. Clearly, he implied that he was the one to lead the country back to its former glory, not the man who was vice president during its decline.[139]

Despite Nixon's claim that the United States was enjoying an all-time high in prestige, the public had a sense at the end of the 1950s and into the early 1960s that the country was in decline and losing the Cold War. The launch of the Soviet satellite *Sputnik* in 1957 was a wake-up call for those who believed America was technologically superior to other countries. The U2 spy plane incident in May 1960, in which the Eisenhower administration first said the plane was not on a spying mission and then, when Soviet leader Nikita Khrushchev exposed the facts, admitted it had lied, seemed to suggest that perhaps the United States was not morally superior either.[140] The situation was compounded when, in April 1961, the planned overthrow of Fidel Castro in Cuba was bungled. In the aftermath of the incident, *New York Times* columnist Cyrus Sulzberger wrote, "We looked like fools to our friends, rascals to our enemies, and incompetents to the rest."[141]

Americans, it seemed, had become complacent with their prosperity, and like Rome before it, the country appeared doomed to collapse from moral decay. Two editors of small-town newspapers speaking to two different press associations recited a litany of examples of America's decline. According to those editors, "behavioristic psychology," progressive education, Hollywood's licentiousness, *Lady Chatterly's Lover,* and the plays of Tennessee Williams had all contributed to the country's "debilitating philosophy of permissiveness."[142]

Others saw a decline in excellence fostered by the conformity of the 1950s. Earle Johnson, a professor of speech at the University of Alabama, told a meeting of Alabama broadcasters that the news media were part of the problem. "A newspaper reporter is sent out on the street to collect the news of the various passers-by on such a question as 'Should the United States defend Formosa,'" he said. "The answer of the barfly who doesn't know where the island is located, or even that it is an island, is quoted in the next edition just as solemnly as that of the college teacher of history."[143] For the chairman of the board for the *Louisville (Ky.) Courier-Journal* and *Louisville Times,* it was time for print journalists to move away from the superficial and to fulfill their obligation to interpret the news to the public. What was needed, he argued, was more "depth reporting and serious editorial writing."[144] But he also acknowledged the constraints with which editors were dealing. By 1962, the percentage of cities with competitive newspapers had shrunk to just 5 percent, with twenty-three states having no such cities. One hundred and nine chains controlled nearly a third of the daily newspapers and half of the daily circulation.

Despite the difficulties, newspapers were still under an obligation to report the information people needed in a democratic society, not only the sensational. But according to editorial writer Alan Barth, newspapers "to an alarming degree, [had] become a mouthpiece and partner of the government."[145] Reporters were, he said, generally "less inquisitive, less probing, less insistent upon being told what's going on than they used to be."[146] The result was that the federal government was being allowed to keep secret information in the name of national security.

Charges of governmental secrecy had surfaced during the Eisenhower administration, and they continued under Kennedy. From Eisenhower and Kennedy's perspective, the Cold War raised threats to national security that were different from the ones associated with a regular war. Troop movements and military readiness were obviously matters of national security, and journalists had traditionally cooperated by not disclosing details about such matters. But the Cold War was being fought through covert operations and intelligence. Labeling something as a matter of national security was less a clear-cut process. Kennedy even went before the American Newspaper Publishers Association to ask that members exercise self-restraint on occasion. He understood his audience well enough to know better than to come right out and say he would tell them what they could and could not print. Instead, he asked them to ask themselves whether the story to be printed was in the interest of national security.[147] But at the time, journalists tended to defer to the president on matters of foreign policy. Although Kennedy appeared to be giving journalists ultimate control over the news, what he was really doing was maintaining control by linking foreign policy and the Cold War with national security.[148]

Kennedy was very much a Cold Warrior, and he was sincere in his belief that the country was facing a pending crisis. And in

October 1962, the Cuban missile crisis erupted.[149] Using television to reach a national and international audience, Kennedy informed the world that the Soviets' actions in Cuba were unacceptable and that the missiles they had positioned there had to be removed. Kennedy had also used television the previous April to warn Americans about the possibility of military confrontation in Laos if a peaceful settlement of tensions there could not be reached.[150] Media historian Mary Ann Weston suggested that the downside to Kennedy's use of television in such situations was that the individual in the presidency became more important than the government. It was Kennedy versus Khrushchev, rather than the U.S. government versus the Soviet politburo. That positioning gave Americans, Weston argued, an "inflated expectation" of what a president was empowered to do.[151] Regardless, the Kennedy administration appeared to show a bias toward television from the start. Press Secretary Pierre Salinger, for instance, was quicker to answer television reporters' calls than print reporters' calls, and he established a relationship of daily telephone conversations with the networks' Washington bureau chiefs.[152]

One of Kennedy's innovations in terms of television was turning press conferences into live televised events. Eisenhower was the first president to have his remarks at press conferences on the record. But Kennedy took that one step further: not only were his remarks on the record, they were also presented to the American public completely unfiltered by journalists. Members of the Washington press corps did not like the change because they felt physically removed from the president. Moreover, the addition of television cameras and crews required an even larger room for the conferences. Over the years, the press corps had grown in size, requiring a periodic change in location for these events. When

Roosevelt was in office, he met with reporters in the Oval Office. Truman dealt with about twenty-five reporters at a time. By the time of Eisenhower's administration, the press conferences had to be moved to the three-hundred-seat Indian Treaty Room of the Executive Office Building next door to the executive mansion. Yet even that room was outgrown by the time Kennedy took office, requiring another move, this time to the auditorium in the new State Department Building.[153]

In addition to opening up the press conferences to live television, Kennedy opened up his personal life to reporters. As one public relations practitioner noted in 1963, he exhibited "a willingness, even anxiousness, to live and work in full focus of public attention."[154] He allowed interviews of family members and photographs of his children. He also posed for or permitted cover shots for nearly every major magazine. In the spring of 1961, he even modeled a suit on the cover of GQ, the men's fashion magazine. And he had an article in the Saturday Evening Post, with the byline indicating he wrote it in his capacity as president.[155]

Despite being obviously open with and accessible to reporters, Kennedy still managed to keep the upper hand in the relationship. He apparently liked television because, as he supposedly told Washington Post journalist and friend Ben Bradlee, "when we don't have to go through you bastards, we can really get our story to the American people."[156] Therefore, he was available for interviews and photographs but only when it suited his purpose. One such occasion occurred in December 1962 after the Cuban missile crisis. Kennedy offered the three networks a joint sixty-minute interview, with one reporter from each network. The stipulation, however, was that they had to tape ninety minutes and then edit the material down to an hour. The administration agreed that Kennedy would have no input into the editing process; the networks together could edit as they saw fit. What they did not realize until later was that Kennedy had, in fact, exercised a great deal of indirect editorial control during the interview. Whenever he was asked an unfriendly question, he would give either a one-sentence response or a very boring answer. He knew that with thirty minutes being edited out, those questions and answers had a good chance of being cut.[157] He was right.

As with the networks, Kennedy exercised control over photographers too. Being photographed with his wife, Jackie, on their yacht or playing touch football on the lawn with his brothers reinforced the image he wished to create, that of a virile leader. It was conscious planning on Kennedy's part, especially considering how ill he actually was, as we now know. In fact, Kennedy was called "America's No. 1 unhidden persuader," and a poll of members of Congress gave him a higher rating for his public relations skills than for any other ability. John Hill, the founder of the PR agency Hill & Knowlton, suggested in 1963 that Kennedy's skill in image building was perhaps an indication that public relations was coming of age.[158]

It was not long, however, before allegations of a "managed news" policy surfaced in the media. The concept of managed news first arose in the Eisenhower administration, but in the March 1963 issue of *Fortune* magazine, Arthur Krock, a Washington correspondent with the *New York Times,* criticized Kennedy for managing the news. A month later in *Atlantic Magazine,* Hanson Baldwin raised questions about the administration's methods of controlling information flow. A House government operations subcommittee even started hearings into the allegations.[159] Regardless of the criticism, Kennedy's PR abilities worked to such an extent that when he was assassinated in November 1963, his death took on greater symbolic meaning than it might otherwise have.

The devastating event was not just the assassination of a president, as tragic and profoundly affecting as that was, but the end of Camelot as well.

Of course, the United States of the 1960s was not Camelot. The seeming consensus and conformity of the 1950s had shattered in the next decade. For some, the changing social mores were a sign of America's moral decay. For others, they were a symbol of hope, a sign that the American dream might be open to everyone.

Although the 1960s are considered the decade of civil rights, the movement's modern roots can at least be traced to the middle of the 1950s and the 1954 Supreme Court decision in *Brown v. Board of Education* that said separate was not equal when it came to education. The decision did not result in immediate integration of the South, but it paved the way for it, as did the Montgomery bus boycott of 1955. Yet in some ways, it was four black students at North Carolina A&T State University who really started it all. When Franklin McCain, Ezell Blair Jr., David Richmond, and Joseph McNeil sat down at a Woolworth's lunch counter in Greensboro, North Carolina, on February 1, 1960, they did not know their actions would ignite a movement. Soon, sit-ins were taking place around the country.[160]

The sit-ins galvanized young people and produced the Student Non-violent Coordinating Committee (SNCC) and the Students for a Democratic Society (SDS). SNCC began in the South as a group of black students with close ties to Martin Luther King Jr.'s Southern Christian Leadership Conference (SCLC), while SDS was originally a group of white students from the North, the Midwest, and the West Coast. But even though the groups were successfully holding demonstrations and sit-ins and gathering members, the majority of Americans remained unaffected by their activities. Without public support for government interference, the federal government chose to leave matters in the hands of local authorities.[161]

In May 1961, the freedom rides—integrated bus trips into the South—took place with the hope that they would provoke confrontations and publicly expose the failure of desegregation. It was also hoped that the southern authorities would use violence on the riders, forcing the federal government to take a stand. At each stop, the riders faced escalating violence. Finally, in Montgomery, Alabama, a federal officer was assaulted. Kennedy had no choice but to send in federal marshals.[162] But while many decried the violence, public opinion still had not shifted. Integration was still deemed a southern problem, not an American one. It took a man named Bull Connor to change that perception.

On May 2, 1962, Connor, police commissioner for the city of Birmingham, Alabama, ordered the use of fire hoses and police dogs on well-dressed marchers who were between the ages of six and sixteen. The world watched in horror as scenes of dogs attacking little girls and streams of water capable of taking the bark off trees rolling people down the street played out on their television sets.[163] CBS commentator Eric Sevareid wrote of the event, "A newspaper or television picture of a snarling police dog set upon a human being is recorded in the permanent photoelectric file of every human brain."[164] Public opinion began to turn because the national media had finally decided the violence in the South was newsworthy.

News is made up of significant events. The sit-ins and demonstrations were events, but they were mostly reported on the local or regional level at the beginning of the civil rights movement. Reporters initially focused on the arrests because police reports were official sources and therefore were relied on in objective reporting. The demonstrators themselves had no standing as sources.

But as sociologist Todd Gitlin noted, "Arrests allow non-celebrities to become news-makers."[165] As the groups became newsmakers in their own right, their events took on greater significance as news in the eyes of the media. The freedom rides were more significant events, for example, and hence more newsworthy because they involved several states and had a symbolic name. The deliberate emphasis on nonviolence on the part of the civil rights workers also served to upset the traditional view of the police as agents for restoring order. Television coverage of the events clearly showed that the authorities themselves were the violent ones, not the demonstrators. Such coverage, in psychological terms, would have created cognitive dissonance in the viewing public and forced at least some people to reconsider their position on civil rights. The use of children in the Birmingham marches was also a concerted effort to leverage news coverage and produce a greater reaction from the nation than would have been prompted by the sight of adult men and women being attacked.

While leaders of the civil rights movement were doing what they could to manage the news and influence public opinion, Woolworth's was trying to do the same. The Woolworth's company was drawn into the civil rights struggle unwittingly when the four students chose to sit down at the store lunch counter in Greensboro. In the months following that event, Woolworth's found itself in the middle of the controversy. Although other stores and restaurants were targets of sit-ins, Woolworth's became the main focus because of its size and prominence. Blacks and whites alike bombarded the company with letters, telephone calls, boycotts, and pickets. A regional office in Boston received some forty-five thousand letters demanding the lunch counters be desegregated immediately. Meanwhile, the Atlanta office received fifteen thousand letters threatening a boycott if the company did desegregate. The company's sales revenues for 1960 dropped by 35 percent. It was apparently in a no-win situation. So in November 1960, the company called in outside public relations help and hired the Carl Byoir and Associates agency.[166]

One of the agency's first moves was to make the media stop using Woolworth's as a symbol. Press leads such as "F. W. Woolworth's and six other store chains were picketed by student demonstrators today" had become commonplace.[167] For the media, the name Woolworth's had come to represent the sit-ins and demonstrations. A letter written by the Byoir staff and signed by Woolworth's vice president of public relations went out to editors and publishers of leading newspapers around the country, asking them to please stop singling out Woolworth's as a symbol of a nationwide problem. According to the account executive at Byoir, the practice was stopped within a few weeks.[168]

The Byoir people also helped Woolworth's slowly desegregate its lunch counters, taking a page from the civil rights movement's own playbook to do so. While the process involved a number of steps each local store manager was to take before actually desegregating the lunch counter, it was suggested that on the day of desegregation, only two blacks should show up to be served. Specifically, the two blacks were to be girls no older than twelve. It was also recommended that they be the only ones to show up for the first month, to help diffuse the situation. In most towns, the process was followed, and desegregation occurred relatively peacefully.[169]

Evidence that the desegregation process the company implemented had been a success came, ironically, when a riot broke out in a Woolworth's in Jackson, Mississippi, in 1963. There, two young black women and a black man, all students, sat down at the lunch counter, which had not yet been desegregated. A group of angry whites confronted the trio and assaulted them. When more blacks came to help the trio, the store manager realized he had a full-scale riot on his hands. The incident lasted for more than two hours and garnered the attention of reporters and television crews. Woolworth's immediately issued a statement to the press, saying that it regretted the incident, that the violence had been instigated by people unconnected with the company, that the store manager had not ordered any arrests, and that he had closed the store as soon as he could to reduce the violence. Virtually all of the media covering the event quoted from the company statement, and none blamed Woolworth's for the violence.[170]

In many ways, the media were vital to the civil rights movement. They gave the movement a voice and extended its reach to the nation. Movement leaders understood that and used events and symbols to ensure media coverage. Woolworth's PR agency also understood the media's role in shaping public opinion and sought to influence media coverage by removing the company as a symbol and encouraging the idea that civil rights was a national problem, not a corporate one, which it was. In the second half of the decade, activists, corporations, and politicians all seemed to become aware that the media were a powerful political force that could not be ignored.[171]

With the rise in the prominence of the media came a decline in public confidence in institutions. In a 1975 study of the governability of democracies, political scientist Samuel Huntington argued that the media focus on controversy and violence and the themes stressed in their coverage tended to promote unfavorable attitudes toward established institutions.[172] While the civil rights movement was part of that development, the Vietnam War contributed significantly to the decline in public confidence in the federal government.

At the beginning of the Vietnam War, journalists tended to rely on official government sources for information. According to historian Daniel Hallin, Americans probably became aware of Vietnam in 1964 with the Gulf of Tonkin incident, in which U.S. naval ships were purportedly fired on by South Vietnamese troops. President Lyndon Johnson sent troops to South Vietnam in response to the attack. Journalists dutifully reported the administration's statements that military action came only after and in retaliation for attacks by the Viet Cong. It is now known that that was not true. But President Johnson's ability to frame the story that way was the result of reporters not having direct access to the details of the incident. They had to rely on the administration for information. And by controlling the information, Johnson effectively controlled the news coverage.[173]

Control of the information about the situation in Southeast Asia began with Kennedy. Wanting to keep American involvement in Vietnam off the political agenda, he framed policy decisions as routine and incremental. Thus, Kennedy announced he was sending just a few hundred advisers to the country. He was careful not to call them troops and not to reveal that he already knew more would be needed. President Johnson kept up the appearance of a consistent policy regarding Vietnam. For instance, in July 1965 when he approved the deployment of an additional 100,000 troops to join the 75,000 troops already there, he announced publicly that 50,000 would be sent, with more to be added as requested. The administration believed that dispatching 50,000 men would not raise any concern but that sending 100,000 might.[174]

Television has often been blamed for causing the country to lose the Vietnam War. It was, of course, the first war that was televised. In the beginning, the news anchors supported the administration and its effort in Southeast Asia. Although it certainly delivered news, television did not lend itself to objective journalism. The anchors did not present themselves as disinterested observers, especially in the case of the Vietnam War. Instead, they were patriots who tended to reinforce the official view of the war. That situation was due in part to the newness of the medium; it was also partly due to the fact that news on television had to be simplified to fit within a thirty-minute program. Consequently, there was a tendency to present a themed story line that promoted a particular worldview.[175]

According to Daniel Hallin, television news provides "ideological guidance and reassurance for the mass public. It, therefore, deals not with issues but with symbols that represent basic values of the established political culture."[176] It was perhaps not surprising, then, that during the 1960s, the anchors themselves became celebrities with loyal followers, especially after CBS and NBC expanded their nightly news broadcasts from fifteen to thirty minutes in September 1963. Walter Cronkite was the evening news anchor on CBS, and Chet Huntley and David Brinkley anchored for NBC.[177] All three men served as influential opinion leaders for many Americans.

The power of those men and of television to shape public attitudes became clear after the Viet Cong launched their Tet offensive in 1968. The offensive was defeated by American troops, but it was a costly military victory. More than sixty million Americans watched the news each evening and saw images from Vietnam that directly countered the government's claims of victory. President Johnson is supposed to have realized he had lost public support for the war when Walter Cronkite told his viewers, "It seems now more certain than ever that the bloody experience in Vietnam is to end in stalemate."[178]

For the first few years of the war, Kennedy and then Johnson were able to control the information about the situation in Vietnam. Reporters tended to accept press conferences as presenting the real story. But as the military involvement grew, so did the coverage of the war and the number of sources cited. More sources meant less control, especially when those sources were providing information that was not in complete accord with the official line. The administration was not able to maintain control in part because it could not restrict reporters' access to sources. Since the official position was that the country was not at war, the administration could not censor the press or restrict its activities. And as time went on, there was less consensus within the administration and Congress over the policy decisions being made on Vietnam. Thus, reporters were able to find official sources who were critical of the president and willing to speak out about the situation. By 1968, the country was deeply divided on the issue.[179]

Of course, antiwar groups also shared some of the credit for destroying the consensus. As civil rights groups such as SNCC had learned, it could be difficult for activist groups to get news coverage because they were not considered legitimate newsmakers. Staging an event at which members were arrested was certainly one way to get coverage, but in itself, that did not necessarily accomplish much. The civil rights groups had an advantage over the antiwar groups in that they were able to align their events with their message. Anyone hearing that a black man was arrested for the simple act of sitting at a lunch counter and expecting to be served would understand the message: blacks wanted equal rights. But staging a sit-in at a university president's office and getting arrested for it, as the antiwar protesters did, would not have the same effect. The message—that the Vietnam War was wrong for a number of reasons—was lost. To get that message out, antiwar groups needed reporters willing to do more in-depth research into their cause.

Students for a Democratic Society got that chance in 1968. In one of their columns, syndicated columnists Rowland Evans and Robert Novak accused SDS of organizing a national draft-dodging campaign for the purpose of sabotaging the war effort. The day before the column ran in newspapers such as the *New York Herald Tribune* and the *Washington Post,* Senator Thomas Dodd of the Senate Internal Security Subcommittee released a report that claimed the antiwar movement had been taken over by Communists. The Evans and Novak column seemed to confirm the report. Suddenly, the SDS found itself the subject of media attention. SDS leaders responded by issuing press releases and holding press conferences in which they used attacks on their group to attack the war itself.[180] Evans and Novak had unwittingly made SDS a newsmaker, and SDS used that opportunity to its advantage.

As more voices joined the criticism of the war effort in the media, the Johnson administration increasingly appeared to be suffering from a credibility gap. The reality of what was happening on the ground in Vietnam did not reflect the official account from the president. And the greater the gap, the more the media investigated. People lost confidence in Johnson, and in 1968, he announced that he would not seek reelection. It had been a long four years from his winning campaign against Barry Goldwater in 1964.

Goldwater's television planning during that campaign suggested that the advice of professional communicators, if sought, was not relied on by the Republican camp. Ironically, it was the Democrats who had learned the lessons from Eisenhower's 1952 and 1956 campaigns and who parlayed that information into a winning campaign strategy for Johnson. Nixon's people realized that their candidate had lost the 1960 campaign because he had not understood that politics had changed, but apparently, they did not share that insight with the Goldwater camp.[181]

Johnson hired the New York ad agency Doyle Dane Bernbach (DDB) for the campaign. The agency had never handled a political campaign before, but that was not seen as a detriment. By that point, it was clear that voters did not vote for a president but rather accepted him or, to use marketing terms, bought him. Therefore, a high-profile and expensive agency such as DDB was considered necessary. From voter formation research and national opinion surveys, DDB decided the best strategy was for Johnson to take the offensive and come out strong against Goldwater and the Republicans, forcing them to be on the defensive.[182]

DDB was used again in the 1968 campaign. Hubert Humphrey hired the agency for the primaries. The account was given to Arie Kopelman, a young man who was known for his specialty packaging for products such as Joy, Bold, and Zest. Kopelman treated the campaign as a product launch. Fifty-seven people worked on the account, plus twenty media planners. A computer was used to determine the placement of television ads by calculating rotation patterns, or the value of repeating certain ads in a market for so many days after originally airing.[183]

The Nixon camp also drew heavily on the latest techniques of the advertising industry. When adman Rosser Reeves created a television ad for Eisenhower in 1952, there was some discussion in the media about the merits of marketing a presidential candidate like a bar of soap, but by 1968, that was an acknowledged practice. Nixon's advertising people were told to reach every voter in the United States who owned a television or radio. The focus was on television because it was believed that the print media were irrelevant.[184]

But unlike their counterparts in the Humphrey camp, who relied on advertising alone, the Nixon people also turned to public relations, and pseudo events became a prominent feature of the campaign. Television was vital because it reached more people than newspapers did; therefore, public events were held simply for the purpose of providing television with something to report. Historian Daniel Boorstin was the first to call such staged events pseudo events. The underlying feature of a pseudo event is that it has no purpose but media coverage.[185] Nixon's people ensured that each of his days contained such an event. And these events were completely staged, right down to having the audience told when to laugh and when to applaud. Another feature of the Nixon campaign was the use of computers that were programmed with the candidate's positions on sixty-seven public issues. People could go into his campaign offices, ask a question into a tape recorder, and get a computer-generated printout of Nixon's response, signed by a signature machine.[186]

Melvyn Bloom suggested that Nixon's advisers in the 1968 campaign represented a new breed of political consultant. These consultants were public relations practitioners first. As such, they used a broader repertoire of tactics, including polls, pseudo events, direct mail, and advertisements, in behalf of their client than did the advertising agencies, which relied on their marketing skills to promote politicians. The focus of the political PR consultants was on having their client appear to interact with voters, such that voters would come to feel they had a relationship with the candidate. As a result, polls and opinion surveys became important to the process of determining how voters were reacting to the candidate's image.[187]

While public relations was making headway in the political realm, it was also gaining ground in the corporate sector. Big business had become an accepted part of the American economy by the 1960s, but a number of ethical breaches, including price fixing and conflicts of interest, were committed by some well-known and established companies at the end of the fifties and threatened to revive hostilities toward business.[188] At least one journalist noted the irony of those falls from grace. Public relations practitioners had "engineered" the image of Westinghouse, personified by the actress and consumer advocate Betty Furness, as "warm and vibrant." Now, however, several of its executives had been indicted for committing the not so warm and vibrant act of conspiring to violate the antitrust laws. Similarly, the *Saturday Review* had recognized the General Electric Company (GE) for its outstanding public relations campaign titled "Progress Is Our Most Important Product." But, of course, that was before the allegations of conflicts of interest on the part of GE's executives.[189]

By 1966, there was evidence that major corporations were paying serious attention to public relations, at least in the short term. A survey of the chief executive officers (CEOs) of *Fortune*'s 750 largest companies revealed that 31 percent of them gave their person in charge of PR a part in policy decision making. Eighty-four of the companies had a separate public relations department, with the principal functions involving press relations, community relations, and annual report preparation. The downside was that the CEOs saw PR as vital in the near term, especially for publicity, but did not consider their public relations people competent to make a contribution regarding long-term planning and influencing public opinion.[190] A survey of public relations practitioners a year earlier supported those findings. Sixty-seven percent of the respondents said they were responsible for product publicity, and 96 percent said that the preparation and distribution of news releases was their number one job.[191]

Churning out press releases did not guarantee coverage, of course. A 1965 edition of a standard PR textbook cited research indicating that 74 news releases out of 339 received by the city desk of a typical daily newspaper (or 22 percent) were used; 32 of them were used exactly as received. Of the nonwire, nonsyndicated news content of the *Milwaukee Sentinel,* 30 percent was based on news releases. At the *Milwaukee Journal,* the proportion was 24 percent, and at the Wisconsin state AP wire, it was 12 percent. The president of the Public Relations Society of America, J. Carroll Bateman, found these statistics to be "surprisingly large" and indicative of how indispensable PR practitioners had become both to their clients and to the mass media.[192]

As the decade wore on, however, and activist groups became more adept at using pressure tactics to achieve their goals, corporations came to see the need for public relations practitioners to advise them on dealing with such groups. Corporate leaders began to realize they needed more than just publicity. As Philip Lesly, a public relations practitioner, observed, "No stunt will solve a company's anti-trust problems, its Negro hiring policies, its inability to attract future executives, or the impression that its products are shoddy."[193]

FOUR

POWER TO THE PEOPLE

In 1969, *Newsweek* described a storm "brewing in the minds of millions of Americans": "It is small now, a cloud no bigger than a vague dissatisfaction, but it may swirl up angrily on the horizon for American business management."[194] The storm was the consumer movement, and *Newsweek* was right, for it did hit businesses hard. In 1969, 58 percent of Americans surveyed agreed that business achieved "a good balance between profits and service." A year later, public support for that statement had dropped to 29 percent, with 46 percent agreeing that "big business is dangerous to our way of life," an increase of 18 percent in five years. And 68 percent believed that new federal laws were needed to protect the consumer.[195] But it was not just businesses that suffered from declining public support. Vietnam, Watergate, and inflation, among other factors in the early 1970s, caused consumers to lose faith in all institutions, including government, education, and journalism.

Although institutions felt the effects of consumerism most strongly in the 1970s, the movement itself had its roots in the late 1950s. In 1957, Vance Packard wrote *The Hidden Persuaders,* an exposé of the advertising and marketing industries.[196] In disclosing the techniques of depth interviews and motivational analyses employed by advertisers and marketers to fuel consumption, Packard suggested that consumers were being used and manipulated by big business. John Kenneth Galbraith's *Affluent Society* furthered and reinforced the sentiment, arguing that too much attention had been paid to the private sector of the economy and not enough to the public sector.[197] But it was President John F. Kennedy who really crystallized the discussion. On March 15, 1962, he sent a message to Congress that he wanted legislative action taken to protect consumers. He called for a consumer bill of rights that included the rights to be safe, to be informed, to choose, and to be heard. Kennedy noted that consumers were the only group in the economy that did not have a lobbyist. He intended to become that lobbyist because, he declared, "consumers, by definition, include us all."[198] And with that, he launched the third wave of the consumer movement in the twentieth century.[199]

Like the first wave in the Progressive Era, this one was fueled by muckraking journalism. Rachel Carson would probably not have called herself a muckraker, but her *Silent Spring* is a work in the muckraking tradition. Serialized in June 1962 over three issues of the *New Yorker* magazine and then published in book form three months later, *Silent Spring* took on the chemical industry and agribusiness, academic researchers, and the government for their failure to adequately research the harmful effects of pesticides. Although the book is considered to have launched the environmental movement, conservation, as it was then called, already had proponents. As media historian Priscilla Coit Murphy so ably pointed out, Carson did not start the movement, but her book propelled the discussion about the environment onto the media agenda and into the consciousness of the general public in an unprecedented way.[200]

Carson's purpose in writing the book was to inform the public and to mobilize her readers into taking action. She believed people had a right to know what was going on with pesticides, but even more than that, she wanted them to do something about it. Thus, her book was not balanced in the journalistic sense; she did not present the chemical industry's view, for example. She used emotional appeals (through a fable about a town with a silent spring because there were no birds) and rational appeals (through scientific data) to persuade her audience to take a stand. The strength of her argument can be seen in both the success of the book in terms of sales and the reaction of those she pilloried in its pages.

One chemical company tried to stop publication of the third installment in the *New Yorker* series. When that failed, the company attempted to intimidate the book's publisher, Houghton Mifflin, into not publishing. That effort, too, failed. At that point, the chemical industry as a whole took an aggressive stance to discredit Carson and her information. According to Murphy, the industry, through the National Agricultural Chemicals Association (NACA), launched a public relations effort, armed with a budget of $250,000. For one official at Monsanto, a prominent chemical company, it was "an opportunity to wield our public relations power."[201] Not everyone, however, thought public relations was the solution. An editorial in an industry trade publication asked, "Have our modern public relationship techniques made mutes or sissies out of all our business executives?"[202] The answer was no, judging by the comment from the Manufacturing Chemists Association's PR director, who said, "If we don't take charge now, we're going to be buried, pure and simple."[203]

Why such fear of just one book? Perhaps it was because businesses were starting to sense a shift in public attitude. There were, of course, the growing civil rights movement and other signs of emerging social activism in the first years of the decade, which made them nervous. There were also signs that President Kennedy might be more open to regulating business than Eisenhower had been. No doubt, Kennedy's call for a consumer bill of rights just three months before Carson's work appeared in the *New Yorker* did not help. Thus, the threat of increased regulation was probably the industry's greatest fear, warranting an aggressive and quick response.

Those preparing the chemical industry's response knew the *New Yorker* was an influential magazine that was read by others in the media. They also knew that the major newspapers and magazines would review a best-selling book, as *Silent Spring* would presumably be. As Murphy remarked, "From the start, Carson's opposition sought to match if not outdistance the reach provided by the book form and compounded somewhat by its appearance in a national magazine."[204] The goal was to gain the media's attention and then to shape its treatment of the book. One approach was to focus on the benefits of pesticides and to make clear that research was an ongoing process. The second approach was to attack Carson's credibility.

To get the message out about the positive side of pesticides, the industry used traditional PR techniques, distributing articles, fact sheets, reprints, policy statements, and direct mail pieces to the media and those sympathetic to its view. As a result, articles about the safe use of pesticides starting appearing in the mainstream press in the summer of 1962. The articles did not mention *Silent Spring,* nor were they identified as having come from the chemical industry. However, they were similar enough to the ones contained in the direct mail packages sent out by the industry, according to Murphy, to suggest that they may well have been influenced by those efforts.[205]

The industry's spokesperson, Robert White-Stevens, went on a national lecture tour between the summer of 1962, just after the *New Yorker* articles appeared, and June 1963, when the issue faded from the media's agenda. Frederick J. Stare, head of the nutrition program at the Harvard School of Public Health, became the unofficial spokesperson for agribusiness. And whenever White-Stevens or Stare gave a lecture or a speech, the industry's PR practitioners made sure the event was covered in the media.[206]

More indirect ways of influencing and managing the media were also used. Individual and group letter-writing campaigns were organized to target local and national government officials and editorial pages in local newspapers to create the impression that Carson did not have popular support. Even subtler was the use of the concept of objectivity to shape the media's reporting on the book. As indicated earlier, Carson did not include opposing views in her book. The work was, spokespeople for the chemical industry cried, a one-sided attack on pesticides and therefore unbalanced and unfair. Their purpose in responding was simply to get the other side out so that the public could evaluate the whole issue. That approach, of course, played into journalism's desire for objectivity.[207] By that point, objectivity had come to mean fairness and balance in reporting. Journalists had learned their lesson after reporting McCarthy's biased attacks in the early 1950s. Reporting just McCarthy's comments was not fair, journalists soon realized, nor did the reports give McCarthy's victims an opportunity to respond. Thus, fairness and balance, in the sense of presenting both sides of a story, came to be the hallmarks of objectivity. Including the chemical industry's views in a story about *Silent Spring* just seemed to reflect good journalistic standards, exactly as the industry hoped it would.

The other strategy used by the chemical industry, in addition to promoting the positive side of pesticides, was to discredit Carson by questioning her credentials, her scientific data, and her motives. The challenge to her science and arguments ensured that coverage of the issue would continue because now there was a real debate for the press to cover.[208] Monsanto ran a parody of Carson's fable in its corporate magazine. Titled "The Desolate Year," it told the story of what would happen if no pesticides at all were used. Monsanto's PR department widely distributed reprints to editors and syndicated columnists. The parody was an effective tool. *PR News,* a trade publication for the public relations industry, described Carson's writing as "hysterical, dangerous extremism" but Monsanto's parody as "admirable, persuasive prose."[209] Another PR executive, in a speech to businesspeople on an unrelated topic, said he agreed with the scientists that her book was full of exaggeration.[210]

While *Silent Spring* became a media symbol for environmentalism, the debate between Carson and the chemical industry largely faded from the public agenda after May 1963 and the release of the president's Science Advising Committee's report on pesticide abuse. Kennedy had directed the committee to look into the matter after reading Carson's articles in the *New Yorker.* The report essentially vindicated Carson, and the media declared her the winner of the debate, though she had for the most part stayed out of the media spotlight and above the fray.[211]

Carson's *Silent Spring* touched off a public discussion about the use of pesticides and raised public awareness of the possibility that the U.S. Department of Agriculture (USDA) was not taking consumers' health and welfare into consideration. The book was in the tradition of the Progressive Era muckraking in that it sought to inform and mobilize the citizenry with regard to a social problem. In time, *Silent Spring* receded from the public agenda, but the issue of the environment did not. It continued to grow in importance over the next few decades, but it did not grab consumers' attention quite the way the issue of automobile safety did. Ralph Nader's 1965 book, *Unsafe at Any Speed: The Designed-In Dangers of the American Automobile,* and his subsequent use of the media to leverage his influence accelerated the consumer movement, making it a force with which to be reckoned.[212]

In the early 1960s, it was commonly believed in the automobile industry and among experts that cars were as safe as they could be made. If accidents occurred, it was attributed to human error, not a flaw in the engineering or design of an automobile. Justin Martin, in his biography of Nader, summed up the sentiment of the time: "Cars don't kill people, people do."[213] And they were killing them to the tune of almost fifty thousand per year by the mid-1960s, with injuries suffered in automobile accidents reaching four million. Senator Abraham Ribicoff (D-Conn.), chairman of the Subcommittee on Executive Reorganization of the Committee on Government Operations, which was tasked with researching issues of potential interest to senators, thought auto safety might be something his subcommittee could explore. When he suggested the topic to his aides, one contacted Nader.[214]

Nader was concerned about "body rights" or the right not to be harmed physically by a product. He was one of the few people who did not buy the argument that automobiles could not be made safer, and he had written an article for the *Nation* in 1963 claiming that some automobiles were more likely to be involved in accidents than others.[215] Although that article generated no further interest about the topic among the media, he had made a name for himself around Washington as an expert in auto safety by 1965. He agreed to help Ribicoff's aides with their investigation, and in the summer of 1965, the senator officially announced that he would be holding hearings to look into the "fantastic carnage" on America's highways.[216]

At the time, Nader was already working on his book, which was finally published in November 1965 by a small publishing house. In *Unsafe at Any Speed,* he argued that automobile manufacturers chose style over safety because of financial considerations. Like Carson before him, Nader also questioned the impartiality of university researchers, but unlike Carson, he added the press to his list of accomplices. It was normal practice then not to identify the makes of automobiles involved in accidents. Thus, university studies into crashes would indicate the number of fatal auto accidents, for instance, but not whether one make was involved in a greater share of those accidents. Similarly, newspapers would not identify makes or models in accidents, which meant, as Nader saw it, that the public had no way of independently or even anecdotally assessing the relative safety of vehicles. He argued again that the whole thing was a matter of finances. Automobile manufacturers were funding the university research, and automobile dealers were heavy advertisers in newspapers. Nader devoted an entire chapter to the Chevrolet Corvair because, according to him, the car's design made it prone to flip even at low speeds. To support his contention, he cited the number of lawsuits against General Motors (GM) for injuries or deaths as a result of rollovers involving Corvairs.[217]

At first, the publisher had trouble generating media attention, and sales of the book were low. *Life* magazine chose not to review the book, but the *San Francisco Chronicle, Scientific American,* and *Book Week* did review it and positively. In fact, the *Chronicle* called it the *Silent Spring* of the auto industry. But those reviews alone were not enough to make the book newsworthy. Then a Broadway agent suggested a publicity stunt. The publisher called a press conference at Detroit's Sheraton Cadillac Hotel, deliberately picking the hotel because of its name, and sent telegraphs inviting the heads of the major American automobile makers. The conference was held on January 6, 1966, and attracted many reporters. Not surprisingly, none of the automakers were represented. Given Nader's criticism of the press, in which he suggested that the wall between the business and editorial sides of newspapers either broke down or did not exist when it came to the auto industry, the reporters in attendance were rather hostile. But Nader acquitted himself well and showed a talent for dealing with the media, although no further coverage came as a result of the press conference.[218]

Now that Nader was a published author, Ribicoff could call him as an expert to testify at the subcommittee hearings on auto safety, which Nader did on February 10, 1966. Since his book was not generating sales or media attention, most automakers did not feel threatened and did not mount an aggressive response, as the chemical industry had for Carson's book. But GM chose to respond anyway. Unfortunately for GM, the company did not recognize the value of public relations and opted instead to use intimidation and harassment to shut down Nader. The result was the media coverage and attention GM had hoped to avoid.[219]

Shortly before Nader testified in front of Ribicoff's subcommittee, he started receiving mysterious phone calls. Then, on the day of his testimony, he became convinced he was being followed. He took his concerns to a *Washington Post* journalist he thought would be sympathetic, and on February 13, 1966, the *Post* ran a story under the headline CAR SAFETY CRITIC NADER REPORTS BEING "TAILED."[220] Shortly thereafter, Nader's friends let him know that a private investigator had been asking questions about him. The investigator claimed he was simply checking references for a company that wanted to offer Nader a job. But the kinds of questions he asked, especially those about Nader's personal life (including his drinking habits, sex life, and driving record), made the friends suspicious. Nader took this information to journalist James Ridgeway of the *New Republic*. Ridgeway's story on March 4, 1966, set off a media firestorm. Within hours, all of the major metropolitan daily newspapers were covering the story. Ford, Chrysler, and American Motors all issued official denials, but GM remained strangely silent. Late on the evening of March 9, 1966, five days after Ridgeway's story appeared, GM issued a press release that said its general counsel had initiated a routine investigation to determine whether Nader was involved in the Corvair lawsuits. In Ribicoff's eyes, the so-called routine investigation was nothing short of harassment of a congressional witness. He ordered GM's CEO, the general counsel, and the private investigator to appear before the subcommittee on March 22 to explain their actions.[221]

At the March hearing, GM's CEO argued that the company was concerned Nader had something to do with the Corvair lawsuits and was using the information he gleaned in those cases contemporaneously in a book. Such behavior, the CEO argued, was unethical and needed to be reported to the American Bar Association (ABA). But the subcommittee did not buy that argument. The investigator had looked too deeply into Nader's personal life for this simply to be a question of ethics. When Nader testified, he said he had nothing to do with the Corvair lawsuits; further, he suggested that the fact GM thought otherwise showed how out of touch its executives were. Striking a blow at GM and, by extension, at corporate America, he said, "General Motors executives continue to be blinded by their own corporate mirror-image that it's 'the buck' that moves the man. They simply cannot understand that the prevention of cruelty to humans can be a sufficient motivation for one endeavoring to obtain the manufacture of safer cars."[222] He continued with a statement that encapsulated what many consumers were feeling: "People sitting in executive suites can make remote decisions which will someday result in tremen-

dous carnage, and because they are remote in time and space between their decision and the consequences of that decision, there
is no accountability."[223]

The effect of the day's events was swift and sure. That evening,
Nader was on every network news show, and the next morning,
every major newspaper carried the story on the front page. Public
opinion had been galvanized around auto safety almost overnight.
President Johnson declared the week of May 15 National Transportation Week.[224]

At first, the automakers thought the whole thing would blow
over, and they chose not to respond publicly. But then, Ribicoff
held a news conference to announce the results of the data on auto
defects he had sought at Nader's urging from the automakers. The
results, as Nader's biographer Martin noted, were staggering. Between 1960 and 1966, there were 426 recall campaigns involving
8.7 million cars, or one out of every five. The sheer size of the
problem was all the more surprising because the public was rarely
told about any recall campaign. The auto company would quietly
tell a dealership to fix the problem when an owner happened to
drop by the premises. Suddenly faced with the imminent threat of
legislation, the automakers reacted. They hired Lloyd Cutler, a
lawyer and lobbyist, to make the best of a bad situation. But it was
too little, too late. On September 9, 1966, President Johnson
signed the National Highway Safety Act, which created the National Highway Safety Bureau and forced the automakers to adopt
certain safety features on all new automobiles sold after January 31,
1968.[225]

In just ten months from the publication of his book, Nader had
managed to get major legislation on auto safety passed, a remark-
able feat—but one in which he was aided by GM's response, the
media, and President Johnson. The media had essentially ignored

Nader and the issue of auto safety and would have continued to do so, no doubt, had it not been for GM's actions. Suddenly, Nader was newsworthy. With the media now following the story, the public became aware of his investigations. Automobile safety became a hot topic and politically viable. For his part, Johnson had been mired down by Vietnam and was unable to accomplish much in terms of domestic policy. But consumer legislation was relatively easy to pass. Few politicians were willing to run the risk of alienating the electorate by voting against consumer protection legislation. And such legislation was relatively inexpensive to enact: it called for some governmental oversight, but the real costs were borne by the offending companies. Johnson jumped at the chance to pick up some political capital, declaring 1966 the Year of the Consumer.[226]

Nader moved on from the issue of auto safety to uninspected meat, which resulted in passage of the Wholesale Meat Act of 1967. He also assisted in getting passed the Natural Gas Pipeline Safety Act, the Wholesale Poultry Act, and the Radiation Control for Health and Safety Act.[227] According to Martin, Nader's heyday was from 1969 to 1976, and the key to his success was his relationships with the press and Congress. Nader was an avid student of the media, reading six newspapers each day. He cultivated print reporters, providing his home telephone number to a select few and making himself available to reporters for interviews on weekends and slow news days. He had clearly established his credibility and was sought out by reporters for quotes on consumer issues. He also understood the personal preferences of the reporters, giving complete stories to some and tips to those he knew would do their own investigating.[228]

Although newspapers such as the *New York Times* and the *Washington Post* did their own investigative work in those days, most newspapers had neither the staff nor the money to send reporters out to investigate. For those journalists who could not do investigative reporting, writing up a Nader report gave them a sense of being part of the process. They were investigative reporters vicariously through Nader; he had done the legwork for them. Thus, he gave reporters what they needed—well-researched, newsworthy stories (often based on official documentation), access to a credible source, and colorful quotes. For example, in 1969, he analyzed the fat content of commercially sold hamburgers and hot dogs. He found that labels indicated a lower fat content than what was actually present. At a press conference announcing the results, he criticized the companies for selling "fatfurters" and "shamburgers." The media used the terms repeatedly in their coverage.[229]

As Nader's interests in a wide variety of corporate behaviors grew, he found he could not do all the investigative work alone and sought the help of some young people, who became known as Nader's Raiders. Their first project was taking on the Federal Trade Commission (FTC), an agency that had gained a reputation for deference to big business. Nader thought the FTC was not doing enough to protect consumers from false and misleading advertising. The resulting report on the FTC led President Nixon, in 1969, to ask the American Bar Association to conduct its own independent investigation of the agency. When the results of the ABA investigation matched those of Nader's Raiders, the FTC chairman stepped down, and Nixon appointed Caspar Weinberger in January 1970 to take over the FTC and revitalize it.[230]

Also in 1969, Nader set up the Center for the Study of Responsive Law. Through the center, lawsuits were brought against companies for a variety of corporate missteps, forcing businesses to change their behaviors and become more socially responsible.

Nader had empowered young people to seek social reform through the courts and Congress but also through innovative means. Two young law students approached him about assisting them with a plan they had in mind. They each had purchased stock in General Motors. Their plan was to attend the annual shareholders meeting and demand that GM change its ways. Although they were not successful, shareholder activism became increasingly important and more effective over the next few decades.[231] Of course, Nader had also shown his followers how to use the media.[232]

The media were not only useful for getting the story out, though. On occasion, they were on the receiving end of the consumer movement's thrusts. A twenty-nine-year-old lawyer by the name of John F. Branzhaf III took a "citizen's complaint" to the Federal Communications Commission in 1969, demanding that television stations provide free airtime for antismoking messages. The television and tobacco industries were stunned when the FCC agreed. Invigorated by his victory, Branzhaf formed a pressure group and antismoking lobby. At George Mason University, he taught a law course on unfair trade practices, and his students became known as Branzhaf's Bandits. Their motto was "Sue the Bastards."[233]

The consumer movement sparked by Nader was different from the other movements of the 1960s in two important ways. For one, Nader's young people and later Branzhaf's were working within the system to bring about change, unlike their counterparts in groups such as the Students for a Democratic Society, who used demonstrations and protests to force change from the outside. Working within the system meant the consumer activists did not have to fight as hard to get media coverage because reporters routinely covered aspects of the system, such as the courts. And being within the system, those activists had greater credibility from the outset than did their more militant counterparts. Beyond that, the consumer movement reached a broader cross section of society than the other movements. Illinois Bell's vice president of public relations called those in the consumer movement antibusiness activists and said their group consisted of a "weird coalition." He noted that not only were there liberals, idealists, Democrats, and Republicans but also that "we are quite likely to see our wives or our children marching along with those who believe there is something drastically wrong with the way business is being run."[234] Consumerism, then, impacted everyone, which made it useful to journalists and to legislators.

The tangible result of the consumer movement was that by 1970, every state had consumer protection laws in place and forty-three had consumer protection agencies. In the entire decade of the 1960s, 20 major pieces of consumer legislation were passed at the federal level. But in the first two years of the seventies, more than 150 consumer bills were introduced.[235] The effects were wide-ranging, but many of the bills involved false or misleading advertising. The Federal Trade Commission recommended counteradvertising, that is, advertising that would rebut controversial product claims made in commercials and that would be run on television and radio for free. The Food and Drug Administration (FDA) put increased pressure on companies that made questionable advertising claims about over-the-counter drugs. Banks and mortgage companies were required to adhere to truth-in-lending practices, by which consumers were to be told the real cost of a loan up front, and marketers were forced to include more information on product labels.[236]

The initial response of businesses to the developing consumer movement was defensive. "There ought to be a law" had become a national slogan, resulting in too many laws being passed needlessly, business leaders felt.[237] Some argued that, worse than not being needed, consumer protection laws violated the American way of doing business. Laws deprived consumers of their freedom of choice and interfered in the workings of the marketplace. Others said that businesses already acted in the public interest, including giving millions of dollars a year to higher education and charities. One individual was even indignant that consumers would criticize business. "I shall not apologize for our country's wealth or the pursuit of the profit motive," an advertising executive cried. "Business has never made rich a man who could not produce something the public wants. And business *knows* what consumers want. Consumer goods businesses spend millions each year to find out."[238]

The answer to the antibusiness sentiment, it was suggested by business leaders and public relations practitioners alike early on, was greater communication in order to create "consumer understanding and appreciation of business efforts in consumer protection."[239] Such thinking was a throwback to an earlier time, however, when PR was used simply to inform the public about business policies. According to this view, information equaled understanding and acceptance. But that position missed the point of consumerism. Consumers did not really care how much it cost to produce a product or how much a business had contributed philanthropically; what they wanted was a business that produced a quality product in a socially responsible manner. "We are operating in a new climate where the *demand* for quality is coupled with a far higher *expectation* of quality," a Ford Motor Company executive told a group of quality control experts in February 1970.[240]

But as the 1960s drew to a close, there were signs that some public relations practitioners recognized times had changed and so had their roles. For example, there was a growing recognition that businesses needed to take into consideration a broader array of publics than just employees, customers, and shareholders. A business's consumers included everyone. Moreover, it was now understood that in addition to the role of informing the public about businesses policies, the PR practitioner should keep management informed about social trends and opinions.[241] That added role reflected the difference between publicity and public relations, which two journalism professors summed up in simple terms: "A publicity office is called in to sell a policy to the public. A public relations office represents the public while the policy is being debated, and then explains the policy and the reasoning behind it to the public."[242]

Some even saw the 1970s as a heady time for public relations, calling the decade "the dawning of the age of communications."[243] The reason was that businesses were operating in an increasingly fragmented and contentious environment. It was argued that traditional advertising and promotional techniques, tied as they were to sales and therefore focused on consumers, were not flexible enough to handle the many disparate groups with which businesses were now concerned. Public relations practitioners, who were used to taking into consideration many publics at once, were more skillful at recognizing and responding to changes in public attitudes. There was still a place for advertising and promotion, but those activities should be under the supervision of a PR practitioner.[244]

Consolidation of the advertising and public relations functions started among major corporations in the early 1970s. The *Gallagher Report,* a communications newsletter, stated in August 1972 that corporate executives were merging the functions to allow PR practitioners to approve advertising claims. The report cited General Motors as an example of a company that had taken steps to consolidate these functions. The reasons given were consumerism and increased regulation.[245]

Clearly, public relations had become more professionalized and more institutionalized by the 1970s. In the 1950s, PR involved primarily publicity—getting the corporate message (most often about products as opposed to policy) to the public. But in 1963, the Securities and Exchange Commission (SEC) held hearings into the use of hyperbole in news releases to tout the benefits of a company's stock, issuing an indictment of the practice on the part of public relations agencies at the conclusion of the hearings. The hearings were followed in 1965 by the SEC lawsuit against the Texas Gulf Sulphur mining company. The case arose from a press release issued by the company, on April 12, 1964, to squelch rumors that it had found "one of the wealthiest bodies of copper, zinc, and silver ever discovered." The SEC contended that the release had misled investors even though the company's officers issued it with good intentions and had not profited from it, a novel position for the time. As a result of the SEC's actions in the early 1960s, PR practitioners gained greater access to upper management and the decision-making process.[246] Regardless of the gains in the sixties, one practitioner, looking back on the decade and the consumer movement from the vantage point of 1972, said, "Empirical evidence suggests that public relations either was not positioned to warn and advise countermeasures, was not capable, or—sadly—was quite ignored in top management strategy councils."[247] But in the seventies, the public relations literature began focusing more on planning and evaluation, suggesting that the practice was moving toward even greater professionalization and a standardization of approach. While the industry may not have responded well to the consumerism of the 1960s, it was, in many ways, poised to be called on by businesses in the 1970s to go on the offensive in an effort to stem the rising tide of dissatisfaction.

Although there were now approximately one hundred thousand individuals who classified themselves as PR practitioners, only seven thousand belonged to the Public Relations Society of America. PRSA created a study group on consumer relations in the early 1970s, a recognition of the effect consumerism was having on businesses and of the fact that public relations would be called on to play a role in dealing with its impact. The purpose of the group was to provide practitioners with information on the latest developments and trends in consumerism and thus better equip them to advise their clients.[248] Of course, keeping management informed about what consumer groups and government agencies were investigating so that it could respond more quickly was an ever more vital role for PR practitioners.

Despite the growing number of regulations and laws arising from consumerism, businesses tended not to learn from the mistakes of others. They failed to recognize the early warning signs that would have allowed them to address issues and make changes before those issues became contentious.[249] One executive's comment reflected the situation: "I don't understand it. I'm doing the very same things now that I did in the early 1960s. Yet, then, I was applauded as an enlightened and progressive business statesman; now I'm vilified as a stubborn defender of the status quo."[250] But for one PR practitioner, it was not so much that business failed to heed the warnings or did not understand how things had changed but that the top executive was not getting the right information in the first place. "He is fully prepared with production records, personnel reports, financial records, sales charts and profit figures," Hale Nelson said. "What he doesn't get is adequate *socio-political* data."[251]

Adequate trend information would allow corporate executives to react more quickly and avoid potentially reputation-damaging news coverage and legislation. In 1975 in the *Harvard Business Review*, Joseph Nolan set out the life cycle of an issue.[252] An issue, he wrote, moved from the dormant phase when it was recognized by only a few to the opinion development phase in which it garnered media coverage and became a topic of conversation; then it proceeded to the institutional action phase, which occurred when Congress, the state legislatures, and the courts got involved. The problem was that in the past, corporations had not seen any need for a response until the issue reached the last stage. Citing environmentalism and consumerism as examples, Nolan noted how issues could be in the dormant phase for a long time but be propelled quickly into the opinion development and then the institutional action phases by a triggering event, as the publication of Carson's *Silent Spring* or Nader's *Unsafe at Any Speed* proved to be. Had the auto industry recognized there was a safety problem, for instance, they could and should have made safety a priority before it became a national issue. Although Nolan recognized that public relations was the natural corporate function to watch out for developing issues, he also admitted that many PR practitioners were reluctant to speak out to their CEOs. Few practitioners wanted to tell those in upper management that they had to change corporate behavior.

The approach that Nolan was describing became a strategic focus of businesses in the second half of the 1970s. W. Howard

Chase is credited both with coining the term *issues management,* on April 15, 1976 (with the first issue of his newsletter, *Corporate Public Issues and Their Management*), and with proposing a model for the management of issues. The first two companies to adopt a formalized process for issues management were Allstate Insurance Company and Stauffer Chemical Company in 1977. Both the insurance and chemical industries had been subject to investigation and regulation as a result of the consumer movement, and they probably felt a need to take a proactive stance.[253]

Not all companies realized the importance of issues management, although all suffered from a decline in public support in the seventies. Opinion Research Corporation reported in 1972 that "big corporations face the worst attitude climate in a decade."[254] A Louis Harris study in February 1972 for *Life* magazine noted that "the image of industry continues to deteriorate."[255] In fact, public trust in major companies had fallen to an all-time low of 19 percent by 1975.[256]

One reason for the antibusiness sentiment was the more intense media coverage of business. In a 1975 study, more than two-thirds of the business editors surveyed said that general interest in financial and business news had increased substantially in the previous ten years. The cause appeared to be, in part, the economy. Between 1965 and 1970, the economy boomed, encouraging ten million new investors to enter the stock market. But in 1970, "the froth evaporated," and the total number of shareholders started to decline. Vietnam, escalating oil prices, the Watergate scandal, budget deficits, and grain, sugar, and paper shortages caused confusion and concern among Americans. By 1973, the public was declaring the economy the most serious problem the nation faced. In 1974, inflation climbed to double-digit levels and the most serious recession since the Depression started.[257] The result was a greater interest in business and financial news—and not just at the national level.

A 1975 study of business editors found that while 22 percent reported a substantial increase in their coverage of the stock market, 50 percent said they had significantly expanded their coverage of local businesses. As one editor put it, "People become bored reading about the titans of industry. They want to know why Joe was laid off from the local widget plant, and why the natural gas company is increasing its rates by yet another 20 percent."[258] Television networks also upped their coverage of economic news, recognizing its importance to their viewers.[259]

Although the economy was obviously a factor in the increased attention paid to business news, so was Nader, with his exposés of business practices and the consumer activists he influenced. One in three business editors responding to the 1975 study said that investigative reporting of businesses had substantially increased, and more than half of those said that it had doubled since 1965, the year of Nader's book. The bad behavior on the part of businesses, involving anything from faulty products to dirty restaurant kitchens, as disclosed by Nader and others convinced business editors of large newspapers they had a responsibility to their readers to find out what businesses in their own community were doing behind closed doors.

The news media had become very powerful through the course of the 1960s and 1970s. They could create heroes or villains virtually overnight or take an issue and put it on the public's agenda in the same short amount of time.[260] Thus, when they turned their attention to business, looking at it in a more skeptical and analytical way, an adversarial relationship developed between the media and business.[261] The press saw its purpose in reporting on business and the economy as providing individuals with accurate information about what was significant to them. But journalists were often prevented from gaining access to such information because businesses refused to be open, despite the growing demand for openness and disclosure. Many business leaders still felt that information about the workings of their companies should stay private. When they did open up, they tended to put out a press release without providing the opportunity for reporters to have their questions answered except through a PR department that was not authorized to go beyond the parameters of the release itself.[262]

On the rare occasion when reporters were allowed to interview the CEO of a company, the interview was typically short and the CEO often unprepared to answer questions. That situation always seemed to lead to charges that the CEO had been misquoted.[263] Reporters also complained that corporations attempted to downplay bad news by deliberately timing the release of their news. A press release issued very early in the morning might get lost in the day's news, or one issued late in the day might prevent reporters from digging deeper.[264]

For their part, business leaders had their own complaints about the media. It is true that executives were initially unsure how to respond to the mounting scrutiny from the press and that they seemed to take it personally. Some attempted to intimidate editors into not running a negative story by threatening to pull advertising dollars or claiming to be a personal friend of the publisher. Many charged that reporters were antibusiness because they reported only the bad corporate news and because they seemed to have adopted the consumer mind-set, always portraying corporations as villains and consumer activists as heroes.[265] And that was unfair, they argued.

Not surprisingly, editors disagreed that their reporters had any-thing against business, but some of them did acknowledge that business reporting had tended to take the consumers' side too readily. The press had allowed itself to be used by activist groups and others either by accepting leaks from them without checking out their stories and sources or by covering them because of their ability to stage pseudo events.[266] Staged events played well for tel-evision, of course, which has always had difficulty covering issues. Even the print media were moving toward greater coverage of people and personalities rather than issues, thanks to the success of *People* magazine and similar publications.[267] Activists received more media attention because they were more likely to be color-ful personalities who courted the press, whereas business leaders tended to shun the media and public attention. But it soon became apparent that hiding from reporters and trying to intimidate them were not effective strategies for dealing with the media.

By 1972 and continuing through the end of the decade, jour-nalists and public relations practitioners alike came to recognize that the CEO had to take responsibility for a business's public image.[268] It was up to the top executive to tell the corporation's story to the media in an effective way. As PR practitioner Robert J. Wood noted, the public wanted to hear directly from the person at the top if there was a business problem: issuing a statement or having a public relations practitioner serve as spokesperson was not enough.[269] But putting the top corporate executive in front of a reporter was not an easy thing to do. Cor-porate leaders had reached their positions because they tended to be focused on the internal workings of the business. Presumably, they were good at management and finances, but they often lacked effective communication skills. Many of them distrusted reporters and were afraid anything they said would be misconstrued. The result was that the interviews often did not go well.

To resolve the situation, PR practitioners began offering media training for the executives. The idea was to teach them how to answer reporters' questions such that the business's story was told in an informative and interesting way. That meant overcoming certain corporate tendencies. For example, some executives became wary when reporters pushed for more information in an interview, which meant their answers made it seem like they were hiding something. Others became impatient or angry with reporters. Another tendency was to be results-oriented and to talk only about achievements or final decisions. Reporters, by contrast, wanted to know about the process. How did the executive reach a particular decision? How was the company able to achieve high earnings? Reporters also needed to simplify what the executive may have seen as a very complex issue, and they typically preferred conflict to consensus, which went against the corporate mind-set.[270]

Part of the training, then, was teaching executives how to answer questions in a compelling fashion. Training also included teaching standard interviewing techniques so that the executive would know what to expect and be better able to manage an interview. Television interviews required more specific instruction, from what color tie to put on to where the individual should look. But most important, media training involved teaching executives how to relax with a reporter, to be seen as open and honest. There had been a prejudice against publicity seeking in the corporate world: it was deemed "unbecoming immodesty."[271] But the importance of serving as the corporate spokesperson and the necessity for training became clear to many CEOs by the end of the decade.

Having the chief executive become more visible was one way to counteract the negative publicity about businesses in the news. Another way was to use advertisements to clarify a business's position on a public policy issue.[272] In the 1970s, some business leaders were concluding that reporters were finding it more and more difficult to cover the complex issues of society within the time and space requirements of their medium. A tendency had developed to oversimplify and reduce everything to black and white. That predisposition was aided by consumer advocates, lobbyists, and political consultants who knew how to use the media—that is, they knew "what hot buttons to push" to generate headlines and advance their causes.[273] As one advertising executive observed, "Often, these newsmakers make their news at the expense of that easiest and most available of targets, the nameless and faceless American corporation. Oil profits are obscene, cars are unsafe at any speed, drugs are a chemical feast."[274] Buying advertising space was one way of getting accurate information out to the public about a corporation's position and giving the corporation an identity. A number of corporations used advocacy advertisements in the 1970s and beyond, but the most successful and best known of the advertising campaigns was that of Mobil Oil.

In 1970, the *New York Times* announced a redesign of its editorial pages. The regular *Times* columnists would be moved to the page opposite the editorial page (or the op-ed page). The op-ed page would also now include space for two opinion pieces daily, written by outside writers, and the lower right-hand quarter of the page would be advertising space, to be used by those who wanted to publish an opinion or commentary.[275] Mobil Oil's vice president of public affairs, Herbert Schmertz, recognized the opportunity the advertising space on the op-ed page provided and began a regular and consistent advertising campaign in January 1972 that would continue through the decade. Every Thursday, Mobil ran an ad in the space that had the look and tone of a traditional opinion piece. Schmertz has indicated that the campaign was in direct response to the media and what Mobil's management saw as "too many attempts by the media to control the agenda and make public policy."[276]

According to media historian Robert Kerr, Mobil ran 332 such ads between 1970 and 1980. Of those, 59.1 percent dealt with oil issues affecting the company, but the remainder dealt with other topics not directly related to Mobil. Kerr found that the most significant feature of the ads was how they "recurringly and forcefully equated the corporate role in democratic processes with the role of the individual citizen."[277] Eventually, the ads even included a call to action, such as the one that concluded, "Write your Senator—before it is too late."[278]

Mobil was the first company to treat corporations as political players in the democratic process, acting not behind the scenes through lobbyists but openly as equal participants with individual citizens in the public discourse. And the company became well known for its advertising campaign. The choice of the *New York Times* ensured that opinion leaders and other influential players would see the ads. The Mobil pieces also generated media coverage, becoming newsworthy in their own right. Schmertz indicated that the campaign won for Mobil "a certain degree of credibility with various key publics," and a survey of Mobil shareholders found that the second-most important reason for buying company stock was a "belief that Mobil will be active in protecting their investment from hostile government intervention and legislation."[279] Other corporations took notice of Mobil's success, and by the end of the 1970s, some 21 percent reported they were discussing public issues in their advertising, up from 11.7 percent two years earlier. Corporate spending on advocacy advertising increased from $154 million in 1970 to more than $500 million by 1979.[280]

Corporations may have been encouraged to speak out on public issues not just because of Mobil's successes but also because, by 1977, there was a changing mood in the country regarding consumerism. John Hanley, the chairman and president of Monsanto, was an outspoken critic of the consumer movement. In speeches he gave around the country, he decried how far the movement had gone. "Why Ban Reason from the Consumer Safety Debate?" he asked rhetorically in the title of one of his speeches. In another, he asked a similar question: "Has Emotion Tipped the Scales on Consumer Safety?" Risks were inherent in society, he argued, and although government and businesses should work together to reduce risk as much as possible, a zero-risk society could never be achieved.[281] Consumers themselves seemed to agree. A bill to create a federal consumer protection agency had stalled in Congress because more and more constituents were not enthusiastic about the idea of additional consumer legislation.[282]

The economy was partly responsible for the shift in consumer mood. In the last few years of the decade, escalating energy prices and inflation became critical issues. As the price of oil soared in 1978, "out of gas" signs appeared at service stations around the country, and President Jimmy Carter wore sweaters to show he was doing his bit to help conserve energy. By early 1979, some 45 percent of people surveyed reported having to cut back on food purchases because of rising prices. Carter suffered at the polls as Americans took their frustrations out on the president and ultimately pinned their hopes on Ronald Reagan.[283]

FIVE

INVESTIGATING POWER

The year 1968 was a watershed in American history. In April, Martin Luther King Jr. was assassinated, and blacks responded by rioting in more than one hundred cities around the country. Students at Columbia University in New York City rioted at the end of April, protesting the Vietnam War. Three months after King's assassination, Robert Kennedy was gunned down as he left a reception held in celebration of his California primary win. At the Democratic National Convention in Chicago, police attacked student demonstrators and candidate Eugene McCarthy supporters alike in a brutal display of pent-up emotion and frustration before network news cameras. Historian Mark Hamilton Lytle noted that "Americans who saw these scenes on television were aghast. Here was a party and a nation at war with itself."[284]

In his 1968 presidential bid, Richard Nixon took advantage of the turmoil, using it as an issue he could ride into the White House. He warned in May 1968 that the disruptions on university campuses, such as the one at Columbia, were "the first skirmish in a revolutionary struggle to seize the universities of this country and transform them into sanctuaries for radicals and vehicles for revolutionary political and social goals."[285] He recognized that the actions of the demonstrators offended most people. The majority of Americans wanted law and order restored, he argued, and he would represent that majority. Nixon declared these people the "silent majority," an apt descriptor, as the statement of one blue-collar worker made clear: "'What I don't like about the students, the loudmouthed ones, is that they think they know so much they can speak for everyone, because they think they're right and the rest of us aren't clever enough and can't talk like they can.'"[286] Media coverage of the riots and demonstrations helped focus the country's attention on the threats to the social order, making a minority of Americans the vocal majority.

Nixon and his advisers believed he had lost the 1960 election because of his image. Now, he portrayed himself as "a new Nixon," a more mature, statesmanlike version of his younger self. Whether he actually was the new Nixon is irrelevant, since his public face was always made up. He did not particularly like people and had to work hard at socializing; nothing was spontaneous about him. In fact, he was ruthless in creating and maintaining his image and destroying that of his opponents. His 1950 Senate race against Helen Gahagan Douglas is considered one of "the most hateful" in California history. His supporters described "the adroitness and calmness with which Nixon and his people executed their hyperbole and innuendo."[287]

To help create and perpetuate his new image, he surrounded himself in the White House with professionals from the advertising field. Nixon's chief of staff, H. R. Haldeman, had been an advertising executive with the J. Walter Thompson agency prior to joining Nixon's staff, as had three of Haldeman's aides. Haldeman also brought on board Jeb Stuart Magruder. Magruder was given the task of developing a public relations program that would circumvent the "liberal" media and allow Nixon to take his message directly to the American people.[288] He might have been hired for his PR expertise, but his background was really sales and marketing. With the emphasis on an advertising approach, the presidency under Nixon became even more image-oriented than it had been under Kennedy. The administration was more concerned with what Nixon had to do to stay in the White House rather than what he could do for the country, at least domestically. Winning over the American people and keeping their support were the paramount objectives.

Nixon did have a public relations practitioner and former journalist on staff, Herbert G. Klein. The president named Klein director of the newly created Office of Communications for the executive branch. Klein's role was different from that of the traditional press secretary. The first press secretary is considered to have been George Akerson, spokesperson for Herbert Hoover. Akerson instituted the twice-a-day press briefings that continued until Nixon did away with them near the end of his first term. Akerson was ultimately replaced by Theodore Joslin, a Washington reporter. For the next forty years, holding briefings was the standard requirement for the position.[289]

Klein was a departure from that norm, as was his new role. He would speak for all of the executive branch rather than just the president, as was typical of the press secretary. The new office was billed as providing an opportunity to streamline communications among the various executive branch agencies and the media. The White House press corps, however, saw it as a way to put distance between Nixon and the press. The centralization of communications also meant more control over the messages coming out of the executive branch. And that is exactly what happened. Klein became increasingly marginalized as Nixon became more dissatisfied with his "crybaby" recommendations, while Ronald Ziegler, the press spokesperson, grew more powerful.[290] Like the others, Ziegler had been an advertising executive and had little understanding of the media. The White House press corps disliked him immensely; they saw him as an obstacle to the flow of information as opposed to a facilitator of it. At one point in 1973, he is supposed to have said to the press, "Look, I know about the way the media work. I bought advertising space for years," a comment that showed how ignorant of the media he really was.[291]

William Porter, in *Assault on the Media,* wrote that Nixon relied on corporate public relations practitioners for media relations as opposed to former journalists and that that reliance upset the traditional symbiotic relationship between political journalists and the president. Corporate PR practitioners are concerned only with issues affecting a single client whose motive is to make a profit. According to Porter, the basic strategy of corporate public relations is to focus media attention on the good and keep out of the media's eye information that makes a company look bad. The strategy is accomplished through the traditional tactics of issuing press releases and giving interviews. But the executive branch is not a single client, and it has many purposes and causes. Press secretaries dealing with the media in behalf of the executive branch must consider the larger public interest and the public's right to information. The serviceable but limited corporate approach, Porter wrote, was what Nixon brought to the executive branch with his advertising executives.

In actuality, Nixon did *not* bring a corporate PR approach to media relations at the White House; he brought an advertising approach. Porter, writing in 1976, erroneously equated Nixon's advertising executives with public relations practitioners. Klein, as a PR practitioner, knew how to build relationships with the media, which was no doubt why Nixon thought he was a crybaby. Ziegler and the boys knew how to buy advertising space and were quite willing to play hardball with the media. As one commentator with 630 WMAL-AM in Washington, D.C., put it in 1971,

"These men think of the media as devices for selling something—whether it's soap or ideas, and their concern of course, is with ideas or perhaps, even non-ideas"; as another wrote, "They thought the message could be bought and paid for and therefore controlled outright."[292]

Ziegler's attitude toward the press reflected that of his boss. Nixon had never liked or trusted the media. When he got into office, he started a campaign intended, in the words of his aide William Safire, "to discredit and malign the press . . . to defame and intimidate Nixon-hating newsmen."[293] Presidents and the media have always had an adversarial relationship, but as Porter explained, the Nixon administration differed in the speed with which it moved to attack the media as well as in the intensity and scope of the attack. "From the Nixon White House there emanated, for the first time, attacks intended to damage the credibility not of a single journalist but of whole classes of them; to intimidate publishers and broadcast ownerships; and, almost unthinkably, to establish in American jurisprudence the legality of censorship," he wrote.[294]

In a series of speeches in the fall of 1969, Vice President Spiro Agnew fired the opening salvo for the administration, criticizing the media, especially television, for its coverage of antiwar demonstrations. The speeches, written by speechwriters William Safire and Patrick Buchanan, were memorable in part for their phrasing. Journalists were "nattering nabobs of negativism" and "troubadours of trouble" who were largely responsible for the "creeping permissiveness that afflicted America" and encouraged antiwar protestors, who themselves were an "effete corps of impudent snobs."[295] But the last speech, given on November 14 before a group of Republicans in Des Moines, Iowa, and broadcast to a national television audience, gave the media the greatest cause for concern.

Two weeks earlier, Nixon had addressed the nation via television on the issue of Vietnam. He asked the "great silent majority" of Americans to support him in his continuation of American involvement in Southeast Asia. He established a clear line in the speech between those who were with him and united for peace and those opposed to his plan who were willing to accept defeat. Immediately afterward, television news commentators noted that the speech offered no new initiatives and concluded that "the President tonight has polarized attitude in the country more than it has ever been into groups that are either for him or against him."[296] Nixon knew the reaction to his words would be hostile and had instructed his aides before he even gave the speech to draft letters to the media complaining about their analysis. Specifically, he wanted "dirty, vicious ones to the [New York] Times and the Washington Post about their editorials."[297]

Agnew kept up the pressure in his speech. He was troubled, he told his audience, by the fact that as soon as Nixon had finished his speech, a "small band of network commentators and self-appointed analysts" had subjected the speech "to instant analysis and querulous criticism." This small group, who all lived in Washington or New York City, had acquired, through no democratic process, "a concentration of power over American public opinion unknown in history." How wise was it, he asked, to leave this "concentration in the hands of a tiny, enclosed fraternity of privileged men elected by no one and enjoying a monopoly sanctioned and licensed by Government?"[298]

Agnew's speech received considerable coverage, especially since the media sought to denounce the charges. But the media were also struck by how much the speech had resonated with the public. Early in 1970, a Harris Poll showed that 56 percent of those surveyed thought "Agnew was right 'in criticizing the way the television networks cover the news.'"[299] Before Agnew's speech, more than half of Americans thought television news was fair and impartial in its coverage of political and social issues. A Gallup Poll in December 1969, a month after Agnew's speech, showed that only four in ten respondents thought television news was fair. Perhaps most important from the media's perspective was that the percentage of Americans who supported the First Amendment dropped from over 50 percent before the speech to 42 percent by March 1970.[300]

Thus, the speech and the public's reaction to it produced a period of quiet reflection on the part of many in the media. They were particularly stung by Agnew's allegations that they were all liberal, with no accountability. In an effort to show its fairness and balance, CBS established a new program called *Spectrum* for radio commentary. The show included two commentators on the right, two on the left, and two in the middle. In a concession to fairness, the *New York Times* balanced its liberal columnists, such as Tom Wicker, Anthony Lewis, and James Reston, with an op-ed page that was opened up to independent voices and to those on the right. It also became the forum Mobil Oil used to enter the public discourse through issue, or advocacy, advertisements. Later, the *Times* hired William Safire, a Nixon speechwriter, to be its resident conservative columnist.[301] Also at this time, the newspaper instituted a correction policy. (Previously, it had not acknowledged corrections, as was the custom in the newspaper trade.) Other newspapers followed suit, although the network news shows did not.

In this climate of distrust and dissatisfaction, the administration was able to go after the media with more force than it might otherwise have been able to muster. Magruder, the aide who had been hired ostensibly to create a public relations plan for the pres-

ident, had suggested in a memo to Haldeman that the administration ought to engage in concentrated efforts to force the media
to "look at things somewhat differently."[302] His recommendations revealed how little he knew about public relations and how
much the philosophy of the ends justifying the means permeated
the administration. His suggestions took full advantage of the executive agencies at Nixon's disposal, including having the Federal Communications Commission monitor television coverage
of the president; the idea was that if the monitoring proved the
networks were biased against Nixon, he could make an official
complaint to the FCC. Moreover, the Justice Department could
bring an antitrust action against the networks. Even "the possible
threat of anti-trust action I think would be effective in changing
their views," Magruder wrote.[303] And the Internal Revenue Service could be used to harass individual journalists via tax audits.
Magruder's ideas were, in fact, adopted by the administration,
with the FCC receiving a challenge to the license renewal of a
television station owned by the *Washington Post* and the Justice
Department filing antitrust charges against all three television
networks.[304] Network owners started complaining among themselves about restraints on the First Amendment, arguing that television regulations imperiled First Amendment protections for
everyone.[305]

Regardless of the complaints, Nixon's tactics apparently
worked. Network executives began to tone down coverage of the
Vietnam War and demonstrations against it, sensitive to public
opinion and the government's ability to pull licenses. Av Westin,
executive producer of ABC News, told his staff as early as March
1969, "I think the time has come to shift some of our focus from
the battlefield, or more specifically from American military involvement with the enemy, to themes and stories under the

general heading, 'We're on our way out of Vietnam.'"[306] NBC News reacted in a similar fashion in 1969. As a result, Americans believed that the war had wound down by the end of 1969 and that the protesters had died out, although neither was true. As First Amendment scholar Margaret Blanchard wrote, "Factual information, a key ingredient for intelligent participation in government, had fallen victim to the twin forces of economic and political pressure."[307]

With television news brought into line, Nixon instructed the Justice Department to pressure newspapers, specifically the *New York Times* and the *Washington Post,* in an effort to stop them from publishing a classified study. The *Times* and later the *Post* had received the study—the Pentagon Papers, as it came to be known—from Daniel Ellsberg. Ellsberg was an employee of the Rand Corporation, a private consulting firm that did work for the Defense Department and had in its possession the top secret report on the origins of the Vietnam War, which had been commissioned in 1967 by then defense secretary Robert McNamara. Ellsberg had become disillusioned over the Vietnam War and what he saw as a pattern of official deception about it. In the fall of 1969, he and a colleague started photocopying the forty-seven-volume report. They gave thousands of pages of the report first to the *Times* in March 1971, then the *Post,* and eventually several other media outlets.[308]

The first article in the *Times* series based on the report appeared on June 13, a Sunday, under the headline VIETNAM ARCHIVE: PENTAGON STUDY TRACES 3 DECADES OF GROWING U.S. INVOLVEMENT. The article was of no concern to the Nixon people at first. They really thought the report was more problematic for Kennedy and Johnson than for Nixon. The document showed that the two previous Democratic presidents had escalated the war even though convinced it could not be won and then had lied to the American people about the level of the country's involvement. But on Monday, the second article appeared, and the administration decided it needed to react. Nixon was concerned about how such a classified document came to be leaked and how the leak might look to the Chinese government with which he was conducting secret negotiations. Thus, on Tuesday, June 15, when the third installment appeared, Attorney General John Mitchell brought an emergency motion in federal court to stop further publication until the leak could be investigated. The government argued that the document was classified top secret because it involved matters of national security and that publication was therefore forbidden under the Espionage Act.[309]

Government secrecy on the basis of national security had escalated under Eisenhower's presidency. At the end of the 1950s, reporters complained about the expanding practice of classifying documents to protect national security. Traditionally, the press tended to rally around the flag in times of war, willingly abiding by requests not to publish information that might harm troops or the nation's ability to fight the enemy. They readily accepted a claim of national security in those situations. But the Cold War was a different kind of war. On one level, there was a traditional enemy, the USSR, but on another level, the enemy was an abstract concept—communism. There were no front lines because the battles were not for land but rather for the minds of men and women. It was a war of intelligence gathering and subterfuge. That made matters of national security more problematic. In a traditional war, the government could tell the media not to divulge troop locations, for example, and the media would abide by the request. But with the Cold War, the nature of the sensitive information was different, and there was no telling if members of the media were, in fact, Communists. Therefore, there was a tendency on the part of the Eisenhower and Kennedy administrations to say, "Just trust us." Journalists feared, however, that national security was a convenient label to slap on documents and other information that might be embarrassing or problematic for the administration domestically or diplomatically. The Pentagon Papers were a classic example of that.

But on June 15, 1971, a U.S. district court judge issued the restraining order the government sought; it was the first time in U.S. history that a newspaper had been enjoined from publishing material. The order made Ellsberg concerned that the rest of the information would not be made public, so he contacted the *Washington Post*. The *Post*'s first article appeared on Friday, June 18. The Justice Department immediately went back to federal court for a second injunction. This time, the judge hearing the case affirmed the right of the *Post* to publish the information, but the next day, an appeals court decided that publication should cease until the government had a chance to argue its case more fully. Although the *Times* and the *Post* were effectively barred from printing further stories based on the Pentagon Papers, articles appeared within days in newspapers around the country, including the *Boston Globe,* the *Chicago Sun-Times,* and the *Los Angeles Times.* On Saturday, June 26, the U.S. Supreme Court held an emergency session to hear oral arguments in behalf of the government and the *New York Times.* Five days later, the Court held, in a six-to-three vote, that the government had not established that the documents were, in fact, a security risk that would justify a restraint on publication.[310]

Nixon's advisers had decided while the case was ongoing that they needed "to explain why this [publication] injures national security and why secret documents must be secure. . . . We need to get across the feeling of disloyalty on the part of those who publish these papers."[311] Apparently, they were successful in getting out that message. Although the government lost the Pentagon Papers case, public opinion was solidly behind Nixon, with the majority of Americans believing the *Times* should not have printed the information.[312]

While the Nixon administration sought to punish the media for their coverage of the presidency, it also sought to take advantage of journalists' coverage of social issues and dissenting groups, turning newsrooms into an investigative arm of the government. Investigative reporting had increased over the course of the 1960s as journalists began covering radical groups and the social movements in greater depth. That coverage offered Nixon an opportunity to accomplish two goals: prosecuting radical groups and stopping journalists from reporting on those groups by jeopardizing their ability to build trust with them. Some government agents even masqueraded as reporters to infiltrate radical groups, which, of course, threatened the ability of real reporters to gather information.[313] But it was the subpoenas that did the most damage.

Between 1968 and the Watergate scandal in the early 1970s, "a cloudburst of subpoenas showered the press," according to media law scholar Donald Gillmor.[314] The Department of Justice wanted journalists to turn over their files, unused photographs, and unused television footage to assist the department in prosecuting drug traffickers and radical groups such as the Weathermen and the Black Panthers. An editor of the *Los Angeles Times* told a subcommittee of the Senate Judiciary Committee that his paper had been served with more than 30 subpoenas and threatened with more than 50 others during the preceding few years. CBS and NBC received 121 subpoenas in a thirty-month period, and a reporter for the *Chicago Sun-Times* was subpoenaed in eleven separate proceedings in eighteen months.[315]

In the most well-known instance, the journalists refused to be intimidated and fought the subpoenas up to the Supreme Court. *Branzburg v. Hayes* came to the Court in 1972 and was a consolidation of four cases. Paul Branzburg, a staff reporter for the *Louisville Courier-Journal* in Kentucky, had written a story describing how he had watched two individuals synthesize hashish from marijuana. Branzburg was subpoenaed before a grand jury investigating drug trafficking. He refused to identify the individuals in his story on the grounds that he had promised them confidentiality. He was subpoenaed a second time after he wrote another article on illicit drug use, but this time, he refused to even appear before the grand jury. The third case involved Earl Caldwell, who was an African American reporter with the *New York Times.* He had befriended the Black Panthers and was called before a grand jury to give testimony about his knowledge of their operation. Like Branzburg, Caldwell refused to even appear. Paul Pappas also had written about the Black Panthers. He did appear before a grand jury in response to a subpoena but agreed to answer questions only about the Black Panthers' activities outside their headquarters.[316]

The greater emphasis on investigative reporting by the media had seen a corresponding rise in the reliance on confidential sources as the basis for stories. The problem that journalists have with appearing before grand juries is that the sessions are closed to the public. No one is permitted to know what was said to the jury. Thus, journalists fear that confidential sources will assume they revealed their sources' names. Appearing at such sessions damages the reporter's credibility with existing and potential sources. From the perspective of the Nixon administration, however, reporters had information about drug traffickers and the Black Panthers; as such, they were witnesses to criminal activity and should have been compelled to testify as to what they saw just as an ordinary citizen would be.

The media eagerly awaited the *Branzburg* decision, sure that the Court would affirm their First Amendment rights to protect sources and put an end to the practice of subpoenaing reporters. But the Court did not do that, instead ruling that journalists did not have and never had had a constitutional right to refuse to disclose confidential sources in the context of grand jury proceedings.

The media were stunned; they also felt a sense of panic, given Nixon's increasing use of subpoenas. The trade publication *Editor & Publisher* responded immediately to the decision. Investigative reporting over the years had revealed many instances of bribery and corruption in city and state governments, it stated. "If those reporters had not protected their confidential sources under the then 'unwritten law,' most of those stories would never have been written. Very few more of them will be written in the future, it is almost guaranteed," the magazine editorialized.[317] Robert Fichenberg, chairman of the Freedom of Information Committee of the American Society of Newspaper Editors, called the Supreme Court's decision "a direct blow at the right of the people to be fully informed without hindrance by the government." Sigma Delta Chi, the professional journalistic society, went even further, arguing that "a free press cannot exist without protection for the reporter and his sources."[318]

Members of Congress reacted to appease the nervous media, introducing more than twenty bills to protect reporters from having to disclose confidential sources. While the subcommittee of the Senate Judiciary Committee held hearings on the various bills, Peter Bridges, a reporter for the *Newark (N.J.) Evening News,* was sent to jail for failing to answer five questions before a grand jury on a story he had written about bribery. New Jersey actually had a shield law protecting journalists from having to disclose the names of their sources, but Bridges was jailed for not disclosing confidential information, something not covered by the state law. When a second reporter, also from a state with a shield law, was jailed in late 1972 for refusing to divulge sources, *Editor & Publisher* made a dire prediction: "Malfeasance and misfeasance in public office will go unreported because no public-spirited person will dare to tell a reporter what he knows. . . . The role of the press as the watchdog of government will surely disappear unless the newsman's power of independent inquiry is guaranteed and protected by Congress."[319]

Although the media were clearly incensed at the Court's ruling, polls showed that the public's reaction was mixed. A Gallup Poll released in November 1972 revealed that 57 percent of respondents agreed with reporters who chose not to identify sources. *Editor & Publisher* saw the results as an indication that the public would strongly favor a federal shield law.[320] But the *Quill,* a monthly magazine owned and published by the Society of Professional Journalists, was more circumspect. Since 43 percent were not on the side of reporters, the public did not fully understand the issue and would not necessarily support a law protecting journalists, the magazine warned.[321]

Regardless of the polls, the Nixon administration kept up its intimidation of journalists, arresting investigative reporter Les Whitten in January 1973 and charging him with possession of stolen documents. Whitten was the chief investigative reporter for syndicated columnist Jack Anderson, who in turn was a particular thorn in Nixon's side. Several journalists whom Nixon did not like had had secret wiretaps put on their phones, but it was the efforts to control Anderson that really showed the extent to which the president would go to quiet his critics. Anderson was subject to surveillance and character assassination, but Nixon aides also approached the Central Intelligence Agency (CIA) about possibly "drugging or poisoning the columnist, staging a fatal mugging or car crash, or simply shooting him in a direct assassination."[322] Fortunately for Anderson, none of those things came to pass, perhaps because he soon became the least of Nixon's worries.

On July 17, 1972, the Democratic National Headquarters in the Watergate office complex was burglarized. Actually, the five burglars had been intending to check on a bug in the headquarters but were stopped by an alert security guard. Nixon's Committee to Re-elect the President, better known as CREEP by the media, had been employing some heavy-handed tactics to ensure Nixon's reelection in November. Clearly, the philosophy of the ends justifying the means was firmly entrenched in the Nixon administration. The maintenance of the president's image, his hold on the presidency, and his desire to take down his enemies were the only things that mattered.

As early as 1971, CREEP had gone after Senator Edmund Muskie of Maine, the most likely Democratic challenger for the presidency in 1972. The committee infiltrated the Muskie camp by having one of their own pose as his driver. Through their informant, CREEP received a copy of a memo in which Muskie's advisers were urging him to take a more left-wing approach to foreign policy. CREEP passed the memo on to columnist Robert Novak, who wrote a column on December 12 that accused Muskie of surrounding himself with left-wing advisers.[323] CREEP also arranged for a forged letter to be sent to William Loeb, publisher of the *Manchester* (N.H.) *Union Leader* and a fierce critic of Muskie, knowing Loeb would feature the letter prominently in the paper. The supposed author of the letter claimed to have heard Muskie make derogatory comments about Franco-Americans, a major Democratic voting bloc in New Hampshire. In defending himself at a news conference, Muskie choked up, although he later said that his voice broke from anger and that he had not cried. Nonetheless, the damage had been done. Media reports of the incident included the emotional display and effectively put an end to his presidential bid.[324]

David Broder, in his 1987 book *Behind the Front Page,* wrote that he would have reported the incident differently had he known at the time that CREEP was behind it. As it was, he had unwittingly helped Nixon's people destroy Muskie's credibility and thus his candidacy. But Broder also acknowledged that he and many of the other reporters following Muskie's campaign had come to question whether the candidate had the temperament to be president. His volatility had come through in semiprivate moments, which, following the tenets of objectivity, the reporters could not or would not report. Thus, Muskie's open and public display of emotion in response to the letter's allegations was an opportunity for Broder and the others to report what they already sensed.[325] In that regard, the coverage was fair, although the incident itself had been manipulated and provoked by Nixon's people.

CREEP often tried to manipulate the press and thus public opinion. When it decided to move the Republican National Convention from San Diego to Miami Beach because of fears of antiwar demonstrators, Magruder again contacted Novak. This time, he gave Novak an exclusive: they were going to move the convention because of San Diego's inadequate hotel and arena facilities. Novak's resulting column said exactly what CREEP had hoped it would say. Magruder described the episode as a good example of how his group could often achieve their ends by effective leaks to the press. A good leak must go to "a writer who had both credibility and mass circulation."[326] Leaks, of course, are commonplace in Washington and are used for a variety of purposes, but Nixon's people leaked false information in an effort to manipulate coverage and control public opinion.[327]

Not all of CREEP's actions were nefarious. In the 1972 California primary, the committee experimented with direct mail and telephone calls rather than the traditional advertisements. They did follow-up evaluations to determine the effectiveness of each tactic—personalized versus nonpersonalized letters, one-page versus longer letters, one mailing versus two or more, and so on.[328] Magruder did, however, remark in his book, written shortly before he was sentenced for his contributions to the Watergate cover-up, that overall, "we may have become too confident that we could manipulate public opinion in a hard-line, rally-round-the-flag way."[329]

At first, the Nixon administration seemed to have the Watergate problem under control. Press Secretary Ziegler told the press corps it was just a "third-rate burglary." Nixon publicly denied any knowledge of the bugging and said that a full and complete investigation was being conducted. The media, except for the *Washington Post,* largely ignored the episode before the election. As Mark Hamilton Lytle asked rhetorically, "Why should the media want to embarrass Nixon when over 753 out of 809 daily papers endorsed him?"[330]

Carl Bernstein and Bob Woodward of the *Washington Post* were the sole reporters who had doggedly kept on the story since the burglars' arraignment, piecing the details together as best they could, but by November, they had run out of leads. In January 1973, however, prosecutors charged Gordon Liddy, Howard Hunt, and their five accomplices with burglary. Although the jury returned a guilty verdict against all seven men, the presiding judge, John Sirica, was unhappy. He thought too many questions remained unanswered, and he threatened the men with stiff sentences if they were not more forthcoming. One of the men caved in and admitted to the judge that they were under political pressure to remain silent.[331] Matters escalated quickly after that. On April 30, 1973, Nixon announced to a national television audience that he had accepted the resignations of John Ehrlichman and H. R. Haldeman, his two top aides, although he still denied any personal involvement. The Senate held televised hearings into the Watergate incident through the summer of 1973. In July, it was disclosed that Nixon had taped all Oval Office conversations. He refused, however, to produce the tapes, claiming executive privilege. Later, he turned over the tapes except for a crucial eighteen minutes that had been miraculously erased.

In a November 4, 1973, editorial, the *New York Times* called for Nixon's resignation. The November 12 issue of *Time* magazine, which hit the newsstands the following day, also urged the president to resign. Over the same weekend, the *Denver Post,* the *Detroit News,* and the *Atlanta Journal* issued the same call.[332] Opinion polls, however, suggested that 62 percent of the American people surveyed were against resignation at the time. In fact, the majority of Americans did not favor resignation until approximately April 1974, although those who watched the hearings on television were more inclined to believe Nixon should resign or be impeached than those who did not.[333] Finally, on August 8, 1974, Nixon went on national television to announce that he would step down the next day and that Gerald R. Ford would be sworn in as president.

Gerald Ford came to power under difficult circumstances. The country had just gone through the long and trying Watergate scandal, the economy was moving into a recession, and public distrust of government was at an all-time high. Usually, an incoming president has an opportunity between the November election and the January inauguration to assemble a team and ease the transition. Ford did not have that luxury. Of course, Johnson had taken over after Kennedy's assassination without the benefit of a transition period, but he had been the vice president for three years, whereas Ford had not been in that position for a full year. And although he was popular in Washington, he did not have a close-knit group of advisers who had been battle-hardened in a presidential campaign and who had a clear idea of how to work together and what they wanted to accomplish. Thus, Ford's team was a mixture of new people he brought in and people left over from Nixon's days. Ron Nessen, his press secretary, said that Ford's administration was plagued by infighting.[334]

Despite not having a media strategy other than emphasizing the idea of a new, open presidency, Ford received fair press coverage in his first thirty days. He was personable and open with the media, and despite the drawbacks he faced, he handled the transition into office smoothly. Two events changed that coverage: the pardon of Nixon and the resignation of Ford's first press secretary, Jerald terHorst.[335] Ford had told the media at a press conference that he would not pardon Nixon, at least not for a while. But a week later, he did exactly that. The media felt they had been deliberately deceived, and the press secretary was furious. TerHorst, who had been a White House correspondent for the *Detroit News* before becoming press secretary, complained that he was not in on the discussion about whether to pardon Nixon and that because he was not, he had been misled into deceiving the media, compromising his credibility with them. Although some in the administration questioned terHorst's motivations for resigning when he did, he was correct that the way the pardon was handled affected the media. TerHorst believed that Ford had considered the pardon from a legal and political standpoint and not from a public relations perspective.[336]

Members of the White House press corps were particularly sensitive to being misled, believing they had been deceived by Nixon. They were determined not to have it happen again and set new standards for how they covered the presidency. After Watergate, they were less inclined, for instance, to treat press conferences as the story. Because of their experiences with Nixon and, to some extent, Johnson before him, they came to see press conferences as performances; they would get the real story from their sources behind the scenes. They were also more willing to challenge statements made by the president.[337] Ford had come into office promising his presidency would represent a new day and a new era of openness, and to his credit, he had instituted the practice of allowing follow-up questions at his regular press conferences.[338] But his actions in pardoning Nixon after telling the press he would not made it look as if he was lying.

TerHorst's replacement, Ron Nessen, had been a correspondent for NBC-TV News. He was the first television correspondent to be a press secretary, although by this point, television was the most influential news medium. Both men came directly from the press corps and had a difficult time making the transition to the press secretary role, as the title of Nessen's book, *It Sure Looks Different from the Inside,* makes clear.[339] Ironically, Nessen was not particularly well liked by the media. For one thing, they criticized him for not facilitating the flow of information reliably; he responded to the criticism by instituting daily press briefings in 1975.[340]

Any president following Nixon would have had a rough time

with the media because of their skepticism, but Ford had a particularly difficult time. Because he had been relatively unknown by the public before becoming president, he was a new subject for political cartoonists. They found his looks lacking in distinctive features to caricaturize and therefore focused on his athleticism. Ford had played college football and was still a golfer, skier, tennis player, and swimmer. But his athleticism was soon used against him. In October 1973, the *New York Times* wrote a story about the newly selected vice president in which they quoted Lyndon Johnson saying that Ford was so dumb "he can't chew gum and walk at the same time."[341] Although the media thought nothing of the comment at first, Ford himself contributed to the belief that there might be something to Johnson's statement through his verbal and physical gaffes. On June 1, 1975, he stumbled coming down the steps of his plane onto the tarmac for a meeting with Egyptian president Anwar Sadat. Over the next couple of months, Ford seemed increasingly accident-prone.[342] Part of his problem was that in an effort to be open and accessible to the media, he allowed reporters to see him in unrehearsed and unguarded moments.

At first, the White House blamed the physical gaffes on Ford's "football knee." But the story had taken on a life of its own. Whenever Ford's aides tried to present him in a more presidential light, the media, especially columnists, claimed he was "acting presidential." The effect of the media's coverage was that Ford was forced to declare over and over, "Your president is no dummy."[343] The bigger problem from a public relations perspective was that the media's portrayal of Ford as a bumbler had come to be a metaphor for the way he was handling the real issues.[344] It was a problem that his advisers seemed unable to fix, despite the impact it was having in the polls. Ford even taped the opening line "Live, from New York, it's Saturday Night" for the television comedy show *Saturday Night Live* (*SNL*) in an attempt to change his image.

SNL debuted on NBC on October 11, 1975, blending "political satire, social commentary, and outrageous humor" and ultimately reaching some thirty million viewers per week.[345] Part of the show involved the "Weekend Update" segment, a parody of nightly newscasts. Lorne Michaels, the show's creator, insisted that the material for the fake newscast had to come from real footage and current stories. Comedian Chevy Chase was the first anchor. Known for his slapstick humor, he also played a hapless, clumsy Ford in skits. Michaels believed that people were ready for a playful look at the president after the oppression of the Nixon administration and Watergate, and he was apparently right in that belief.[346] Another member of the *SNL* cast, Al Franken, said that it was Chase's portrayal of Ford as clumsy and not very smart that gave the president his reputation as a bumbler.[347]

To help defuse the show's portrayal of Ford as clumsy and to reach out to a younger audience, Ford's press secretary hosted the show in early 1976. Nessen thought that if the president could be seen poking fun at himself, the media might back off. For *SNL,* it was a coup to be in the middle of its first season and already a force to be reckoned with in political circles. Although only Nessen appeared in person on the show, Ford taped the signature "Live, from New York" opening. Unfortunately for the president, Nessen's appearance did nothing for Ford's reputation, as the *SNL* writers took advantage of the knowledge that Ford would be watching and featured some very raunchy material.[348]

Initially, Nessen had been in charge of the press office as well as the Office of Communications, but the latter was an unwelcome reminder of Watergate and Nixon. As a result, Ford stopped using the name and downscaled its operation. By 1976, with an election approaching and polls showing that he rated poorly among voters in terms of his competency, strength, and intelligence, Ford named David Gergen, a former Nixon speechwriter, as head of the Office of Communications. Gergen did not serve under Nessen, however. Instead, he reported to Chief of Staff Richard B. Cheney. With Gergen in charge, the office became more involved in strategizing and developing campaign themes. Although some criticized Gergen's operation as too political, he saw that as a necessary component. "If you've got a president running for office, you've got to do it," he said.[349]

But the addition of Gergen was too little, too late. Ford was never able to mount an effective campaign to establish his image as a leader, and he did not win the 1976 election. That honor went to Jimmy Carter. Carter had campaigned as a Washington outsider. He was a southern peanut farmer who promised to bring greater openness and transparency to the White House. He eschewed the traditional ceremonial trappings of the inauguration, choosing instead to walk down Pennsylvania Avenue holding hands with his wife and daughter. Two weeks after assuming the presidency, he told the American people in a television address that he would "conduct an open Administration, with frequent press conferences and reports to the people and with 'town hall' meetings across the nation, where you can criticize, make suggestions, and ask questions."[350]

Mark Rozell, a professor of public policy, suggested that presidents who are concerned with image and take their public relations seriously fare better in the media than those who do not. He argued that Nixon, until Watergate, and Reagan received more favorable media coverage than Ford and Carter because public relations did not play an important role in either of their administrations.[351] Of course, both Ford and Carter were in the unfortunate situation of following Nixon and Watergate. They were put into positions where they had to adopt a policy of openness and transparency. The problem was that they did so without the benefit of public relations advice, which left them vulnerable to an aggressive and antagonistic press, also a product of Watergate.

Watergate influenced a whole generation of would-be journalists. Journalism departments swelled with an influx of students who envisioned themselves as the next Woodward or Bernstein. To them and to many in journalism in the post-Watergate era, investigative reporting was the "begin-all and end-all of newspapering," by "seeking out evildoers in government and bringing down high officials."[352] But some warned that assaults on government would go too far. Walter Wriston, chairman of Citibank, for example, suggested that the media had come to believe that the end justified the means—an ironic twist, since the same philosophy had brought about Nixon's downfall. Wriston argued that some in the news business believed the "truth" must be revealed, "no matter how obtained or how irrelevant, or how . . . adverse to the public interest."[353]

Matters that reporters of an earlier time had kept private were seen now as fair game. Thus, the editor of the *Detroit News,* Martin Hayden, noted how journalists were now willing to discredit Lyndon Johnson not only for his Vietnam War position but also for his "alleged love of confidential political bedroom gossip passed on by J. Edgar Hoover" of the Federal Bureau of Investigation (FBI); similarly, John F. Kennedy had been revealed as a promoter of the war in Vietnam, "as a misuser of both the FBI and the CIA, as an alleged sanctioner of assassinations, an unsuccessful Bay of Pigs adventurer, and most recently as a bed-hopper."[354] And many of these and other exposés were being reported without objectivity in the sense of fairness and balance. Hayden contended that "such objectivity is necessary if we are to discriminate between the evils within our system and the worthiness of the system . . . itself."[355]

Even a public relations practitioner warned about the shift away from objectivity and toward advocacy journalism. In addition, he saw two other trends in journalism that disturbed him. One was a growing belief among some journalists that they had to abandon their neutral stance and take a position in behalf of the "little people" against major political and corporate institutions. The other was a trend toward adversarial journalism. The net result of these two trends was that public confidence in major institutions was being undermined. And that was the third trend—a greater animosity toward the media, "a deepening distrust of their credibility, a mounting contempt for their power."[356] In fact, a 1978 Harris Poll revealed that in a listing of twenty professions, the people "running" the press came in sixteenth in public esteem, just ahead of law firms, Congress, organized labor, and advertising agencies.[357]

SIX

BLAMING THE MESSENGER

The post-Watergate era was a heady time for the media. After all, investigative reporting had brought down a president. As columnist David Broder wrote in *Behind the Front Page,* "[Bob] Woodward and [Carl] Bernstein became symbols of the new Washington reporters—those who could make things happen by what they wrote."[358] Enrollment in journalism schools tripled after the movie version of Watergate made the two reporters heroes.[359] Meanwhile, Ed Asner reflected the popular image of an editor in the *Lou Grant* TV series—"an image of fierce devotion to truth and justice."[360] But some were concerned with the apparent growing power of the media, especially the Washington press corps.

A series of events that seemed to reveal an arrogant and occasionally dishonest press eventually led to a fall from grace. A presidential commission looking into the March 28, 1979, Three Mile Island accident, in which the nuclear power plant near Middleton, Pennsylvania, experienced a partial meltdown of its reactor core, found fault with the coverage of the incident, citing the media for exaggerating the radiation threat. One example referred to by the commission was a story by *New York Daily News* columnist Jimmy Breslin. Breslin wrote that "steam drifted out of the tops of the four cooling towers and ran down the sides like candle wax. The steam was evil, laced with radiation."[361] Definitely a descriptive and effective piece but hardly what one would call objective reporting.

Then came Janet Cooke's "Jimmy's World" story for the *Washington Post* in 1981. The problem with the article was that Jimmy, the eleven-year-old heroin addict at the center of the narrative, did not exist. The *Post*, after having basked in the glory of its dogged and determined reporting of the Watergate story, returned the Pulitzer Prize it won for "Jimmy's World." Shortly thereafter, the *New York Times* revealed that one of its reporters had fabricated a story about conditions in Cambodia: not only had the reporter not been in Cambodia, he had also taken part of the story from a novel.[362]

Old-time journalists called for a return to the basics of journalism, or objectivity, and in certain cases, even a return to some form of partisanship.[363] As early as 1979, George Reedy, a former Lyndon Johnson aide and the Neiman Professor of Journalism at Marquette University, argued that although people believed the press had become too powerful, as evidenced by Watergate, it had actually lost real political power. Concentration of media ownership meant centralization, which in turn meant standardization. Journalism had become a service profession. As Reedy phrased it, "On the whole, it seeks to provide its readers with unexceptionable information which they need to function in their daily lives."[364] What was missing was the political leadership that the media, especially newspapers, used to exhibit in communities. Editors and publishers had political clout and used the editorial pages of their papers to raise issues of importance and foster debate. But no room existed in a standardized and centralized press for "contentious communication."[365] Reedy even suggested that the lack of such discussion was partly to blame for the label of liberal bias that had been affixed to the media. When newspapers were openly partisan, most people could find one paper in their community that expressed views similar to their own and that they therefore felt was "objective."[366]

Whether Reedy was correct in his assumption, there is no question that the public had lost faith in the media by 1983. That fact was made clear by the public's response to the U.S. invasion of the island of Grenada. On Tuesday, October 25, 1983, President Ronald Reagan announced at a press conference that American troops had invaded Grenada that morning after "an urgent, formal request" was received from the Organization of Eastern Caribbean States (OECS).[367] The request came after a Cuban-connected military junta murdered the Grenadian prime minister. However, the primary rationale for the invasion, according to the government, was to rescue the five hundred Americans who were students at the St. George's University School of Medicine on the island. The problem for the press was that the military imposed a blackout for the first four days of the invasion. Actually, as consumer advocates Jeff and Marie Blyskal made clear, it was not a blackout per se. It really amounted to a deliberate attempt on the part of the Pentagon to make reporting the invasion difficult by refusing to transport journalists, especially television reporters, to the island or assist them in getting there. The military turned back those who tried to enter the military zone via yachts or airplanes, although some print reporters did manage to make it to the island.[368]

For the first four days, television coverage carried only video provided by the Pentagon. Journalists tried to cover the invasion as best they could, but the story of the blackout itself was not reported, at least not at first. John Chancellor, anchor of NBC's *Nightly News,* referred to the administration's attempts at censorship on Wednesday evening, one day after the invasion. ABC's

World News Tonight viewers heard about the blackout indirectly on the next evening when reporter John McWethy noted that "Pentagon sources say one of the reasons the press was kept off the island during the early stages of the operation had to do with the presence of the super-secret Delta Group."[369] And CBS ran "Cleared by Defense Department Censors" over Pentagon-released pictures of the invasion the following night, after the restrictions had been relaxed somewhat.[370]

Later, the editorial pages of the leading daily newspapers criticized the administration's no-media policy, and representatives of all three networks appeared before a congressional subcommittee to formally protest the press ban. But it was too little, too late. The battle for public opinion had already been won by the Reagan camp. The press had carried uncritically the administration's version of events and in doing so had bolstered Reagan's image. Before the invasion, his approval rating was 46 percent, with 37 percent disapproving of his handling of the presidency. But his approval rating rose to 53 percent and his disapproval rating fell to 31 percent in the weeks following the invasion. Meanwhile, in a poll by the *Los Angeles Times,* Americans supported by 52 percent the policy of denying unrestricted press access during the Grenada invasion.[371] Other polls reflected similar findings.[372] As journalist Mark Hertsgaard put it, "The press had become, without knowing it, a passive accomplice in its own censorship."[373]

But it was not simply a matter of carrying the administration's version of events uncritically. In reviewing the Grenada incident, Jeff and Marie Blyskal, in their book *How the Public Relations Industry Writes the News,* painted a picture of a very carefully planned and executed public relations campaign, of which press censorship was only a part. Reagan's advisers recognized some PR problems and opportunities with the invasion from the outset. First, it was an opportunity to boost the president's falling ratings. Americans were demoralized after Vietnam, Watergate, and the Iranian hostage crisis. A quick, successful military action would raise national morale, and certainly, invading the tiny island of Grenada would be a quick and successful operation. The massacre of 225 U.S. Marines in Lebanon two days before the invasion also lent urgency to the Grenada action. Dividing the public's attention between two hot spots would help defuse the Lebanese situation. At the same time, however, the invasion posed a problem, given Reagan's reputation for being trigger happy: the whole thing could blow up in their faces.[374]

To take advantage of the opportunity and reduce the problematic aspects, Reagan's public relations advisers came up with three strategies. The first was to push the idea that the invasion was a hastily prepared operation rather than the planned move of a warmongering president. Thus, at his October 25 press conference announcing the invasion, Reagan said he had received an urgent request for assistance from the OECS on October 23. Reagan's advisers made sure that the prime minister of Dominica, who was also the head of the OECS, was present at the press conference so that the president would appear to be helping out an ally in a time of need, as opposed to attempting to remove a government he did not like. In reality, although the prime minister of St. Lucia had made an informal request for assistance on October 20, the military had started preliminary planning for the evacuation of Americans almost two weeks prior.[375]

The second strategy was to use the rescue of the American students at the medical school in Grenada as the primary rationale for the invasion, since it was a much easier "sell" than the ousting of an unfriendly government. The PR advisers made sure that message was stressed in all information coming from the government.

But were the students really in danger? The government leaked a story to the *New York Times* that the military had found documents in Grenada showing that the new leaders there planned to hold U.S. citizens hostage. The article went on to quote a "senior official" who said, "It looks like we got there just in time to prevent a tragedy."[376] Since no reporters were allowed on the island, the contents of the documents could not be independently verified. According to the Blyskals, the documents were never referred to again and were not disclosed with other documentary evidence released in November 1983. Nor were they mentioned in a report on the invasion that was prepared by the Department of State and the Department of Defense. The Blyskals' conclusion was that the documents were part of the public relations strategy to support the students-as-hostages theme and discredit the school's chancellor, who had been quoted by the *Washington Post* criticizing Reagan for saying the students were in danger.[377]

Regardless of the reality of the situation, the government public relations people took full advantage of the student angle. They alerted the media in ample time to cover the arrival of the plane carrying the students back to American soil. At the photo op, one student kissed the ground, much to the delight of the PR people. The gesture made for a great visual, although the student later said he did it because of a running joke with one of his friends. In fact, the 5:00 P.M. photo op was deliberately timed to follow a press conference given by the Joint Chiefs of Staff at 4:30 P.M. to talk about how well the invasion was going. The arrival of the students visually and conveniently reinforced the message of the press conference. The arrival of the bodies of the U.S. Marines killed in Lebanon was also deliberately timed—for 3:00 A.M.—in order to minimize media coverage.[378]

The third strategy was to make it difficult for the media to report the story. The point of the strategy was to keep television cameras from the scene. Print reporters were not a problem, but the Pentagon had been wary of television since the Vietnam War. They were well aware that reading a story about the horrors of war in a newspaper does not carry the same emotional impact that watching pictures of it on television does. But the government knew that reporters could not be kept off the island indefinitely. The window of opportunity to frame the story was small. The government public relations people also knew they needed to fill the news hole that was created by the strategy. Reporters would be more aggressive in trying to get to Grenada themselves if they had nothing to report. Thus, the Defense Department provided the media with footage and photographs, which the media used without mentioning, at least initially, that they came from the government. Not surprisingly, the video and pictures reinforced the PR themes established at the outset: that the students were in danger, that the invasion was launched at the request of the OECS, and that the situation in Grenada was volatile enough to warrant invasion. Senior officials made the rounds of talk and morning shows to further support those frames. And to keep journalists away from Grenada, the administration centralized information flow in Washington. All information came from the office of the assistant secretary of defense for public affairs.[379]

Finally, in November, material captured by the military in Grenada was put on display for the media at Andrews Air Force Base. The display was to reinforce the idea that the situation was volatile and dangerous prior to the invasion. A UPI story included the following lines: "Passing a table full of Soviet-bloc sidearms and machine guns, [Vice President George] Bush picked up a new Russian AK-47 assault rifle. He shook his head and said, 'I guess everything we heard is true. This is pretty stark evidence.'"[380]

The success with which Reagan's public relations advisers handled the Grenada invasion was typical of their work for him in his first administration. Reagan has been described as the first public relations president. In fact, Leslie Janka, a deputy White House press secretary who resigned over the banning of the press from Grenada, went so far as to say, "This was a PR outfit that became President and took over the country."[381] Nixon set up much of the communications apparatus that Reagan's people used, but Nixon had surrounded himself with advertising people who did not understand the media or know how to build relationships with them. Reagan brought with him into office public relations practitioners who knew how to carefully cultivate his image and the business of the presidency.

Many at the time saw the election of Reagan in 1980 as more of a rejection of President Carter than as widespread support for the Republican candidate. And it is true that only 27 percent of eligible voters actually voted for Reagan. But his ascendancy signaled the rise of the New Right as a power player. The emergence of the New Right in the 1970s can be traced, in part, to the fact that politicians had shifted from mass appeals to segmentation in the 1960s.

Marketers began focusing on segmented markets rather than a mass market in the 1950s, thanks to psychological research.[382] In the 1940s and early 1950s, psychologists applied their findings from experiments in which animals were taught behaviors through exposure to certain conditions in order to explain parallel human behaviors. Humans, they found, could be trained to respond in specific ways to particular stimuli. But by the end of the 1950s, psychologists had come to see humans as individuals who had different motivations. Put another way, not all humans would respond the same way to the same stimuli. For marketers, the information meant that not everyone could be persuaded to buy a product with the same appeal. For politicians, it meant that voters might be attracted to a particular candidate for different reasons.

Dwight Eisenhower was the first president to bring the full panoply of the then current mass-marketing techniques into the political process in the fifties. Richard Nixon, with his promise to campaign in every state, continued the practice of mass marketing in the 1960 presidential campaign. But John Kennedy chose to move away from mass marketing and appealing to the lowest common denominator and instead followed the new marketing trend of segmentation. Kennedy hired Louis Harris to conduct state-level public opinion polling so that he could tailor his message to meet the interests of citizens in each state. His advisers used the polling data to create special interest groups, such as Senior Citizens for Kennedy. Members of those groups would then go out and target other voters just like them.[383]

Barry Goldwater took the idea of targeting audiences to a new level in his 1964 campaign with the implementation of a direct mail strategy. Political direct mail had begun as a technique of the Left in World War II. Harold Oram used direct mail to raise money for Loyalist refugees of the Spanish civil war. One of the people working for him was Marvin Liebman. After the war, Liebman made a political shift to the right, and in 1960, he started raising funds for Young Americans for Freedom (YAF), a conservative group. Liebman hired Richard Viguerie to help out with his direct mail campaign for YAF. Liebman and Viguerie then helped Goldwater with his fund-raising, the first successful large-scale political solicitation.[384] Fifteen million letters were sent out, raising $5.8 million.[385] After Goldwater's defeat in 1964, Viguerie left YAF and went to Washington, D.C., to open his own direct mail company to promote conservative causes, taking with him the names of the 12,500 people who had given more than $50 to Goldwater's campaign. At the time, Viguerie said, "there really wasn't a conservative movement worthy of the name."[386] He believed that many people would contribute to conservative causes if they were asked.

Nixon did not use Viguerie's company in his 1968 election campaign, but he did use segmentation. His campaign strategists employed the latest polling and marketing research techniques to divide voters into groups that would receive different images of Nixon. For example, television ads airing in the South, where Nixon was facing George Wallace in the primaries, used terms and images that had special resonance in the region, such as busing, crime, and the Supreme Court. Black voters were courted in November 1972 with an ad in *Ebony* magazine that outlined Nixon's record: "He has made possible more loans to black businesses than any President before him. He is the first President to ask for governmental funds to fight Sickle Cell Anemia. . . . Don't be taken for granted. Make your vote count."[387] Kevin Phillips, just twenty-seven years old in 1968, became Nixon's "ethnic specialist." It was his job to identify groups, locate them, and decide how to reach them.[388]

The effect of such segmentation on the political process, as historian Lizabeth Cohen noted, is that presidential candidates since Kennedy have attempted to avoid the common ground, rather than find and appeal to common factors among all voters as Roosevelt, Truman, and Eisenhower had done. There is no attempt to establish a shared political agenda. Marketing research suggests that it is too difficult to change people's attitudes during the short period of a campaign, and so, politicians seek to "appeal to voters' existing attitudes and views without offending them with contrary positions."[389] What is sought is "high interest, low backlash" communication. Political direct mail exacerbates the polarization. To be effective—to get an individual to send in $1, $10, or $100—the direct mail appeals must bring out strong emotions in the recipient, especially fear. Claims are sensationalized, and the other side is demonized.[390] Done right, direct mail will bring in funds for the cause and translate into votes.

Regardless of the potential negative effect on democracy, direct mail campaigns became a necessity for candidates and causes after 1974. In that year, campaign finance reform laws were passed that limited the amount of money single donors could give to a campaign. The result was that grassroots fund-raising became crucial, and Richard Viguerie's direct mail company became lucrative. In 1974, he helped create the Committee for the Survival of a Free Congress, among several other such groups. In its first year, the committee raised more than twice as much money as the Conservative Victory Fund, an Old Right organization. By 1977, Viguerie had a computerized list of thirty million conservative donors.[391]

Lizabeth Cohen argued that the segmentation of the 1960s in both marketing and politics led consumer-citizens to view the marketplace and government as existing to meet their personal needs and interests. Government was judged by the benefits it provided to individual citizens rather than to the public interest. The expansion of the federal government under Johnson's Great Society and the rise of consumerism fueled this "politics of consumption."[392] But when the economy took a downturn in the 1970s, it seemed that the excesses of the liberal 1960s had brought about the fall, and Reagan's election in 1980 suggested that the country had shifted to the right ideologically.

Reagan came to power at a time when the public was losing

faith in the media. Cries of liberal bias even from some within the media could be heard in the late 1970s, but concerns about that bias became apparent in public opinion polls in the early 1980s. Reagan's public relations advisers exploited this situation. Reagan, of course, had an advantage over Ford and Carter in that on entering the presidency, he had a public image independent of his portrayal by the news media. He was an actor and a celebrity, which meant he had star appeal. Nixon had created the image of a new Nixon, which the media for the most part accepted, at least initially. Ford had no image on taking office, and so, the media created one for him—first that of athlete and later that of bumbler. Carter portrayed himself as a Southern Baptist, a warm, nice man. The media knew him to be cold and manipulative, and by the end of his term, according to columnist David Broder, few reporters covering Carter bothered to disguise their dislike of him.[393] This would not be Reagan's fate. Former Reagan press aide Leslie Janka said, "The difference between Reagan and Carter is that Reagan fundamentally understands that politics is communication with leadership, and he probably puts communication above substance. Carter was just the flip side of that. He put substance ahead of politics."[394] To that end, Reagan's advisers sought to carefully manage his image and consistently present it to voters and reporters alike.

Jeff and Marie Blyskal argued that the real success of the Reagan PR operation was its ability to involve reporters "as knowing partners in the business of building favorable opinion for the President."[395] Similarly, Mark Hertsgaard observed that the "objective was not simply to tame the press but to transform it into an unwitting mouthpiece of the government."[396] Unlike Nixon and Carter, who sought to go over the heads of the White House press corps and communicate directly with the American people, Reagan's advisers understood that Americans got most of their information about the president through the media and that the way to reach the voters was *through* the press, not over or around it.

Reagan's major public relations players were Michael Deaver and David Gergen. Deaver had been responsible for Reagan's public appearances and press work when Reagan served as governor of California. After the second gubernatorial session ended, Deaver opened a public relations firm whose primary client was Ronald Reagan. Therefore, when Reagan was elected president, it was natural that Deaver was installed as deputy chief of staff. Gergen started out as an assistant speechwriter for Nixon, stayed on through the Watergate years, and later became Ford's director of White House communications. He held the same position in the Reagan administration. Deaver and Gergen shared an appreciation for the power of the press, especially television, to make or break the president. They believed that press–White House relations had deteriorated under Johnson and Nixon to the extent that the situation was destructive to both the media and the presidency. Their top priority was reestablishing positive media relations so that Reagan could communicate with the American people through the filter of the press and build a consensus.[397] As both men saw it, "To govern successfully, the government has to set the agenda; it can't let the press set the agenda for it."[398]

Deaver and Gergen saw television as the key to power. Presidents could not hope to reach the American people with their message without going through television, but the medium was a double-edged sword: it could help or hurt a president because of its power to influence public opinion. Mark Hertsgaard used the example of a lion tamer to describe the nature of a president's relationship with television. A lion tamer can control the lion, but he never forgets that the animal could kill at any time.[399] It was this

balance of control and respect for television that Deaver and Gergen brought to the White House.

While they handled the daily PR activities for the president,
they were joined by, among others, James A. Baker III, Reagan's
chief of staff, and Richard Darman, the deputy chief of staff, in
determining the longer-term public relations strategies. According
to Hertsgaard, those strategies followed basic news management
principles: "plan ahead, stay on the offensive, control the flow of
information, limit reporters' access to the President, talk about the
issues *you* want to talk about, speak in one voice, repeat the same
message many times."[400] Planning was the key. To that end, the
four men and other senior White House aides would meet every
Friday to determine the communication strategy that would set
the media's agenda for the next week. The concern was the big
picture—Reagan's overall policy agenda and how to sell it. Specific tactics to implement the communication strategy were decided by the communications group.

In addition, Reagan's PR team would meet daily to discuss
what they wanted the press to cover that day and establish "the line
of the day."[401] This was immediately transmitted to the other
senior administration officials and executive branch press spokespersons. The line of the day ensured that everyone was saying the
same thing, according to Deaver, but it also represented the
amount of control over the news the White House felt it could
wield. Reporters would first get the line at the 9:15 A.M. mini-
briefing, along with Reagan's schedule for the day, and then have
it repeated at the noon briefing.

Controlling the day's news did not stop with the briefing. All
reporters' telephone calls to White House officials were routed
through Gergen.[402] The practice was to centralize the information
flow so that Gergen could direct reporters to the appropriate indi-

viduals. But reporters found the practice intimidating.[403] Gergen, however, did work behind the scenes to get them what they needed and to supply further information. He also used the relationships he built with reporters to see that the daily coverage was framed as the administration wanted it to be. He called reporters working on stories to make sure they understood the White House's position and to answer questions. And he routinely called the networks close to their final deadlines to find out how they would be reporting a story. He would then spend time trying to influence that coverage, to shape how the story was framed. That kind of behind-the-scenes cajoling of individual reporters would become known as spin.

The term *spin doctor* first entered the American lexicon in 1984 in an editorial in the *New York Times* about the Reagan-Mondale televised debates. The editorial talked about how seconds after a debate ended, "a dozen men in good suits and women in silk dresses will circulate smoothly among the reporters, spouting confident opinions."[404] These men and women, the *Times* noted, were no ordinary "press agents." They were "the Spin Doctors, senior advisers to the candidates, and [they were] playing for very high stakes."[405] According to William Safire, Elisabeth Bumiller of the *Washington Post* adopted the term four days later, defining spin doctors as "the advisers who talk to reporters and try to put their own spin, or analysis, on the story." The term's place in the lexicon was sealed.[406] Safire acknowledged that the word *spin* probably came from the slang meaning of the verb *to spin,* which meant "to deceive" in the 1950s, but he suggested that the phrase *spin doctor* was coined from *play doctor,* or one who fixes up a boring second act.[407]

While Gergen was the spin doctor, the reporters' contact and advocate inside the White House, Deaver was the master of the visuals. When the president visited South Korea in November 1983, Deaver arranged for Reagan to be photographed dressed in a flak jacket and looking through field glasses at North Korea to reinforce his image as commander in chief. On another occasion, Deaver had Reagan drink beer with some blue-collar workers in an Irish pub in Boston to emphasize he was just one of the boys. Deaver left nothing to chance, however, usually traveling to a site in advance and planning every detail, right down to toe marks so that Reagan would know where to stand for the optimum camera shot.[408]

Deaver understood well two tenets of modern marketing: that repetition is necessary to break through the clutter and that visuals are more influential than oral arguments. "If you only get your message across in 30 or 40 seconds on the evening news, then it's important that you restate that message in as many ways as you can," he told a *Los Angeles Times* reporter in 1984.[409] To that end, Reagan would travel the country giving the same speech on a topic over and over, but the visuals with each stop would change. For example, one day he would visit an auto plant and talk about how the economy was growing. The next day, he might give the same speech at a high-tech plant. As Deaver explained, "Pretty soon it begins to soak in, pretty soon people begin to believe the economy *is* getting better."[410] The approach produced effective results, at least when it came to the issue of education. Polls indicated in 1983 that Americans disapproved of Reagan's policy of reducing federal aid to education by a two-to-one margin. The president's strategists decided to emphasize three themes to shift public opinion: excellence in education, merit pay for teachers, and greater classroom discipline. Reagan made approximately twenty-five public appearances on the issue. Afterward, polls showed that people *favored* the policy two to one, a complete reversal.

The visuals orchestrated by the White House were problematic for reporters, especially those in television, in two ways. First, even when the stories were negative, the pictures always showed a smiling Reagan in front of adoring (carefully screened) crowds. As newscaster Sam Donaldson noted, "It's what people see that counts"—and, he might have added, that is what they remember.[411] The second problem was that although Reagan appeared to be highly accessible to the media, the opposite was, in fact, true. His advisers deliberately kept him away from reporters. In his first six years in office, the president held only thirty-nine press conferences, although he did have several brief exchanges with reporters on very narrow and specific issues.[412] But because he was so visible in terms of television coverage, reporters could not complain about not having access. People would not believe them.

That the White House could generate a consistent flow of news while at the same time keeping reporters at bay showed the extent to which the president was a newsmaker. A study comparing coverage of the president and Congress over a sixteen-year period showed that the president's ability to generate media coverage increased from 1958 to 1974 whereas Congress's ability declined. "Presidential news, as a portion of total national government news, increased from 61.9 percent in the period 1958–1963" to 73.1 percent between 1970 and 1974. In the same time span, congressional news steadily declined from 33 percent between 1958 and 1963 to 17.8 percent in the early 1970s.[413]

Unlike the Nixon administration, which controlled coverage by controlling information flow, the Reagan administration chose to inundate the media with information, providing actual prepackaged stories with great visuals that made for appealing coverage. Television wanted and needed pictures of the president; in turn, the White House wanted and needed positive images of the president to be communicated to the American people. In that sense, the two had a symbiotic relationship. But for the White House, the strategy of giving television what it wanted also accomplished something else: it kept reporters from seeking out their own stories. For the most part, the Washington press corps was too busy following Reagan around to search for and develop their own story lines. They knew that most of what they covered were pseudo events rather than hard news, but they had little choice. Competition among the networks and the influential dailies meant they all had to cover the same thing or explain to their editors and publishers why they did not have the story.[414]

Mark Hertsgaard argued that it was the media's allegiance to objectivity that put them at a strategic disadvantage when it came to dealing with the Reagan White House.[415] Objectivity meant a reliance on official sources, which in turn meant that the range of views on a topic was limited to those expressed by officials. Thus, if members of the Democratic Party were not publicly criticizing Reagan's policies, then journalists could not do so in their stories. Journalists were restricted to what Daniel Hallin called the sphere of legitimate controversy.[416] That sphere had taken a decidedly rightward turn with the Reagan presidency, in part because there were no official voices on the left in Washington. No politician could afford to be seen as "liberal" and soft on communism.

In practical terms, that meant Reagan could repeat false or misleading statements over and over and no one would challenge them. Eventually, through repetition, those statements would become accepted as the truth. For instance, in May 1984, Reagan gave a nationally televised speech in which he said that Communists were supplying guerrilla groups in Central America with weapons and that if the United States did not act, "our choice will be a Communist Central America with additional Communist military bases on the mainland of this hemisphere and Communist subversion spreading southward and northward."[417] None of the networks' summaries after the speech or the newspaper accounts the next day noted that many of Reagan's contentions were either unproved or false.[418] Objectivity required the assertions to be reported uncritically because to do otherwise would mean the media had adopted a political stance. It would also mean accusing the president of being a liar, something the media hesitated to do, especially when that president was as well liked as Reagan was.

The media were particularly sensitive to accusations that they were liberal and out of touch with the average American. In the mid-1970s after Spiro Agnew attacked the media for its liberal stance, the *New York Times* and the *Washington Post* broadened the scope of discussion on their op-ed pages by bringing on board the conservatives William Safire and George Will, respectively. Neither man had journalism experience, the traditional background for a columnist. Media critic Eric Alterman, in *Sound and Fury: The Making of the Punditocracy,* suggested that the *Times* and *Post* had to go outside the journalism circle because there were no conservatives among the journalists they might otherwise have considered for the job. Such political columnists, or pundits as some of them came to be called, are important to political discourse because they are the only journalists in newspapers who are allowed to provide the context necessary for people to make informed opinions about what is going on in the world. Freed from the constraints of objectivity, pundits can challenge policies, expose official sources who are playing with the truth, and generally help people understand what actions mean.[419]

Earlier pundits, such as Walter Lippmann and James Reston, tended to be centrists who contributed to the public debate through rational discussion. The world was viewed as a complex place, and the pundits were just one voice among many. Reston had been promoted to pundit from the ranks of journalism and took his role as public informer seriously. Lippmann was only a journalist for a short time; he was actually a political philosopher. He believed an elite group of intellectuals was needed to translate political events to people, and he took that approach in his writing. But Safire and Will came from a different perspective. Safire had been a speechwriter for President Nixon, and Will was a former professor and a Republican aide. Safire was considered by many at the *Times* as just a paid manipulator, and when Will first started at the *Post,* the editor of the editorial page said that "Will had not as yet developed even an 'elementary sense of journalistic propriety.'"[420] For both men, their columns served as a means of political partisanship, as a way for them to espouse their conservative ideology. They did not seek to inform or educate, just persuade.

Safire and Will were part of a group of pundits who grew in stature and power during the 1970s when, according to Alterman, "television discovered punditry and vice versa."[421] Ironically, the process began with Lippmann, the political philosopher, when CBS News aired a program entitled "Conversation with Walter Lippmann" on August 11, 1963. Lippmann did not have much use for television, but he agreed to do annual broadcasts. In 1969, a weekly television show, *Agronsky and Company,* debuted, devoted to the opinions of journalists. A whole series of such shows followed over the years, such as ABC's *This Week,* CBS's *Inside Washington,* and NBC's *The McLaughlin Group* and *Meet the Press.* Television gave the pundits wealth and celebrity status, but it also deteriorated the discussion. By the early 1980s, the trend of hiring nonjournalists such as Safire and Will escalated. As Alterman remarked, "No longer a means of rewarding the profession's most distinguished members, the jobs opened up to political deal makers, speechwriters, press flacks, and professional ideologues."[422] Television became a no-holds-barred venue, where ethics and the public took backseats to persuasion. For example, Will found no ethical problem with coaching Reagan prior to his debate with President Carter in 1980 and then going on *Nightline* as an impartial observer, declaring that the Republican challenger had given a "thoroughbred performance."[423]

The growing power of the pundit class coincided with the rise of the New Right in the 1970s. The neoconservatives took the grievances of the middle class, Nixon's silent majority, and blamed all of the country's problems on liberal elites, "scientists, teachers, and educational administrators, journalists and others."[424] These elites were said to be engaged in a vast conspiracy to promote socialism. Everything that was wrong with the country, especially the social changes brought about by the civil rights, women's, and student movements, was the fault of those on the left. Richard Viguerie's direct mail campaigns promoted the ideology at the grassroots level, and Safire and Will, among others, promoted it at the influential Washington pundit level.

When Reagan came to power, the power was complete. Will, for example, made no attempts to hide his friendship with the new president; in fact, he wrote his first column after Reagan's inauguration from the Oval Office. During the 1980s, Will was a regular presence on the network news shows, such as *Agronsky and Company*, *This Week with David Brinkley,* the *ABC Evening News,* and *Nightline,* as well as on the *Washington Post*'s op-ed page. An NBC official explained the attraction: "Someone had to explain why Ronald Reagan's conservatism was sweeping the country and he filled the vacuum."[425] In the mid-1980s, the *Wall Street Journal* described Will as "perhaps the most powerful journalist in America."[426]

What made him seem powerful was his inside track to the president. The new pundit class always claimed to have inside information about what official Washington was going to do. During Reagan's presidency, that was true. Reagan's advisers understood the importance of television punditry and used it to the president's advantage. They held special pundit briefings on Friday mornings, in which White House officials would give "not for attribution" information. The pundits would then go off to their tapings, where, according to Alterman, "the tidbits and leaks were repeated verbatim, either in the form of predictions or inside scoops."[427] The pundits, then, became simply another group through which the Reagan camp could control and frame the debate.

While the public may not have known about these efforts on the part of the Reagan administration to control information flow, the media did alert them to other ways that control was exerted, although people seemed not to care. Americans did not appear concerned, for example, that the media were kept from covering the Grenada invasion. Nor did they seem concerned about Reagan's executive order in 1983 subjecting all federal employees with access to classified information to polygraph tests or his efforts to narrow the scope of the Freedom of Information Act by expanding the kinds of information that could be classified and kept from public view. During the Carter years, officials had been directed to classify material only on the basis of an identifiable harm and to use the lower level of classification if they were not sure in which category the information belonged. Reagan did away with both requirements.[428]

The administration also sought to require that more than one hundred thousand government employees with access to high-level classified information had to sign prepublication contracts that were enforceable for the rest of their lives. The contracts were onerous in that they were not restricted to writings about classified information. Any information about intelligence activities had to be submitted for government approval.[429]

The Reporters Committee for the Freedom of the Press called the administration's various efforts a "systematic censorship campaign on government information." In 1983, First Amendment lawyer Floyd Abrams wrote in the *New York Times Magazine* that the administration "seems obsessed with the risk of information, fearful of both its unpredictability and its potential for leading the public to the 'wrong' conclusions." Even William Safire, arguably of the same conservative ideology as the administration, described its "obsession with secrecy" as its "Frankenstein's monster."[430]

But things were to get worse in the second Reagan term. David Gergen, Michael Deaver, and James Baker III all left the administration at the end of the first term. Under their stewardship, the White House had maintained a press policy in which the lines of communication were kept open even with journalists who had criticized Reagan or his policies.[431] The administration did not want to close off media outlets and thereby lose the opportunity to frame the coverage. And according to David Broder of the *Washington Post,* although Reagan personally was not accessible to the media, "the access to senior White House staff was so constant and their responses so full during the first term that . . . readers of papers like the *Post* were often better informed about presidential decision making than ever before."[432]

But when Donald T. Regan replaced Baker as chief of staff at the start of Reagan's second term, the tone changed, and the

White House became closed, sometimes even hostile, to the media. Regan came from the brokerage business, not public relations, and he treated information as the investment industry did. Power was centralized, and the number of people involved in policy decisions was reduced. Fewer people meant fewer sources of information for journalists. And even as the potential for leaks was decreased, penalties for leaking information increased. Where Baker, Deaver, and Gergen had tried to manage the news and frame coverage often behind the scenes and "on background," Regan provided information on a need-to-know basis, although it was usually on the record. He also adopted a top-down management style in which policy decisions were presented as faits accomplis. In the first administration, Baker, Deaver, and Gergen had sought to make reporters understand why and how a given policy had been chosen.[433]

Shortly after the 1984 election, the Reagan administration launched an aggressive policy to stop unauthorized leaks of information, including wiretapping of government officials and reinstating the polygraph requirement for federal employees. In one instance, Secretary of Defense Caspar W. Weinberger requested that the *Washington Post* withhold a story about the space shuttle containing a satellite that would monitor Soviet electronic signals. When the *Post* published the story anyway because it contained information already in the public record, Weinberger accused the paper of lending "aid and comfort" to America's enemies and said the story was "the height of journalistic irresponsibility."[434] Floyd Abrams, in a speech before the College of Communications at Boston University in 1985, complained that the use of the language of treason in such situations was an attack on the legitimacy of the press, not on what the press reported.[435] It was as if once

Reagan did not have to worry about reelection, his true contempt for the media could be allowed to reveal itself.[436]

Despite the changes in attitude between the first and second administrations, the media continued to show relative deference to Reagan—until the Iran-Contra affair, that is. In 1986, a small Lebanese newspaper reported that the United States had been secretly shipping arms to Iran in an effort to get the Ayatollah Khomeini's help in arranging for the release of three Americans held hostage in Lebanon. Previously, Reagan had publicly said he would not bargain with terrorists for the release of the hostages, and he had imposed an embargo on arms shipments to Iran, which he asked other nations to observe.[437]

Reagan attempted to repair the damage caused by the Lebanese paper's report by giving a televised speech in which he tried to explain his actions. When that tactic was not successful, he held a news conference to deny that he had sanctioned arms sales by Israel to Iran on behalf of the United States. But senior officials had already told reporters that Israel agreed to supply Iran with the arms on the condition that its stock would be replaced from Pentagon supplies. Then it was discovered that millions of dollars from the arms sales to Iran had gone to support the forces fighting the Sandinista government in Nicaragua, without Reagan's approval and in violation of American law.[438]

Mark Hertsgaard asked rhetorically whether the "Reagan administration officials [would] have risked trading arms for hostages had the U.S. press been more of a watchdog in the preceding months and years." It would also be fair to ask whether the trade would have occurred had Baker, Deaver, and Gergen still been around.[439] As David Broder noted, Baker's view was that "no policy of any scope, significance or duration could be maintained unless it could enlist support of sensible people in Congress and be explained and defended to sensible people in the press and public."[440] It is unlikely that Baker would have approved such a secret deal. But his replacement in the second term, Regan, operated on the assumption that the president had a mandate and therefore did not have to defend himself or his actions to anyone.[441] The strict control of information in the second term and the closing off of the White House from media access created an atmosphere and an opportunity that allowed the administration to engage in risky behavior.

For its part, the media became more aggressive in their coverage of Reagan, but they also were careful not to be seen as out to get the president, as some had accused them of doing during Watergate. By the 1988 presidential election, it was clear that both George Bush and Walter Mondale had learned how to run campaigns from Reagan. Both focused on photo opportunities and kept their distance from reporters. The media in turn continued to focus on the horse-race aspect of the election rather than on issues. Ratings took priority, and news was treated as "a commodity to be sold rather than an educational trust to be fulfilled."[442]

SEVEN

CONTROLLING THE MESSAGE

In 1976, the ABC network hired interviewer-reporter Barbara Walters for a record $1 million. News of the salary sparked a debate among people in and out of the media about how much television reporters should be paid.[443] It was not a question of whether ABC could afford the salary; after all, the combined pretax profits of the three major networks went from $268 million in 1961 to $1 billion in 1985 (in 1986 dollars).[444] Rather, it was a question about the relative worth of such reporters. By 1976, the network news anchors had become highly paid celebrities, as Walters's salary revealed.

Television news had been considered a headline service until the 1970s. Print reporters gathered the news, which was then made available to all media via the news services.[445] But in the last half of the decade, television news made improvements that elevated its stature. News departments grew in size, and reporters became more specialized, allowing them to do their own reporting. Technological advances such as electronic news gathering (ENG) equipment allowed for live transmission from an event, greatly enhancing television's ability to "show" the news as it happened, rather than just telling people what had occurred. Of course, this also meant that reporters were now part of the story, since they were "live at the scene."[446] The "eyewitness news" approach lent itself to what CBS's *60 Minutes* called tabloid news, especially at the local level.[447] A 1974 study of the weekly news programs produced by a top-rated San Francisco television station revealed that the tabloid news category of "fire, sex, tear-jerkers, accidents, and exorcism" accounted for more than half of all the stories presented.[448]

The show *60 Minutes,* which started on CBS in 1968, was not without its own tabloid news problems. Media critic David Shaw accused the program of ignoring serious issues in favor of stories that had an emotional impact. Much of the show consisted of "sex, crime, [and] consumer rip-offs," Shaw charged.[449] And the technique used to exploit the entertainment value of the stories was often "trial by television," in which the production team acted as accuser, judge, and jury of individuals and institutions.[450] In trial by television, the accused was usually offered the opportunity to respond to allegations through an interview for the program, but the editing process put the producer in complete control of what the accused could say in his or her own defense. Consequently, the program was more about entertaining rather than informing.[451] The show was also accused of practicing "checkbook journalism," in which sources were paid for their information or interview, a questionable ethical practice. Apparently, CBS paid H. R. Haldeman, Nixon's former aide, $100,000 for an interview.[452]

At the syndicated programming level, tabloid news found its niche in *Entertainment Tonight,* which focused on celebrities, television shows, and movies. Its success spawned copycat shows, such as *A Current Affair, Inside Edition,* and *Hard Copy.* But to their credit, the networks did try to elevate their news coverage to balance the sensationalism of the syndicated shows. Both ABC and NBC ran longer pieces over several evenings to cover in more depth ongoing stories of significance. For example, ABC ran a series of twenty-minute updates on the 1979 Iran hostage crisis every evening after the nightly news. The series eventually turned into *Nightline* and became an established presence in the nightly news market.[453] And in the early 1980s, CBS offered an expanded late and early morning news service for its affiliates that provided seven hours of continuous news.[454]

Part of network television's efforts to be taken seriously as a provider of news came about because of the competition from cable. Cable technology allowed for a vastly increased number of stations and expanded programming. The number of cable subscribers in the country jumped from approximately five million in 1970 to thirty-five million by 1985. The multichannel nature of cable meant that all-news channels and channels targeted to specific markets could be developed.[455] In fact, cable made the term *broadcasting* seem obsolete: *narrowcasting* was more appropriate.[456]

Ted Turner launched the first twenty-four-hour television news service, Cable News Network, in 1980 and shortly thereafter began airing *Money Line,* the first nightly half-hour business news program on television.[457] When CNN proved successful, others followed suit with their own brand of cable news. The Financial News Network (FNN) focused on market developments and business news.[458] C-SPAN, the nonprofit public service network, began broadcasting twenty-four hours a day in 1982. NBC started CNBC to compete with CNN, and in an example of niche marketing, the Christian Broadcasting Network (CBN) began providing news coverage of issues important to Christian evangelicals.[459]

The growth of television as a news outlet created significant competition for newspapers. At first, publishers saw cable as more of a problem for the networks than for newspapers. It was believed that people would still need newspapers as a source of information, even if just to tell them what was on television. But cable did pose a threat. The number of daily newspapers had remained relatively stable at 1,750 until 1980, when 50 dailies closed. Chain ownership of dailies had climbed dramatically since 1960, when 114 chains owned 563 dailies, or 32 percent of all the daily papers. By 1977, however, chains owned 60 percent of the total. Not coincidentally, the number of cities with competing dailies decreased in the same period until 1990, when only thirty-four cities had two daily newspapers.[460]

Increasingly in the 1980s and 1990s, newspapers experimented with ways to make themselves more relevant. *USA Today,* the first national newspaper, came out in the early 1980s in an attempt to mimic the television format. With its colorful graphics and "sound-bite" articles, it led other newspapers to update their own look.[461] In the 1990s, newspapers became even more consumer friendly, adding reader hotlines, shopping discount cards, and personal computer links.[462]

Despite, or perhaps because of, the increased competition among the news media, news coverage was surprisingly uniform. The networks were afraid not to cover an event their competitors were covering even if the event's newsworthiness was questionable. For instance, the networks routinely covered President Reagan's daily activities even though his appearances involved calculated photo opportunities more often than developing news. For newspapers, chain ownership meant shared resources, such as international and national news stories, making the front pages of papers around the country similar in terms of coverage.[463] But competition and shared ownership do not account fully for the standardization, since a similar uniformity could be found among the newsmagazines. *Time* and *Newsweek* had identical cover subjects four times in 1961; by 1985, the number of identical cover subjects had quadrupled to sixteen, an average of nearly one in

three issues.[464] In the case of newsmagazines, the growing professionalism of reporters seemed to provide an explanation for the
uniformity.

College programs in journalism had been in existence since the
beginning of the twentieth century, but the number of journalists
holding degrees was finally making an impact on the field.[465] In
the mid-1950s, to cite one example, fewer than 20 percent of the
staff of Texan newspapers had been to college.[466] But by the early
1970s, that figure was approaching 90 percent.[467] A 1978 survey of
Washington journalists found that all had college degrees and one-
third had advanced professional or graduate degrees.[468] Journalism
education helped create a shared value system and a set of standards
for what constituted news and how to report it. The college training and the self-scrutiny found in professional journals such as the
Columbia Journalism Review helped cement the belief among reporters that the media's role in society was that of watchdog of
established institutions and protector of the underdog.[469] The
watchdog metaphor grew out of the Vietnam and Watergate eras
and consumerism. Protecting the underdog was the purpose, and
investigative reporting was the method.

By adopting the watchdog metaphor, the media put themselves
into an adversarial position vis-à-vis the institutions of government, business, and, in some cases, religion. Scholars have suggested that the press was probing but relatively supportive of the
presidency until Vietnam, when it became obvious that President
Johnson had been not just selectively disclosing information but
also deliberately misleading the American people.[470] The Watergate scandal pushed the media over the edge into an openly
adversarial stance. A similar process occurred with the relationship
between business and the press. Journalists, for the most part, left

corporate America alone until Ralph Nader's probes revealed the extent of bad corporate behavior and the power of the press to produce positive changes in that behavior.

As the watchdog role was conceived in the 1970s, it was not enough to simply keep an eye on government. Now, those in the media, especially television, believed that their "chief duty [was] to put before the nation its unfinished business."[471] As one lobbyist observed, the old journalistic standard of "getting the story and getting it right" was being replaced by "getting the story and *using* it right," that is, to influence public policy in the media's capacity as watchdog and protector.[472] The media's power in terms of setting the political agenda by influencing public opinion had risen with the growth of television news. By 1985, two-thirds of Americans said television was their major news source; for almost 60 percent of that group, it was their only news source.[473]

Although the media assumed their role as protectors of the underdog, the average American in the 1970s came to see the media as a whole as a liberal institution out to undermine his or her way of life.[474] President Nixon helped fuel the idea of the liberal media bias through the speeches of his vice president, Spiro Agnew, who accused the press of being "nattering nabobs of negativism."[475] For many people, the adversarial stance the media took with Presidents Ford and Carter seemed to confirm that they were, in fact, liberal and antiestablishment. Surveys of reporters also suggested that the majority of journalists were Democrats or independents. But the same could not be said about editors and publishers. Actually, studies showed that newspapers traditionally supported conservative presidential candidates. In 1976, some 84 percent of daily newspapers supported Gerald Ford over Jimmy Carter, and four years earlier, 93 percent had supported Richard Nixon over George McGovern.[476]

In 1981, when President Reagan came to power, the majority of media outlets in the United States were owned or controlled by fifty large corporations. Six years later, that number had been reduced to just twenty-nine. Half of the media corporations ranked among the Fortune 500.[477] As Mark Hertsgaard put it, "Contrary to right-wing mythology, the press was not an institution dominated by leftists but a creature of the very richest of the rich and mightiest of the mighty in American society."[478]

As the media took on the characteristics of big business, corporate executives tried to take advantage of that situation and forge greater understanding between the press and business.[479] As the chairman of Standard Oil Company told a group of journalists in 1982, "Business and journalism—for better or worse—are locked together in a symbiotic relationship."[480] Another individual described the two as "inextricably intertwined."[481] Business executive Irvine Hockaday told editors that businesses and the media were both subject to the whims of society. The corporate charter was granted by the public and could be taken away by the public, he noted, but so was the First Amendment. He argued that business and the media had to both respond to and reflect the values of society unless they wished to lose their legitimacy.[482] Hockaday also questioned the adversarial relationship between business and the media. "Where does the line between objectivity and adversity lie?" he asked. "When does coverage cease to be comprehensive and start to become relentless; ultimately to become an invasion of privacy?"[483]

Business professor Wilmar Bernthal, in a *Business Forum* article, noted with irony that business and media seemed locked in an adversarial battle even though neither sector was seen as very credible. A 1983 Gallup Poll revealed that public confidence in big business was at 28 percent, while newspapers enjoyed a 38 percent confidence level. Television received the lowest rating, with just 25 percent of respondents expressing confidence in that medium.[484]

Bernthal sought to explain the tensions between business and the media. He observed that business executives who had been steeped in capitalistic values tended to want media coverage "that waves the flag for free enterprise, equates business leadership with motherhood, celebrates the good news, and suppresses scandals and failures."[485] Naturally, these executives felt betrayed when the media reported the "bad" news. For their part, the media had what Bernthal described as "mixed motives." They saw themselves as having a special role in society, but at the same time, they were businesses.[486] As such, audience share and profits were sometimes more determinant of what news was covered than was the value of the information itself. On one hand, that situation led to superficial reporting and personality pieces, driven by the success of *People* magazine and similar publications. On the other hand, it also produced what one businessman described as "overzealous" investigative reporting or "the post-Watergate syndrome."[487] In both cases, sensationalism, which the public appeared to want, seemed to be the determining factor.

But on an individual basis, the problem between business and media seemed to stem from a failure to understand one another. When it came to business reporting, journalists felt hampered by businesspeople they felt were lying to them or at least not telling the whole truth. And businesspeople, for their part, were convinced that reporters were out to get them. A study for the American Management Association showed that both sides were frustrated with the relationship.[488] But change was occurring. Journalists were beginning to understand business better, and businesspeople were beginning to understand the limitations under which reporters worked.[489] Some in the media recognized that the problem was the CEO, but others put the blame squarely on the PR practitioner.[490] A former editor of *New York* magazine said, tongue in cheek, "Corporations should eliminate every public relations person who ever was born," suggesting that PR practitioners got in the way of the flow of information.[491]

But in some cases, corporations took a more aggressive stance, striking back at what they perceived as negative media coverage. Businesses started monitoring media performance in areas such as energy, the environment, and consumerism, on the lookout for evidence of antibusiness bias or at least news inaccuracies. When inaccuracies were found, companies took out full-page ads in newspapers to reveal what they considered the real facts. Mobil Oil went so far as to boycott the *Wall Street Journal* after the newspaper accused the company chairman of nepotism. Mobil refused to answer inquiries from the *Journal*'s reporters, issue releases to the newspaper, or place ads in it.[492] When asked about the boycott decision, Herbert Schmertz, Mobil's vice president for public affairs, said that the *Journal* was "not interested in business stories but in gossip and innuendo."[493] The consensus of a group of public relations and media executives asked to comment on the boycott by the *Business and Society Review* was that it was a childish and ineffective strategy.

Schmertz, by contrast, described the boycott as "creative confrontation" and said that inaccurate or distorted reporting posing an immediate threat to Mobil required such a strategy.[494] Mobil also used its op-ed page ads to voice criticisms of media coverage and correct what it saw as inaccuracies in news stories. The company engaged in a strategy of "discretionary confrontation" against critics when they posed no immediate threat but were still adversaries. For instance, when consumer activist Ralph Nader decided to hold a "big business day" to point out the problems caused by big business, Mobil held its own "growth day." As Schmertz put it, "We need to use the same techniques as our adversaries."[495]

While Mobil took on a major newspaper for what it considered biased reporting, dealing with inaccuracies on television was more problematic for companies. Because the majority of Americans got their news from television rather than newspapers, buying ad space in a newspaper was unlikely to reach the people who had seen the original program. Nor could a print ad compete against the immediacy and emotional impact of television. But when *60 Minutes* aired a segment on Illinois Power Company, claiming its nuclear power plant project was over budget and mismanaged, causing the utility's stock to fall, the company decided to fight back on the show's terms via videotape.[496] The utility had taped the entire three-hour CBS interview with Illinois Power's executive vice president, William Gerstner. Using that footage along with the *60 Minutes* segment, the company produced its own forty-two-minute counterprogram, "60 Minutes: Our Reply."

The slickly produced show mimicked the style of *60 Minutes*, complete with a public relations staffer, Howard Rowe, serving as the reporter-narrator. The show took a point-counterpoint format, with Rowe interrupting the *60 Minutes* segment at every contested part. As one industry observer said of the film, "It's very effective. There's nothing like direct contrast."[497] The *60 Minutes* segment had contended that "the cost of building the plants has gone crazy . . . a China syndrome of cost."[498] But viewers were not provided with specifics to justify the allegation that this project was "'well ahead of the pack' in cost overruns."[499] Nor were viewers allowed to see Gerstner's explanations for the costs, although they were part of his original interview. Gerstner's three-hour interview had been reduced to two minutes for the show; Illinois Power's critics dominated the remaining fourteen minutes. In the reply program, the critics were revealed to have had personal agendas and questionable motives. One critic— Mr. X—had been shown in the shadows, with his voice disguised to protect his identity. According to *60 Minutes,* that was because he feared retribution, but Sandy Graham, in a piece on the Illinois Power counterprogram, called it "good theater."[500]

Clearly, Illinois Power was unable to reach the same number of people with its program as the original *60 Minutes* program did, but the company contended that was not the purpose. The counterprogram was sent to its main publics—employees, customers, shareholders, and the investment community. When word of the videotape got out, however, requests for copies came from all over the country. "As a means of reaching the thinking people and thoughtshapers, this is just an excellent medium," the utility concluded.[501] The reply program was also an effective intimidation tactic, potentially forcing broadcast journalists to be more careful with their editing.

Particularly problematic in terms of the relationship between business and the media were the oil crises experienced in the 1970s. Polls showed that Americans did not believe the crises really existed. They blamed the oil companies for creating an artificial shortage to raise prices.[502] The Media Institute, a nonprofit research organization, conducted a study of the news coverage of the 1973–1974 and 1978–1979 oil crises. The study found that solutions such as conservation and price controls received three times more coverage than did market solutions; that the networks used government sources for information on solutions 77 percent of the time and oil industry sources 9 percent of the time; and that when causes were discussed, the oil industry was accused of perpetuating a hoax, profiteering, or other such actions 25 percent of the time.[503]

A 1985 study of the television news coverage of six risk issues had similar results regarding sources. Officials accounted for 54 percent of the sources, while citizens accounted for 28 percent. Scientific experts and members of interest groups made up the remaining 18 percent.[504] Four years later, a study of network television news coverage of environmental risks over a twenty-six-month period determined that because of time constraints, the networks usually showed only two sources for a story. Not surprisingly, they were more likely to pair sources with opposing viewpoints than sources with complementary viewpoints. In all, 67 percent of the stories showed at least one source on the air, and that source tended to be a citizen. The conclusion of the researchers was that the sources themselves were responsible for the coverage. Experts needed to learn to summarize their points in twenty- to thirty-second sound bites and to make their data more visual.[505]

For at least one oilman, however, the inability of oil companies to communicate their position was not caused by television's time constraints or the fact that the oil experts were not media savvy but by the corruption of the public discourse. In a speech before the Houston Association of Petroleum Landmen in 1980, Joseph Reid declared that society had "begun to lose the means of identifying, recognizing and telling the truth."[506] Vietnam and Watergate had caused Americans to question the truth and, in the process, had destroyed the standards of public discourse.

Reid lamented the fact that the public found consumer and environmental groups the most reliable sources on the energy issue, presumably because they were seen as disinterested. Oil companies were considered the least reliable sources, even though, as Reid put it, they were the closest to the problem. Experts, he contended, were losing ground in terms of credibility to those who had a cause but little expertise.[507] As one media person stated, "We're currently in the process of de-frocking all our experts."[508] But at the same time, in an age of twenty-four-hour news channels, a key factor in a media outlet's competitiveness was speed.[509] And when the real experts or the corporate spokespersons who had direct knowledge of a specific event refused or were unwilling to provide the media with timely information, the media would find their own experts to fill the information vacuum. Many of these "instant experts," who had no direct knowledge of the event, provided unsubstantiated and misleading information, leaving the public confused and cynical.[510]

In addition to the credibility problem facing experts, the situation was exacerbated by the less than precise and sometimes even careless use of language in the media. Reid cited the windfall profits tax law as an example: "The president declared it: the media legitimized it: the congress passed it. . . . Everybody in our industry fought the tax. Nobody fought the language."[511] He complained that the concept of a "windfall" profit suggested that the money just fell into their laps and ignored the fact that the companies spent millions on research and infrastructure.

Philosopher David Kelley, in an article in the *Harvard Business Review*, warned businesses about the same thing. Critics of corporations had been allowed to set the terms of the debate on social and economic issues, he said. And unless businesses were prepared to challenge the assumptions on which those terms were based, they could not expect to win any battles for public opinion. The three most important assumptions, according to Kelley, were, first, that the public interest was the most important interest; second, that businesspeople had few or no morals because they were motivated by profit; and third, that corporations were political as well as economic entities.[512] The idea that an industry could experience so-called windfall profits and should be taxed because of those profits exemplified all three assumptions at work.

Slogans and descriptors such as "windfall profits tax" had long been used in politics, but some were concerned about the growing acceptance of euphemisms and slogans as "shorthand for reality," especially given television's need for thirty-second sound bites.[513] The danger was that they threatened to "substitute packages for contents as the medium of communication."[514] Rollo May, in *Power and Innocence,* for instance, noted that words, especially those on television, were being used to sell the personality of the speaker rather than to communicate meaning. "Language bears less and less relationship to the item being discussed. There is a denial of any relationship to underlying logic," he wrote.[515]

These changes in society, along with consumerism, environmentalism, and the growth of governmental regulation, forced corporations and their CEOs to take a more activist stance on public policy issues by the end of the 1970s.[516] For much of their early history, corporations were active in public affairs, but the Great Depression changed that. Business leaders lost their influence when it became clear they did not have a solution to the economic woes facing the nation. People instead turned to the federal government for answers. The result was that for the next fifty years, corporations remained politically quiet, content with philanthropic endeavors such as having a presence on the board of directors of the local art museum or hospital. But that situation began to change in the 1970s as people turned away from government solutions and back to private enterprise.[517]

By 1980, CEOs were spending more and more of their time engaged in public affairs. Indeed, some business leaders suggested that anywhere from 10 to 50 percent of their time was committed in that way.[518] As William May, the chairman and CEO of American Can Company, stated in describing the activities of the modern CEO, "We play an active role in our company's public relations, we make ourselves available to the media, we speak out on current public issues on television, in Op-Ed articles and to audiences of interested citizens."[519] The increased activism was necessary because corporate behavior was coming under greater scrutiny from special interest groups, the media, governmental agencies, and Congress. It was the role of the CEO to equate the corporate interest with the public interest and adapt the corporate interest when necessary to meet external pressures.[520] In other words, CEOs had to resolve the conflict between "their management responsibilities to their stockholders, and . . . their political and public responsibilities to the world outside their own doors."[521] The role of the PR practitioner was to correctly interpret the public will as it emerged so the CEO could ensure the company was in conformity with it.[522]

Public relations practitioner Philip Lesly referred to the public will as the "human climate," which he defined as "the attitudes of people that determine how all segments of society will function."[523] For Lesly, the human climate was becoming the dominant force globally in the last decades of the twentieth century. Invention had been the main force in the first third of the century, followed by the rise of the professional management class.[524] Lesly attributed the ascendence of the human climate to several factors, including accelerated technology, the availability of a higher living standard, mass education, television, a glorification of democracy, the management revolution, and a universal sense of entitlement.[525] Whatever the cause, according to Lesly, "people now have a sense of instability that leads to frustration and fear. That leads to susceptibility to illogic and emotion, which can be fired up for causes or ideologies that happen to arise at the right time."[526]

One consequence of the dominance of Lesly's human climate was that the public will was becoming vital to the policy-making process, as the decision making moved from the legislative arena to a more public one, thanks to special interest groups.[527] These groups had a long political history, but the events of the 1960s and 1970s propelled them to center stage. First came the civil rights movement and then Vietnam, which focused attention on the federal government and taught people "how to disrupt, how to form coalitions, how to seduce the media."[528] In the 1970s, the environment, consumerism, and health and safety became the key issues, concerns that were directed at the business community. These issues and their potential solutions were not simply debated in legislative circles. As PR practitioner Richard Armstrong put it, "Each advocate also took its case 'to the people' through the media, and in many cases took to the streets or to corporate Board rooms to attract the media's attention" and get grassroots support.[529]

And to a greater extent than in the past, advocates were hiring public relations firms to carefully plan and implement their media campaigns. The 1989 alar scare is a case in point. On October 3, 1989, the *Wall Street Journal* printed, on its op-ed page, excerpts from a memorandum written by David Fenton of Fenton Communications.[530] Fenton outlined how his agency had created the scare in behalf of its client, the Natural Resources Defense Council (NRDC). The memo indicated that NRDC hired Fenton to conduct a media campaign for the release of an NRDC report titled "Intolerable Risk: Pesticides in Our Children's Food." One of the pesticides in the report was alar, a substance used to make apples look redder and more marketable.

The Fenton plan called for *60 Minutes* to break the story of the report in late February 1989. The NRDC would then hold a news conference to officially release the report. Exactly one week later, actress Meryl Streep, who had contacted the NRDC and offered her assistance, would hold a news conference to announce the formation of a group called Mothers and Others for Pesticide Limits. The purpose of the group was to "direct citizen action at changing the pesticide laws, and help consumers lobby for pesticide-free produce at their grocery stores."[531] The plan stipulated that the release of the report and the formation of the group were to be separate events, to ensure the media had two stories to report on the issue and not just one. Interviews with major women's magazines were arranged ahead of time.

The campaign was launched, in part, in response to a statement by the Environmental Protection Agency (EPA) on February 3, 1989, that alar did not pose a significant cancer threat to adults.[532] This campaign was designed to keep the pressure on the EPA to ban alar's use by shifting the focus from adults to children, and it went off without a hitch. On February 26, 1989, *60 Minutes* broke the story to forty million viewers. The next morning, the NRDC held its national news conference; local news conferences were conducted simultaneously in twelve cities around the country. Then, on March 7, Meryl Streep announced the formation of the grassroots group at a news conference in Washington, D.C. She also did sixteen interviews by satellite with local television anchors. In all, media coverage included: "two segments on CBS *60 Minutes,* the covers of *Time* and *Newsweek* (two stories in each magazine), the *Phil Donahue* show, multiple appearances on *Today, Good Morning America* and *CBS This Morning,* several stories on each of the network evening newscasts, *MacNeil/Lehrer,* multiple stories in the *N.Y. Times, Washington Post, L.A. Times* and newspapers around the country, three cover stories in *USA Today, People,* four women's magazines with a combined circulation of 17 million . . . and thousands of repeat stories in local media around the nation and the world."[533]

In his memo, Fenton noted that such coverage was unusual for the release of a public interest group's report. But in this case, the coverage was "created by design."[534] "Our goal was to create so many repetitions of NRDC's message that average American consumers (not just the policy elite in Washington) could not avoid hearing it—from many different media outlets within a short period of time," he wrote. The story was to take on a life of its own once given the initial push by Fenton Communications and then continue to "affect policy and consumer habits," which was exactly what happened. Media coverage continued, and some school systems actually banned apples.[535] The apple growers struck back by hiring their own public relations firm, Hill & Knowlton. News stories started appearing that said the alar levels in apples were below federal standards and that the media had exaggerated the problem. But by then, the damage to the apple growers had been done and the public had lost interest in the issue.[536]

Fenton and NRDC were successful not just because of their news management capabilities but also because their message tapped into the attitudes and beliefs of their target public—mothers and others concerned with pesticide levels in food. The message played on the fear of mothers that their children were being exposed to harmful substances and their sense of guilt in being complicit in that exposure. This combination of news management and message creation has been called strategic communication. A strategic campaign is "one that selects and markets through the news those symbols that most effectively resonate with the most relevant perceptions and expectations of the highest priority audiences."[537] What separates a strategic communication campaign from traditional ones is the systematic way it "integrates theory, research, and practice to manage perceptions, preferences, and behaviors."[538]

Strategic communication arose out of social scientific studies done in the 1940s and 1950s on voting behavior. The development of the random-sampling method, borrowed from the agricultural sciences by a group of Michigan social psychologists, allowed for more accurate surveys of attitudes and beliefs. The results of two national studies of voting behavior using the random-sampling method were published in 1960 in *The American Voter*. The book was highly influential among political and social scientists, prompting a collaborative undertaking that produced the Simulmatics Project that same year.[539]

The project was a computer simulation model that was designed to predict voter turnout and party preference using a candidate's position on any given issue. The model was offered to John Kennedy's campaign team in 1960 and was used to test three issues: civil rights, foreign policy, and religion. Although Kennedy's team did not rely entirely on the model's recommendations, the fact that his advisers took it into consideration at all convinced the social scientists that their theories could have practical applications.[540] The Simulmatics Project did not survive, but the growing body of knowledge about human behavior gave political and persuasive communicators an appreciation for theory and research. As the data–collecting techniques became more sophisticated and the theory derived from the data more predictive, the persuasive communicators became more sophisticated and effective. Some of these communicators applied their skills and knowledge in political campaigns; others worked for lobbying or grassroots groups. Still others served unions or even foreign governments seeking advantageous American trade policies. As political scientist Jarol Manheim wrote, these were "a new class of political operatives, working in the streets, but trained in the classroom."[541]

This movement of social scientific theory and research methods from the classroom to the streets was not restricted to politics. It also occurred in journalism, although not until a decade later. The trend of news organizations reporting social science data and conducting their own in-house polls became especially prominent in the 1970s.[542] A 1978 survey of 437 newspapers revealed a marked increase in newspaper polling after 1970, with more than half of those that did poll conducting their first poll since then.[543] In fact, the use of social science methodology by reporters led to a new genre of reporting known as precision journalism. Journalists began using social science methods to explore public opinion on a variety of topics. Suddenly, quantitative data had acquired value as news, making journalism more of an applied science.[544]

David Weaver and Maxwell McCombs, mass communication scholars, traced this merger between journalism, social science methodology, and journalism education. Beginning in the 1930s with the creation of a Ph.D. minor in journalism within the social sciences, journalism schools began hiring Ph.D.'s out of social science disciplines rather than from the humanities. Those Ph.D.'s brought with them a way of looking at the world that was different from that of the earlier English language and history scholars.

The new academics put more emphasis on systematically recording and analyzing observations and on generalizing from those observations in their research. By 1973, a survey of the 17 schools in the country offering a doctorate in journalism or mass communication revealed that communication theory and behavioral research methodology comprised the most common specialization within the programs. Not surprisingly, this social science worldview ultimately reached into the undergraduate journalism classroom. A 1974 survey showed that 64 percent of the 103 journalism schools and departments responding offered at least one communication theory course.[545]

The growing emphasis on social scientific ways of observing the world among journalists, especially from the 1950s on, reflected the changing character of journalism. In the immediate post–World War II era, objectivity required journalists to be passive transmitters of information about events. But the McCarthy era caused journalists to become more active, engaging with the information and interpreting it for the public. As early as 1938, journalist Curtis MacDougall, in a textbook titled *Interpretative Reporting,* wrote that interpreting the news "involves recognizing the particular event as one of a series with both a cause and an effect."[546] And journalist Neale Copple described investigative reporting in his 1964 book as "digging out facts beneath the surface. There is no opinion in truly investigative reporting. It resembles a scientific approach."[547] By 1973, mass communication scholar Philip Meyer was calling on reporters to apply social science methodology directly to news reporting, in what he termed precision journalism.[548]

Public relations took a similar turn toward social science but not because of developments in education. Unlike political communicators, PR practitioners had not recognized the practical value of public relations academic research. Instead, it was pragmatism that prompted the change. When the economy that had been booming since the end of World War II stalled in the early 1970s, companies began cutting costs. Since PR practitioners tended to talk in terms of intangibles such as reputation and image rather than impacts on the bottom line, budgets for public relations were slashed. To protect themselves and make management appreciate their worth, PR practitioners were forced to turn to social scientific methods of research and measurement.[549] Evaluation became the industry's number one concern. Conferences, seminars, articles, and books on how to evaluate and measure the success of campaigns proliferated. By 1978, a survey found that 68 percent of Fortune 1,000 companies used research in public relations planning.[550]

A comparison of two editions of a PR textbook illustrates the changing nature of the practice. *Effective Public Relations* was first published in 1952 and defined public relations as involving "good deeds or good conduct coupled with making those good deeds widely known, or correctly understood."[551] Not yet a part of the practice and therefore not mentioned in the book were the fragmentation of publics, advocacy advertising, activists, issues management, investor relations, and corporate social responsibility. Government public relations in 1952 was simply public relations practiced by the government.[552] By the sixth edition in 1985, however, public relations was defined as helping "organizations anticipate and react to significant publics' perceptions and opinions, new values and life styles in the marketplace, power shifts among the electorate and within legislative bodies, and other changes in the social, economic, technological and political environment."[553]

Despite the changing nature of public relations work, practitioners themselves were still not well understood by journalists. In a study of the perceived roles of journalism and public relations, researchers found that while journalists and PR practitioners had similar perceptions of the journalistic role (probably because the public relations major was most often housed in journalism schools), the two groups differed markedly in their perceptions of the public relations role.[554] In some senses, journalists viewed PR as a mirror image of journalism. Though both groups agreed that journalism involved "accuracy, fairness, objectivity, balance, and informativeness," journalists perceived public relations as involving "advocacy, persuasion, withholding of information and aggressiveness."[555] They also indicated that public relations was not concerned with "objectivity, balance, or fairness" and did "little to protect the public interest or to be 'independent and resistant to favor seekers.'"[556] PR practitioners, by contrast, tended to see themselves as "accurate, . . . able to construct clear messages, and . . . forthright, honest, and informative."[557]

A 1989 article in a public relations trade journal attempted to explain why some journalists perceived PR practitioners as "hired guns running interference for clients, ever ready to bend the truth or manipulate the press to serve those clients."[558] One of the explanations was psychological. In an effort to get their clients' messages to the public, PR practitioners continuously offered unsolicited assistance to journalists. They were always saying, "Here's a story idea" or "Here's an interview." Being given advice on how to do one's job, however, even when that advice is accepted, tends to make the beneficiary feel deficient in some way, as though he or she is incapable of doing the job independently. Thus, journalists had mixed feelings about public relations practitioners.

Another problem was the eagerness of practitioners to help.

Given that journalists tended to think that the job of the PR practitioner was to withhold information, journalistic suspicions about motive were raised when a practitioner was forthcoming. The sheer volume of public relations–created material also made sorting out the truly newsworthy story difficult. And because so much of the information was not relevant, journalists' perceptions about PR seemed to be confirmed.[559]

Public relations practitioners often heightened the tension between the two groups by congratulating themselves on media coverage, implying they had put one over on the journalists. For example, Michael Deaver, former deputy chief of staff for President Reagan, discussed the pack mentality of the White House press corps on *Nightline* in 1989 and said, "The media is lazy. We simply did their jobs for them"—by setting and maintaining the day's news agenda for the press as he and his staff saw fit.[560] Needless to say, the media were not amused.

Most of the tension between journalists and PR practitioners arose in the print media. Television and radio media were more reliant on public relations material because they had airtime to fill. Broadcasting also tended to be more oriented to show business or entertainment than daily newspapers. Although network news programs resisted public relations material and video news releases, local stations with tight budgets and small staffs were more open to such material. The rise of twenty-four-hour news and specialty channels only added to the need and potential outlet for public relations messages.[561]

Advances in communication technology that resulted in cable television, satellites, and computers ushered in a new age. The industrial age of the nineteenth century began to give way to the information age in 1956 when white-collar workers in the United

States for the first time outnumbered blue-collar workers.[562] A year later, the Soviet satellite *Sputnik* signaled the beginning of the era of global satellite communications.[563] By the early 1980s, some 60 percent of American workers held information jobs, and personal computers (PCs) were making those jobs easier. The Apple II home computer was released in 1977, followed by the first IBM PC in 1981. The first Windows operating system appeared in 1985. But it was the Windows system launched in 1990 that made PCs easy to use and accelerated the computer age.[564]

EIGHT

THE POWER SHIFT

On June 3, 1992, sunglass-wearing, saxophone-playing William Jefferson Clinton appeared on *The Arsenio Hall Show.* The appearance would have been unremarkable had Clinton not been a candidate for president at the time. Actually, he was not the first such candidate to appear on a nonnews television show. John F. Kennedy began the practice when he appeared on Jack Paar's *Tonight Show* and Edward R. Murrow's *Person to Person.*[565] Richard Nixon had asked "Sock it to me?" on Dan Rowan and Dick Martin's *Laugh-In* when he was a presidential candidate during the 1960s, and President Gerald Ford had taped the introduction to a *Saturday Night Live* episode in the 1970s.[566] Nixon and Ford did the shows in an attempt to make themselves more relevant to younger voters, while Clinton did *The Arsenio Hall Show* to revitalize a campaign that had lost momentum to Ross Perot.[567] And in contrast to the Nixon and Ford appearances, Clinton's did not seem contrived. He fit the genre of Hall's show; he was hip and completely at home with Hall and his predominantly African American audience. Clinton had an affinity for dealing with people, and his campaign strategists played on that strength, having him interviewed by Phil Donahue, CNN's Larry King, and Tabatha Soren of Music Television (MTV), in addition to Hall.[568] That strategy of going directly to the people was refreshing for many, especially for those on the left, who had become disillusioned with politics during the tumultuousness of the sixties, the scandals of the seventies, and the conservatism of the eighties. Here was a chance to rebuild Camelot.

Many in the media, themselves similar in age and outlook to Clinton, saw great promise in his candidacy. But perhaps because there was such hope, the honeymoon between Clinton and the media did not last long. Clinton's efforts to bypass journalists and go directly to the public, while an effective campaign strategy, were not successful as a media strategy once he became president. Actually, the problems started with his inauguration. Reporters were kept blocks away from the inaugural events, although Clinton's advisers ensured plenty of media coverage. *PrimeTime Live* began the week with pictures of the Clintons packing for Washington; then came Home Box Office (HBO), CBS, Disney specials, and the MTV ball. Howard Kurtz of the *Washington Post* described the coverage, "The *Washington Post,* the *Wall Street Journal,* the *New York Times Magazine, Washington Times, Newsweek* and the *New Republic* published special editions. Clinton fed the media hunger by granting interviews to ABC's Diane Sawyer, PBS's Judy Woodruff, NBC's Tom Brokaw, CBS's Dan Rather, *Newsweek, U.S. News & World Report, The Post* and the *New York Times.*"[569] Despite the extent of the coverage, reporters themselves thought they had been sent a clear message: "You'll be watching this administration through the window."[570]

But just three weeks into his presidency, Clinton was forced to seek the help of his campaign strategists to restore the luster that had surrounded his campaign. Several public relations missteps, including failed attorney general selections and the "don't ask, don't tell" policy regarding gays in the military, had created a negative media atmosphere. The media also became consumed by the notion of a $200 presidential haircut and the shake-up in the White House travel office. After a year, the hostility between the president and the media was as intense as it had been during President Carter's administration. For one journalism observer, both sides were to blame: Clinton and his staff had withdrawn out of paranoia, and for their part, the media engaged in "mean-spirited knit-picking [*sic*]" and "curiously little solid investigative reporting."[571]

Seeking to restore some control over the media, Clinton hired David Gergen, director of White House communications in the first Reagan administration, as adviser to the president.[572] Gergen had had obvious success in controlling Reagan's image and managing his news coverage, but he was unable to do the same for Clinton. The failure was not Gergen's. The fact is that Clinton was not Reagan. Reagan followed direction well and did what his public relations advisers told him to do. But Clinton enjoyed being around people, and he liked the mental challenge of a give-and-take news conference. That made him difficult to control because he had a tendency to get caught up in the moment. He was also faced with an increasingly vocal conservative media outside the traditional newspapers and network news.

Talk radio became an outlet for right-wing commentators who not only espoused their own beliefs but also opened up the airwaves to ordinary Americans, giving them a public forum in which to vent their political views. Rush Limbaugh, perhaps the best known of the radio talk show hosts, kept up a daily diatribe against the "liberals" in the White House, even keeping a running tally of the number of days the country had endured the Clinton administration.[573] Limbaugh's discourse was in keeping with what historian Richard Hofstadter described in a 1964 *Harper's Magazine* article as the paranoid style in American politics, which, he wrote, first revealed itself in 1798 in response to the rise of Jeffersonian democracy and then reappeared periodically. Hofstadter used the term *paranoid* "because no other word adequately evokes the sense of heated exaggeration, suspiciousness, and conspiratorial fantasy that [he] had in mind."[574] Hofstadter was writing about the resurgence of the style in the Goldwater movement of the early 1960s, but the term equally applies to Limbaugh's rhetoric, as does Hofstadter's explanation for why the style reappeared in the sixties.

Writing in 1964, Hofstadter argued that the modern right wing was feeling dispossessed. Bedrock American values were perceived as having been taken over and undermined by intellectuals. Liberals were promoting relativism and socialistic policies that were ruining the traditional market forces of capitalism. It was all seen as part of a vast conspiracy fomented from the centers of power to destroy the American way of life. The various movements for change that arose during the remainder of the 1960s continued to fuel the feelings of dispossession. For Hofstadter, the Goldwater movement showed "how much political leverage can be got out of the animosities and passions of a small minority."[575] But through the remainder of the sixties, that small minority grew in size to the extent that Nixon could claim he was representing the "silent majority." Nixon's presidency, however, did not appease these neoconservatives. They were still convinced a liberal elite conspiracy was afoot and that the new liberal class was engaged in an attack on business. To combat the movement, conservative intellectuals organized think tanks such as the Heritage Foundation.[576]

For many, Reagan's election represented the ascendancy of conservatism, the return of traditional values. But George H. W. Bush, who followed Reagan, was a one-term president; he lost to Clinton, the poster child of the liberal elite. Conservatives feared that a liberal president would roll back the deregulation and other probusiness policies of Reagan, and then Clinton began his presidency with a push for universal health care, surely evidence of a liberal conspiracy. Thus, Clinton's election represented not just a Democratic Party win over the Republican Party but also a clash of liberal and conservative ideologies. Clinton became the enemy in a battle for possession of the American way of life.

In the paranoid style of political rhetoric as enunciated by Hofstadter, "the enemy is clearly delineated: he is a perfect model of malice, a kind of amoral superman—sinister, ubiquitous, powerful, cruel, sensual, luxury-loving."[577] And Clinton was portrayed on talk radio as all of those things. Interestingly, First Lady Hillary Clinton engaged in her own paranoid style of rhetoric when she publicly blamed a right-wing conspiracy for the attacks on her husband. His over-the-top personality, however, no doubt contributed to his portrayal and prompted the glee with which conservatives went after him for the Monica Lewinsky affair.

The Lewinsky affair had the ingredients that made for a great story: sex and politics. For some critics, however, media coverage of that story represented a new low for journalism. *Newsweek* had the story first, but given that the allegations involved the highest office in the land, the editors decided to wait to release the story pending further verification. Shortly thereafter, the story broke in a gossip column on the Internet. Everyone then picked it up and ran with it, often relying on a single, unnamed source in their reportage. For example, the *Dallas Evening News* reported that a Secret Service agent had walked in on the president and Lewinsky. Although the source for that report later said the information was incorrect, the story had gone out over the Associated Press wire service and aired on CNN. Three days later, ABC's *Nightly News* opened with a story about "someone with specific knowledge of what it is that Monica Lewinsky says really took place between her and the president."[578] The majority of the story was based on that single source. In comparison, during the Watergate scandal, the

Washington Post had set the industry standard for the use of anonymous sources, publishing the information only if it was corroborated by two sources with independent and firsthand knowledge of it.[579]

   The networks denied lowering their standards, but critics of the Lewinsky coverage blamed media competition not just for the use of unnamed, single sources but also for excessive coverage.[580] Through the eighties, the networks had faced increased competition from cable and satellite. Now, they also had to compete with the Internet. News by the mid-1990s seemed to be everywhere. And yet, the increase in news had not been accompanied by an increase in the number of journalists. Newsrooms had downsized. Actually, it was not news, or information, that had increased; rather, commentary—talk about news—had grown. As a 1996 article in *Time* magazine noted, "News is chewed over by TV pundits, railed about by talk-radio hosts, nibbled at in gossip columns, debated over the Internet—relentless, insistent, inescapable."[581]

   But at the same time, interest in news from traditional mass media outlets was on the decline. Newspaper readership continued to drop. Most people got their news from television rather than newspapers, although the combined audience for the nightly news on the three networks, ABC, CBS, and NBC, was also dropping.[582] Those under thirty apparently were tuning out the most often. A survey released by the Pew Research Center in May 1996 revealed that the number of under-thirty respondents who said they regularly watched network news had dropped by more than one-third in the previous twelve months. An editorial in the *Nation* suggested young people were becoming disillusioned with the quality of the news.[583]

   The *Nation* blamed the corporate culture pervading network

newsrooms for the emphasis on infotainment rather than hard news. In 1995 and 1996, a number of corporate mergers involving media outlets took place, resulting in the major news outlets being owned by a handful of corporations. Walt Disney purchased ABC, CBS became a Westinghouse property, NBC went to General Electric, and CNN became part of Time Warner. In July 1996, NBC and Microsoft launched MSNBC, a TV and Internet news service; three months later, Rupert Murdoch launched the Fox News Channel, a twenty-four-hour news competitor of CNN. Specialized cable channels offered business news and sports around the clock. In addition, most of the major broadcast stations and newspapers either had or were developing online versions.

Radio talk shows and the proliferation of Web sites on the Internet were democratizing news and information. In the process, the concept of news was changing. More players were honing in on the traditional media gatekeepers, expanding the definition of what constituted hard news and challenging journalistic norms and standards. As the number of news sources grew, the audience became increasingly fragmented. No longer faced with the choice of one or two newspapers and a handful of television stations, people were choosing the news source that interested them personally. In an effort to compete in this consumer-oriented culture, network news and major newspapers were allowing stories historically relegated to the tabloids to seep into their pages. But whenever they did, a debate would arise in media circles about whether the role of the press was to give the people what they wanted or what they needed.[584]

One explanation for the declining interest in "serious" news was that the material seemed to have less relevance to people's lives than it once did. Since the Great Depression in the 1930s, a series of significant events had occurred that directly impacted the lives of Americans. World War II, the Cold War, Vietnam, the civil unrest of the 1960s, and Watergate all came within a relatively short period, just four decades. But through the 1980s and 1990s, the domestic scene was calm, and wars in the rest of the world seemed far away.

Perhaps because there were no truly contentious issues to debate or perhaps because of the changed nature of campaigns, George W. Bush and Al Gore worked the TV talk show circuit during the 2000 election season. Both appeared on the *Oprah Show*, the first candidates to do so; both appeared on *Live with Regis*. Gore also appeared on shows hosted by Rosie O'Donnell, David Letterman, and Jay Leno. The candidates' spokespeople justified the appearances on "pop culture" venues rather than serious news shows on the basis that they could reach men and women (especially women) who did not get their news from the evening news programs. It was certainly true that people were no longer tuning in to regular news programs, but beyond that, as journalist Martha Moore put it, "candidates like these [pop culture] shows for obvious reasons: They have a chance to come across as personable, and the interviews are pretty friendly."[585]

The election of 2000 generated some interest, but that passed quickly. Once in office, Bush initially kept a low profile, avoiding photo opportunities. His goal was to establish himself as the man in charge of a hardworking, professional administration. To that end, Vice President Dick Cheney, who some in the media contended actually ran the country, made the television talk show rounds to spread the message that Bush was "very much in charge of the show."[586] A strategy the Bush administration borrowed from Reagan was to act as though the president had won a landslide victory.[587] In fact, Reagan was elected by just 27 percent of all eligible voters, and Bush needed the Supreme Court of the United States to declare him the winner. Neither had a mandate, but both claimed one. The advantage of such a strategy is that it puts the White House on the offensive and detractors on the defensive. Of course, Bush's people had started to frame his presidency even before he took office, suggesting to the media that they should not focus on the first hundred days. It was far better to judge someone after six months, they argued.[588]

Regardless of the administration's efforts, the media did assess Bush's first hundred days. And generally, he received high marks. His approval rating was at 63 percent, compared with 59 percent for Clinton at the same marker, although Bush was below his father's rating of 71 percent and Reagan's 73 percent. In assessing Bush's first hundred days in office, Eric Cohen of the *Los Angeles Times* wrote, "It seems likely that Bush came to office in a calm-before-the-storm moment in American politics. This age of confusion and bliss will not last forever—good feeling never does—and, sooner or later, Bush will have to make hard choices."[589]

Those hard choices came when the calm was shattered on September 11, 2001. Suddenly, the rest of the world was very important to Americans. One of the criticisms of the Internet was that it destroyed any sense of community and shared experience. But from the moment the first plane struck the North Tower of the World Trade Center, Americans were a community once again. All Americans shared in the horror and heartbreak of that day. And they turned again to the networks for their news. Studies have suggested that they did so because of the familiarity and credibility of the anchors. People needed to hear the news from individuals they trusted. They wanted someone else to wade through the information, synthesize it, and tell them what they needed to know.[590]

In the months following September 11, network news programs focused on hard news, in particular the terrorism threats, the anthrax scare, and military action. But a study revealed that by June 2002, soft news, such as celebrity and lifestyle coverage, had made a comeback, making up approximately 20 percent of the evening newscasts. Interestingly, the morning shows were slower to return to their pre-9/11 formats. Although the amount of hard news those shows were covering had dropped, it was still more than it had been prior to September 11.[591]

The media did focus on news of terrorism threats after 9/11, but the White House framed the coverage. President Bush's promise to get Osama Bin Laden, the mastermind behind the World Trade Center attacks, "dead or alive" was soon reframed by the White House into a targeted attack against Iraq and Saddam Hussein. The country, which had pulled together after the terrorists struck, was in no mood for debate. Its citizens wanted and needed revenge, which the White House took advantage of in framing the invasion of Iraq in terms of an "us versus them" action. To question the president's policy was to be unpatriotic, as one country music group, the Dixie Chicks, found out.

While onstage at a concert in Great Britain on March 10, 2003, just ten days before the start of the Iraq War, Natalie Maines, the lead singer for the Dixie Chicks and a Texan herself, told the audience, "Just so you know, we're ashamed the president of the United States is from Texas."[592] The retaliation at home against the highly successful band was swift and sure. Callers demanded that country music stations drop the Dixie Chicks from their playlists. Right-wing blogs and talk shows denounced the band and fueled the fervor against it. Fox News commentator Bill O'Reilly called Maines's statement "despicable."[593] In some towns, people protested by burning and bulldozing the Dixie

Chicks' CDs. The band even received death threats, especially after a newspaper printed Maines's home address.[594]

The Dixie Chicks were not the only ones to experience the pressure of conformity after 9/11. Cartoonists also came under intense scrutiny. Political cartoonist Steve Benson of the *Arizona Republic* described the situation: "There is immense pressure from readers and advertisers to toe the patriotic line as they define it. I have had editors who pulled my syndicated cartoons because readers marched to their offices and demanded retractions. I have had death threats, efforts to silence me, people who have compared me to traitors."[595] Another cartoonist who depicted the president flying a plane marked "Bush budget" into twin towers labeled "Social" and "Security" saw his editor write a follow-up column after the cartoon ran to apologize for it because of the angry response of readers.[596]

Thus, the assertion that the media focused on hard news after 9/11, while accurate, ignores the reality that objectivity, in the sense of fairness and balance, was at a premium. Journalists were not permitted to perform their watchdog role, in part because the majority of Americans would not tolerate the questioning of the president's policies. Dissenting voices were heard, but they were effectively relegated to the margins of discourse.[597] And the Bush administration had an effective counterpunch to keep the media docile and compliant.

For example, in May 2002, it was being suggested for the first time that the administration might have been warned about the possibilities of a terrorist attack prior to September 11. The allegations did not extend to personal knowledge on the part of the president but implied that he did not receive the intelligence that was available, which raised key questions: Exactly how did this happen? Why didn't the intelligence community know the attacks were coming? To avert the spotlight from such questions, Vice President Dick Cheney and others in the administration went on a weekend counterattack, hitting the Sunday political talk shows. By Monday, the media were, as the *Ottawa Citizen* reported it, "back on the White House message track" with "not if but when" warnings about future terrorist attacks.[598] Although Cheney and the others offered no specific evidence to support the message, it was a no-lose communications strategy for the White House. If another attack occurred, members of the administration could declare that they had warned people. If another attack did not occur, they could take the credit for keeping the country safe.[599] The media, by contrast, were in a no-win situation. Failing to report the message would be to fail in their duty to inform the public.

Murdoch's Fox News Channel capitalized on the patriotic fervor present after 9/11 and during the Iraq War, openly proclaiming its support for the president and conservatism. For thirty-six of the top forty time slots from March 31 to April 6, 2003, Fox News was the highest-rated cable station, even compared to nonnews cable stations. CNN had established itself as a major news player during the first Gulf War, but this time, it was bested by Fox. And for the first time ever during a war, ABC, CBS, and NBC saw their audiences shrink, losing approximately two million viewers a night to cable. In another sign of the times, the Fox morning show, *Fox & Friends,* brought in more viewers than CBS's *Early Show.*[600]

Part of the Fox success stems from the belief fostered by the station's commentators and its owner, Rupert Murdoch, that liberals control the American media. In contrast to the liberal elite media, Fox calls itself "fair and balanced," even as it often engages in baiting liberals. It is the "no-spin zone," as Bill O'Reilly calls it.[601] And polls show that viewers do consider Fox more objective than its network counterparts. Of course, people who watch coverage that reflects their own attitudes are more likely to perceive that coverage as objective than are people who watch news that may, in fact, be more balanced. But Fox understands that dynamic. People who watch twenty-four-hour news coverage of the war tend to support the effort. So Fox gives them the war the way they perceive it. As one commentator remarked, the war is covered like an Olympic event where the Americans have won.[602] More accurately, it is covered like a movie set in World War II, in which John Wayne leads the charge. Freed from the politically correct restraints of objectivity and balance, Fox can be entertaining, and after all, cable television is show business.[603]

Part of Fox News's success can be traced to Roger Ailes, the head of the news division since 1996. Ailes started out as a prop boy for Mike Douglas's program in 1965, but within three years, he was the executive producer of the talk show. He met Richard Nixon in 1967 when Nixon appeared as a guest on the show, and subsequently, he was hired to produce one-hour television programs for Nixon during the 1968 campaign.[604] He went on to serve as a media adviser for Ronald Reagan and George Bush Sr. Ailes had no news experience when he was hired by Murdoch to run his news channel, but he shared Murdoch's conservative views and his belief in the liberal media bias. Ailes is supposed to have come up with Fox News's taglines: "We Report. You Decide." and "Fox News. Fair and Balanced."[605] Despite these slogans, Fox News essentially "has taken the combative ethos of conservative talk radio into the TV studio."[606]

Bill O'Reilly is a case in point. His *O'Reilly Factor* on the Fox News Channel has been the top-rated 7 P.M. cable news program since 2001.[607] But O'Reilly does not conform to the standards of network journalism. When he started, he was, as media critic Jay

Rosen put it, the antianchor, openly eschewing the traditionally cool professionalism of the network anchors of the time: ABC's Peter Jennings, NBC's Tom Brokaw, and CBS's Dan Rather.[608] For one thing, he gives his audience what they want, a person who cares passionately about the stories he covers. And he is political; he has no problem with taking a position and defending American values that he perceives as under attack.[609] With a daily radio program, a syndicated newspaper column, Web sites, and six best-selling books in addition to his Fox program, he is a significant player in the country's political discourse.[610]

O'Reilly's on-air persona also fits Hofstadter's definition of the paranoid style of news.[611] He taps into the resentment of those Americans who feel they have been denied a voice, and he does what they cannot—he talks back to the established liberal media elite. He fuels his supporters' belief in a liberal conspiracy through his paranoid style of rhetoric, and the established media often play into his hands. For instance, he tells his supporters that the mainstream media, such as National Public Radio (NPR) and the *New York Times,* would never review his books; they only review books from authors on the left. If NPR and the *Times* choose not to review the books, he can say, "I told you so." And if they do review the books and do so negatively, as they no doubt would, then he can blame that on liberal bias.[612] Either way, he wins, and his fans have their beliefs reinforced.

O'Reilly warns his viewers that they are entering the "no-spin zone" when they tune into his program, but what they are really getting is propaganda. In 1939, the Institute for Propaganda Analysis (IPA) defined propaganda as *"expression of opinion or action by individuals or groups deliberately designed to influence opinions or actions of other individuals or groups with reference to predetermined ends."*[613] The IPA identified seven devices or categories that can be used in detecting propaganda: "name calling, glittering generalities, transfer, testimonial, plain folks, card stacking, and band wagon."[614] Applying these devices, originally used to study the rhetoric of right-wing radio commentator Father Charles E. Coughlin in the 1930s, to Bill O'Reilly's "Talking Points Memo" editorials, researchers at Indiana University found that O'Reilly is a "heavier and less nuanced user of the devices" than Coughlin was. O'Reilly relies heavily on name-calling, which gives a person or an idea a bad label and makes the audience reject that person or idea without looking at the evidence, and card-stacking, which involves the selective use of facts and half-truths to convince the audience to accept the speaker's point of view.[615]

The researchers also looked at O'Reilly's use of fear appeals. Fear appeals are an effective tool in propaganda and are often used at the beginning of a war to heighten support for the conflict. Journalists have been criticized for creating fear in their audiences by focusing on crime, for example, but they tend to temper the fear by including more lighthearted and uplifting information in newscasts as well because one journalistic value is the promotion of social cohesion. But the research showed that O'Reilly used a fear frame in just over half of the editorials that were analyzed and offered no resolution to the threat 99 percent of the time. The researchers concluded, "This distinguishes O'Reilly from traditional values in journalism, but it also suggests a rhetorical strategy of playing on a primal human emotion to attract viewership."[616]

Despite O'Reilly's refusal to adhere to traditional journalistic standards, a 2005 study revealed that 40 percent of Americans consider him a journalist, the same percentage that consider talk radio host Rush Limbaugh a journalist. Yet only 1 percent of journalists surveyed thought O'Reilly was "very close" to their idea of a journalist; another 10 percent thought he was "somewhat close."[617] Why the discrepancy? Journalists clearly were applying the traditional notions of news and the norms of the profession in their assessment of O'Reilly. They clung to the concept of objectivity as fairness and balance—the notion that journalists should keep their own views hidden and present the news as neutrally as possible to maintain credibility. But the idea of news and what constitutes it is changing, a fact not lost on O'Reilly. Having left ABC in 1989 to join *Inside Edition,* a syndicated tabloid news program aired on local stations, he learned the lesson of television early: it's just show business.[618] And the lines between journalism, opinion, entertainment, and public relations are blurring on television in often unexpected ways.

In March 2004, *USA Today* reported that video news releases produced in behalf of the Department of Health and Human Services by Ketchum, a public relations agency, had been airing on local television stations' news segments. The VNRs praised the new Medicare law without disclosing that the government had developed the footage being aired. The VNRs looked like regular broadcast news segments and included a "reporter" signing off with "In Washington, I'm Karen Ryan reporting." Ryan was apparently hired by the production company to read the script prepared by the government. A government spokesperson said that the practice of using VNRs was common and widespread in both the public and private sectors. Democrats, however, disgreed. Senator Frank R. Lautenberg (D–N.J.) called the practice "a covert attempt to manipulate the press."[619]

VNRs have had a short but troubled history. Public relations practitioners view them as the broadcast equivalent of the print news release. News releases tend to serve as story ideas for reporters rather than as ready-to-print articles. The same applies to VNRs, the practitioners argue. VNRs are an attempt to convince television newsrooms that a certain story can be told visually in ninety seconds or less.[620] But because of newsroom staff cuts, VNRs are sometimes aired during the news just as they are. Critics of VNRs argue that when that happens, viewers have no independent means of judging the accuracy or bias of the video releases. They assume that they are watching a news segment that has been vetted by journalists, when, in fact, an interested party, usually a large corporation, has supplied the footage. The concern is that viewers will not realize they are being shown a one-sided, self-interested perspective. Producers and distributors of VNRs argue in response that what they are producing and stations are airing are informative and entertaining stories. As one such producer noted, "In the 30 or 40 seconds my client's VNR aired on a newscast, attributed or not, the viewer learned that diabetes is a serious health risk, the Postal Service has unveiled a stamp supporting breast cancer awareness, that you can get free tax advice at the IRS or that you should spray cooking oil on your grill so food doesn't stick to the surface." "Who's been hurt?"[621]

The idea of producing VNRs was a logical development once corporations realized the potential of video technology. An early example of the use of such technology by a business to reach its external publics came with the 1980 telecast of the Emhart Corporation's annual report to shareholders in eight states.[622] John Budd Jr., the vice president of public relations for Emhart, argued that two developments made video a viable communication option for corporations. The first was the growth of satellite technology, and the second was deregulation. Until the early 1970s, the Federal Communications Commission had kept tight restrictions on television. But once the FCC removed those restrictions, cable stations especially were "multiplying faster than love-sick rabbits," according to Budd.[623]

He warned, however, that the nature of television "involves the uncritical absorption of the story—the information—portrayed."[624] In addition, with a corporate video, there is no gatekeeper or editor to check facts. Because of those aspects, corporations had to exercise restraint and discipline themselves. Via video, Budd argued, corporations would be able to reach those whose support they wanted through a medium that looked like news and not advertising but at the same time reach an audience that was fragmented and targeted, rather than network television's more homogenized audience.[625]

Two years after Budd's company first videotaped its annual report for shareholders, independent production houses started touting the virtues of video news releases. By the end of the 1980s, United Press International and a private New York firm, Medialink, were transmitting VNRs over their wire services to commercial television stations around the country, although the Associated Press continued to refuse to allow public relations material over its wires.[626] A video news release primer appearing in the 1987–1988 winter issue of *Public Relations Quarterly* gave guidance on how to increase the likelihood that a local station would use a VNR. For example, the article suggested "[keeping] your reporter-narrator off camera. . . . Most stations won't use strange faces and voices."[627]

The use of VNRs first came to public attention in 1992 when *TV Guide* exposed the practice in an article titled "Fake News." Although VNRs grew out of the entertainment business and initially were just long commercials for products or services, by 1992 they were addressing issues such as workplace safety, homelessness, fraud, the first Iraq War, and presidential elections. A study of the 1992 primaries and the use of VNRs by the presidential candidates revealed that "one out of every ten of the 115 television stations surveyed aired at least one VNR from a major candidate, a three-fold increase from the 1988 campaign."[628] Sometimes, the videos were aired without editing or identifying the sources. Candidates used VNRs because they believed the videos would give them some control over the newscasts and allow them to bypass the national networks.[629]

Ironically, the movement away from hype and toward more hard news in VNRs led to more criticism, not less.[630] The problem was that production companies began turning out newsworthy video, raising the question of whether media outlets should clearly identify the sponsor of the footage. *TV Guide* said yes; the Public Relations Society of America said it was sufficient for the video producers to identify the source to the news organization: it was then up to the news outlet to identify the source to its viewers.

The 2004 Medicare VNR brought the subject of so-called fake news back into the public's consciousness. Concerned that public relations had a poor reputation as it was, PRSA announced its position on the use of VNRs. It recommended that an organization producing a VNR should clearly label it as such and disclose who paid for and produced the tape. The association also recommended that the word *reporting* not be used by the narrator if the person was not, in fact, a reporter.[631] The Government Accountability Office (GAO), the congressional investigative unit, ruled that government VNRs such as the Medicare one could constitute "covert propaganda." The GAO declared that federal agencies could not produce VNRs that concealed or did not identify to the viewing audience that they actually came from the government.[632] In response, the Justice Department issued a memorandum to all executive branch agencies telling them to ignore the GAO report.[633]

A March 2005 article by the *New York Times* revealed the extent of the practice. At least twenty federal agencies, including the

Defense Department, the State Department, the Transportation Security Administration, and the Agriculture Department, had made and distributed hundreds of VNRs, called prepackaged news by journalists, since Bush came to power in 2001. The practice of federal agencies producing VNRs dates from at least the first Clinton administration, but the number of releases and the range of topics had increased under Bush.[634]

The *Times* acknowledged that the VNRs avoided overt ideological appeals but suggested they produced "a quiet drumbeat of broadcasts describing a vigilant and compassionate administration."[635] The VNRs often featured scripted interviews with senior administration officials. Critics of the administration's policies or any suggestions of controversy were excluded. The *Times*'s article depicted a shadowy world, "a world where the traditional lines between public relations and journalism have become tangled, where local anchors introduce prepackaged segments with 'suggested' lead-ins written by public relations experts. It is a world where government-produced reports disappear into a maze of satellite transmissions, Web portals, syndicated news programs and network feeds, only to emerge cleansed on the other side as 'independent' journalism."[636] For example, the news director for a cable station in Syracuse, New York, told the *Times* that he thought the Medicare segment had come from a network, not the government. He edited out Karen Ryan, and one of the station's own reporters narrated the piece from essentially the same script.[637]

The *Times* went on to report that a VNR depicting how the U.S. efforts in Afghanistan were liberating Afghan women had aired in 2002 on a Fox affiliate in Memphis, Tennessee. The VNR was the result of a White House initiative to promote American achievements in Afghanistan and Iraq and reinforce the administration's rationale for war. The Office of Broadcasting Services, a State Department unit, was instructed to produce narrated feature reports and distribute them to stations in the United States and around the world. In all, fifty-nine segments were produced, segments the Bush administration considered "powerful strategic tools."[638]

Although broadcasters argue that they rarely, if ever, use VNRs as is, a study by the Center for Media and Democracy, in which thirty-six VNRs were tracked, found that sixty-nine stations, reaching 52.7 percent of the American population, aired at least one VNR from June 2005 to March 2006. In addition, the study found that stations did not disclose the VNRs to viewers, disguised the VNRs as their own reporting, and did not verify the VNR claims.[639] One way broadcasters disguised VNR footage as their own was by editing out the narrator's affiliation. Thus, in a VNR produced by the Agriculture Department, the narrator concluded the segment with "I'm Pat O'Leary reporting for the U.S. Department of Agriculture," a statement that would clarify for viewers the creator of the video. Yet *AgDay,* a syndicated farm news program, introduced the segment as being by "AgDay's Pat O'Leary." The final sentence was edited to "I'm Pat O'Leary reporting."[640]

As pressure mounted on broadcasters about their use of VNRs, Medialink Worldwide, a VNR producer, took video one step further, blurring the distinction between journalism and public relations even more. Instead of sending out a VNR, public relations agencies produced a newscast through Medialink and then bought a spot in which to air it. The thirty-second commercial looked exactly like a network news update, complete with logo and anchor backdrop. One such spot began with "Now . . . News from the Net, with high-tech hearing aids for infants. Hi, I'm Kate Brookes with News Break." Brookes continued on to "interview" an expert in hearing aids for newborns with hearing loss. The expert, of course, and Brookes herself worked for the hearing aid company. Other companies have copied the practice, producing pseudo newscasts with titles such as "Consumer Reports" and "American Scene" and buying time on cable stations to air them. As journalist Joe Mandese commented in *Broadcasting and Cable,* "If viewers were confused before, they'll certainly have a hard time discerning news updates from mini-infomercials now."[641] Critics say the most troubling aspect of the PR paid spot is that while the news content may be genuine, the spot serves as a conduit for a brand mention. In fact, Medialink calls the practice brand journalism, a practice that blurs journalism, public relations, advertising, and marketing.[642] Even more troubling is the practice of pay for play, whereby advertisers buy mentions on TV news programs. For instance, KARE-TV in Minnesota charged $2,000 for a segment on its morning news show, *Showcase Minnesota.* Channel 13 in Phoenix charges guests $5,000 for a six-minute segment on its half-hour *Mind, Body and Spirit* program. A San Francisco station charges advertisers "production integration fees" if they want to be included in a news story. Journalism professor Jill Geisler finds pay for play problematic: "In a news program, the person asking the questions is the advocate for the viewer. In pay for play, the person asking the question is the paid advocate of the interviewee."[643]

In addition to the use of VNRs and pay for play, other practices caused journalists and public relations practitioners to take on interchangeable roles.[644] One was the paying of journalists to support the policies of the Bush administration. In early January 2005, *USA Today* revealed that Armstrong Williams, an African American conservative commentator, had been paid $240,000 by the Department of Education to promote its controversial No Child

Left Behind (NCLB) Act on his syndicated television and radio shows.[645] The deal, which was brokered by the public relations firm Ketchum, a unit of Omnicom Group, required Williams's public relations agency, the Graham Williams Group, to produce radio and television ads featuring Education Secretary Rod Paige; in addition, Williams was "to regularly comment on NCLB during the course of his broadcasts."[646] As a leading black commentator, Williams was also supposed to use his influence to get other black journalists to talk about the act.[647] At no time on his radio or television shows or in his column did Williams disclose the contract. Although he initially defended his actions because the NCLB was something he believed in, he subsequently acknowledged his error: "Even though I'm not a journalist—I'm a commentator—I feel I should be held to the media ethics standard. My judgment was not the best. I wouldn't do it again."[648]

Subsequently, the media revealed that Universal Press Syndicate columnist Maggie Gallagher had been paid $21,000 by the Health and Human Services Department to provide research and write materials promoting the agency's Healthy Marriage Initiative. Although that arrangement was not in itself unethical, Gallagher crossed the line when she promoted the initiative in her own columns without disclosing her relationship with the agency. In her January 25, 2005, column, she apologized to her readers for not telling them about this. She said that at first it did not occur to her to disclose it and then she forgot about it.[649] Columnist Michael McManus took the same tack when it was revealed that he had been paid $10,000 to promote the same initiative. Again, the problem was not the speeches he gave to religious and community groups advocating the initiative but the use of his column to promote it without acknowledging he had been paid to do so. McManus, whose subject is ethics and religion, wrote in his column, "In retrospect, that was a clear conflict of interest. It was not by intent, but by omission."[650]

Democrats jumped on the disclosure of these contracts as another example of the Bush administration's "covert propaganda" techniques and argued that the paying of journalists for favorable coverage of government policies was undermining the integrity of American democracy.[651] The Bush administration is not, however, the first administration to contract with public relations firms to promote its policies. Between 1997 and 2000, for instance, the Clinton administration spent $128 million on outside public relations.[652] But the Bush administration has raised the level of expenditures, spending as of 2004 between $197 and $250 million, depending on the source of the information.[653] For his part, President Bush said in a news conference that he was unaware of the arrangements to pay journalists, and he ordered federal agencies not to make such deals. In its October 2005 report of the incidents, the Government Accountability Office declared the purchasing of favorable coverage a violation of the statutory ban on domestic propaganda.[654]

But a month after that report, the *Los Angeles Times* revealed that the Pentagon had engaged in similar practices with the Iraqi press through a contract with the Lincoln Group, one of three public relations firms awarded part of the overall $300 million budget contract in 2005 to conduct media planning and media-effects analysis for the Pentagon. The Lincoln Group, a strategic-communication firm in Washington, translated Pentagon-written stories into Arabic and then paid Iraqi newspapers to publish the pro-American articles. The stories were accurate but one-sided and omitted any information about the American soldiers or Iraqi government that might be construed negatively. The articles did not include any indication that they came from the Pentagon.[655]

They were part of an effort aimed at "international perception management."[656] Journalists' biggest complaint about the practice was that it undermined the government's efforts to train their Iraqi counterparts and to promote an open and free press in the country.[657]

The government was not alone in using commentators to promote its objectives; corporations have been known to do the same. A policy adviser for the Heartland Institute wrote a column for the *Louisville (Ky.) Courier-Journal* praising Wal-Mart as a positive economic force in the country. He did not disclose to his readers that the Walton Family Foundation, run by the heirs of Wal-Mart's founder, had given his institute $300,000. Similarly, an analyst at Competitive Enterprise Institute who took the side of the oil industry against windfall profits taxes in a column for the *Washington Post* did not reveal that his institute had received money from ExxonMobil. And syndicated columnist James K. Glassman criticized *Super Size Me,* a movie documenting the effects of eating McDonald's food for thirty days, in his column, despite the fact that he is the host of a Web site, TechCentralStation, owned by the DCI Group, a Washington lobbying firm, and sponsored by McDonald's, ExxonMobil, General Motors, and other large corporations.[658] Glassman called the film "an outrageously dishonest and dangerous piece of self-promotion," while failing to disclose his connections to McDonald's.[659] The DCI Group also engaged in questionable behavior when it apparently posted a parody of Al Gore's documentary about global warming on the Web site YouTube.com, presenting the parody as the product of a twenty-nine-year-old from Beverly Hills, California.[660]

Although the agency denied any connection to the YouTube video and refused to speak about any activities it was conducting for its clients, ExxonMobil is known for its attempts to influence attitudes about climate change. One of the company's tactics is to fund groups such as TechCentralStation.[661] Front groups have been used since the early 1940s, but PRSA has considered their use unethical since 1962. Front groups consist of organizations that, by name alone, sound as though they are legitimate and represent beliefs that are widespread. In fact, they are fake groups that have been created by an industry or an organization to create doubt in the mind of the public about the credibility of their opponents. For example, the tobacco company Philip Morris set out in 1993 to discredit the 1992 findings of the Environmental Protection Agency that secondhand smoke was a serious public health threat. The company's objective was to keep cities from passing smoking bans. Its strategy was to create a supposedly grassroots group called The Advancement of Sound Science Coalition (TASSC) to educate the public about the dangers of buying into "junk science." The second part of the strategy was to announce the launch of TASSC in selected local and regional media markets because "this approach . . . avoids cynical reporters from major media: less reviewing/challenging of TASSC messages."[662]

Although the public relations industry made no comment about these ethical lapses in judgment, it did react with anger and indignation to the Ketchum-Williams controversy.[663] Ketchum, after all, is a large and prominent agency, and to have it publicly cross the ethical line in its dealings with the media was unacceptable. PRSA, which is often silent when the PR industry comes under attack, issued a statement denouncing the use of paid endorsements as a violation of the PRSA code of ethics.[664] The Ketchum-Williams matter brought about the strongest reaction from practitioners, but it was not the only ethical breach by a large agency in the news. Fleishman-Hillard, an Omnicom company along with Ketchum, found itself embroiled in civil and criminal lawsuits after allegations that it had overbilled the city of Los Angeles for services.[665]

Some suggested that the consolidation of agencies into global communications giants, which began in the 1980s, contributed to the recent ethical breaches. Publicly traded corporations, such as Omnicom, the WPP Group, the Interpublic Group, and Publicis Groupe, have acquired a number of large, well-known, and formerly independent public relations firms to complement their advertising, marketing, and consulting businesses. Absorbing PR agencies made sense, since their revenues were growing. In 2002, the top ten public relations firms in the United States billed approximately $2.5 billion, compared to just $192 million in 1968.[666] Critics of the communication conglomerates, however, say that at a time when everyone has to work harder to reach audiences because of the new media technologies, pressure for profits pushed firms such as Ketchum to cross ethical lines. Executives of the conglomerates distance themselves from the controversy by saying their public relations units operate independently. And they deny putting pressure on them to increase billings.[667]

But the critics may have a point. In the 1970s and 1980s, a series of takeovers of public relations firms by major advertising agencies occurred. The rationale on the part of the advertising firms at the time was that they sought to turn themselves into full-service agencies. But no real integration took place, and the PR firm Hill & Knowlton, for one, experienced a series of embarrassing ethical controversies after it was taken over by J. Walter Thompson, an advertising agency.[668] As Jack O'Dwyer, who publishes a trade newsletter on public relations, remarked, "The industry began selling its soul when it sold out to these advertising companies because the public relations business should be about the truth, not about sales."[669]

Whatever the cause of the ethical breaches, there is no question that they were coming at a time when truth, trust, and credibility were at a premium in both public relations and journalism. The Pew Research Center for the People and the Press reported that the percentage of people who believed what they read in the newspaper declined from 80 percent in 1985 to 59 percent in 2003. For network television news, believability dropped from 74 percent in 1996 to 65 percent in 2002. When asked which medium had been doing the best job of covering the news, cable was cited by 38 percent of the respondents, more than twice the percentage garnered by the networks, nearly three times that of local television, and nearly four times that of newspapers. More than 50 percent of respondents to a Pew Internet and American Life Project survey said that during the Iraq War, they went to the Internet to get "different points of view from those of traditional news and government sources."[670]

Incidents such as the Armstrong Williams affair do not help restore credibility. Nor do scandals involving plagiarism and fabrication. The Jayson Blair and Rick Bragg episodes at the *New York Times* are the best-known incidents of this type; thirteen cases of unethical behavior on the part of journalists came to light between March and June 2005. One involved the *Boston Globe,* which on April 15 said it would no longer use articles from a freelance writer after it discovered that she had fabricated a story on a Canadian seal hunt. The hunt was delayed because of bad weather, but her article reported that it had already taken place.[671] The media outlets affected took appropriate steps to remedy their particular situations, but some suggest that the rash of ethical breaches is a symptom of problems in newsroom culture. The focus on the bottom line by the megacorporations that own the outlets along with the pressure to produce more with fewer resources result in some journalists cutting corners in their reporting.[672]

Others suggest that the ethical lapses on the part of journalists and public relations practitioners are just the tip of the iceberg and that "communicators are suddenly facing a crisis of truth and integrity like they've never experienced before."[673] The editor of *Slate,* Michael Kinsley, described the year 2000 as a milestone in the manufacture of spin: "Spin is sometimes dismissed as a simple euphemism for lying. But it's actually something more insidious: indifference to the truth. Spinning means describing a reality that suits your purposes. Whether it resembles the reality we all share is an issue that doesn't even arise."[674] The problem is that "when we become adept at deluding audiences, we also become capable of deluding ourselves," and the ability to define what constitutes the truth may be lost.[675] And if no one is what they seem to be, then whom can we trust?

Journalists themselves, once dependable truth-tellers, are being manipulated by those who have an interest in the outcome of their stories—their sources. Kinsley said this is because journalism has bought into spin.[676] Bill Kovach of the Nieman Foundation pointed to the impact of the Internet; Web sites and blogs have shifted the power relationship toward sources and away from journalists. "Increasingly, sources usurp the gate-keeping role of the journalist to dictate the terms of the interaction, the conditions under which the information will be released, and the timing of publication," he said.[677]

Corporations were going so far as to demand advance notice of editorial content so that they could pull their advertising if necessary. British Petroleum (BP) and Morgan Stanley both insisted that their media buyers be told in advance when "objectionable editorial coverage is planned."[678] Chrysler went even further, seeking essentially a veto over "any editorial content that encompasses sexual, political, social issues, or any editorial that might be construed as provocative or offensive."[679] Publishers were already in the habit of pulling airline advertisements in the event of a plane crash, but as Julia Hood for *PR Week* noted, that practice is a matter of taste and media sensitivity in the face of a tragic accident. The question of whether to run an ordinary business story should be decided on the basis of newsworthiness and not commercial pressure. Hood was particularly incensed by the laissez-faire attitude on the part of the advertising industry in regard to the new practice. She quoted a spokesperson for an advertising agency owned by Publicis Groupe as saying that the practice is "not intended in any way to impinge upon a publication's editorial integrity." It is unlikely, Hood wrote, "that executives in the company's PR holdings would agree."[680]

Corporate attempts at controlling information flow did not stop at seeking editorial vetoes. They also apparently extended to stopping leaks, if the situation at Hewlett-Packard is any indication. Someone on the company's board of directors leaked information to the media about the board's discussions. In an effort to find the source of the leak and stop it, the chairwoman of the board, Patricia Dunn, authorized an investigation into the private lives of board members and their families that crossed the line into warrantless searches of phone records.[681] While the Hewlett-Packard reaction to a media leak may seem extreme, the attitude toward leaks was set in Washington.

There is no question that the Bush administration has adopted an aggressive and controlling stance toward the media. The amount of money spent on public relations activities by the government suggests that the Bush White House is in perpetual campaign mode. In fact, one critic said it is as much a media enterprise as a governing one.[682] The federal Office of Personnel Management reported that employment of public relations personnel in government agencies increased 9 percent between 2000 and 2005, although it is difficult to assess the real number because most government PR practitioners do not hold PR titles. A directory of senior executive branch officials, however, suggests that those numbers have climbed. For instance, the Commerce Department listed two public relations positions during the Carter administration. The number of such positions rose steadily in the department through the years, standing at twenty-seven by 2005.[683]

Government public relations practitioners work to get information about their agencies to the people directly "by going over the heads, around the backs, and between the legs of [mainstream media]."[684] The proliferation of Web news sites, blogs, and all-news cable stations has made bypassing the regular news media much easier for PR practitioners. Editor Frank Greve suggested that those nontraditional outlets are prime targets because they are understaffed and their news cycles are so short, which makes them effective agenda-setters.[685]

Of course, not all bloggers are or claim to be journalists, and they do not necessarily adhere to traditional standards of journalism. Therefore, they are free to be partisan and ideological if they choose. And because many of them operate outside the regular news media, they can challenge and criticize mainstream coverage of events. Thus, PowerLine.com started the furor that caused Dan Rather to resign over the use of faked memos in his story about George Bush's National Guard tour of duty. Similarly, Talkingpointsmemo.com revealed the racist remarks made by Senate majority leader Trent Lott, a story to which the regular news media were late in coming. And bloggers brought down CNN news chief Eason Jordan because of claims he made about American soldiers in Iraq.[686] In each case, the mainstream news media looked not just slow and out of touch but also, and more important, not credible. As a result, in one of the 2004 presidential debates when Senator John Kerry made reference to a media report, Bush could say with a straight face, "With all due respect, I'm not so sure it's credible to quote leading news organizations."[687]

While President Bush has relied heavily on public relations to spread his message through the media, he has at the same time worked to rein in and keep control of the mainstream media. Even before 9/11, the administration was known for not returning reporters' telephone calls and losing interview requests. His advisers sometimes call editors and criticize reporters, a tactic used by both Kennedy and Nixon to intimidate the media.[688] That attitude toward reporters is more like the Nixon administration's than either Reagan's or Clinton's; advisers to both these earlier presidents worked at developing a relationship with reporters, even those they knew were ideologically against them. Also like Nixon, Bush has avoided the national media, preferring instead to communicate through regional media outlets. When he has dealt with the national media, he has tended to prefer the Fox News Channel, as has Vice President Dick Cheney.

Cheney's handling of the coverage of his hunting accident reveals much about the administration's attitudes toward the Washington press corps. And the reaction of public relations practitioners to the way the matter was handled speaks volumes about how much media relations have changed. On Saturday, February 11, 2006, Cheney was hunting with friends at a private lodge in Texas when he accidentally shot a member of the hunting party, Harry Whittington. The following day, the ranch owner, Katherine Armstrong, herself a lobbyist and public relations practitioner, gave the story to the local *Corpus Christi Caller-Times* newspaper. From there, it went onto the Internet and then to the Associated Press wire service and CNN. Even though Whittington took a turn for the worse in the hospital, Cheney remained silent. When he finally did speak after three days, it was to Brit Hume of Fox News. Cheney explained that he considered the incident a private matter and felt it would be best for the ranch owner to make an announcement to the local residents at her discretion. "I thought that made good sense because you can get as accurate a story as possible from somebody who knew and understood hunting," Cheney told Hume.[689]

Naturally, members of the Washington press corps were upset at being excluded and preempted by Cheney's decision. About their reaction, the vice president said, "I had a bit of the feeling that the press corps was upset because, to some extent, it was about them—they didn't like the idea that we called the *Corpus Christi Caller-Times* instead of *The New York Times.* But it strikes me that the *Corpus Christi Caller-Times* is just as valid a newspaper as *The New York Times* is."[690] The statement made it clear that Cheney called the shots, not the media. He effectively managed the news by choosing when and to whom to disclose it. The statement also reinforced the view that the national media were liberal and biased and thought they knew better than everyone else.

Public relations practitioners reacted similarly to the Washington press corps. CHENEY'S MISSTEPS TURNED ACCIDENT INTO PR DISASTER, EXPERTS SAY, read one headline.[691] Another said the communications inconsistencies over the accident "haunt" the White House.[692] The former press secretary to Reagan and George H. W. Bush, Marlin Fitzwater, said Cheney should have called his own press secretary, who in turn would have contacted the doctor and the ranch owner and then would have issued a statement to inform the public. Most PR experts agreed: Cheney should have made an announcement Saturday evening after the shooting and issued a public statement of concern for his victim. But Jay Rosen suggested that Fitzwater and the others have not realized that the rules of the game have changed. Public relations as openness is no longer the policy. The Bush administration has indicated it has no regard for the media and therefore no use for it. According to Rosen, "Bush has openly denied that journalists represent Americans' interests in anything, including the public's right to know."[693]

Some would argue that the national media brought about their own power demise by their behavior during the 2004 election season. As the country appeared to grow ever more polarized during the campaigns, the media were drawn into the debate. Media critics complained that advocacy and bias had seeped into news stories. How deeply the media were involved in the partisan struggle could be seen in the CBS News controversy and the fall from grace of Dan Rather. By relying on false reports for its story on Bush's National Guard duty, CBS seemed to confirm the allegations of liberal bias in the news once and for all.[694]

But though CBS was cowed by the controversy, not all media outlets were, forcing the Bush administration to use more heavy-handed tactics, reminiscent of the Nixon administration. After Dana Priest wrote a story for the *Washington Post* on secret CIA prisons, the agency fired Mary McCarthy, an analyst accused of having given classified information to the reporter.[695] Before the story ran, Bush summoned the *Post*'s editor to the Oval Office in an attempt to persuade him not to use the story. The president chose the same tactic to convince the *New York Times* not to do a story on the National Security Agency's program to listen in on domestic telephone calls. As in the case of the secret prisons, the tactic did not work. The *Times*'s story ran on December 16, 2005.[696]

So, six months later, when the *New York Times,* the *Wall Street Journal,* and the *Los Angeles Times* disclosed a program to secretly monitor the financial transactions of suspected terrorists, Bush retaliated by calling the disclosure "disgraceful." Both Cheney and White House spokesman Tony Snow singled out the *New York Times* in their criticism. Cheney said, "Some of the press, particularly the *New York Times,* have made the job of defending against further terrorist attacks more difficult." And Snow said, "The *New York Times* and other news organizations ought to think long and hard about whether a public's right to know in some cases might override somebody's right to live."[697] Snow's choice to call it *a* public's right to know rather than *the* public's right to know was telling. It suggested that the concept of the public's right to know is just a journalistic contrivance to justify reporters' actions. In an effort to further weaken and intimidate the *Times* and other media outlets, protestors rallied outside the *Times*'s headquarters to demand that the government prosecute the newspaper for treason.[698]

Of course, the *New York Times* and the Bush administration have a history of bad relations. In July 2003, the paper published a guest editorial by former ambassador Joseph Wilson, disputing the assertion that Iraq had tried to buy uranium from Niger for use in nuclear weapons, as stated by Bush in his State of the Union address. Wilson had gone to Niger in 2002 to investigate the claim about Iraq at the behest of the CIA. He reported to the agency on his return that the claim was "extremely doubtful." For that reason, he was angry when Bush repeated the allegation in his January 2003 address. Then, eight days after the Wilson editorial, syndicated columnist Robert Novak published the name of CIA officer Valerie Plame, Wilson's wife.[699] The perception around

Washington was that Plame's name was revealed to punish her husband for criticizing the administration's Iraq policy. The Justice Department appointed a special prosecutor to investigate the incident. As part of the investigation, subpoenas were issued to two reporters, Matthew Cooper of *Time* magazine, and Judith Miller, of the *New York Times.* The subpoenas asked for the reporters to turn over their notes and e-mails with confidential sources regarding the Plame matter.

Under the Nixon administration when Bob Woodward and Carl Bernstein's Watergate notes were subpoenaed, the *Washington Post*'s publisher Katherine Graham took possession of the material. Graham was a formidable opponent and was willing to stand up to the government in behalf of her reporters. But this time, Time, Inc., owned by Time Warner, was willing to turn over Cooper's notes (although Miller did go to jail rather than surrender her documents). For journalists, the most troubling aspect of the Plame inquiry was the lack of commitment from the publishers. Where were the modern-day Grahams? Or, as the *Columbia Journalism Review* asked in the title of an article, in the age of corporate journalism "Who Has Your Back?"[700]

NINE

CONCLUSION

In 1985, Neil Postman wrote a book entitled *Amusing Ourselves to Death,* suggesting that television had changed the form and the content of our public discourse.[701] Postman argued that how we communicate affects how we think and the content of our culture. Members of oral cultures, for example, think differently and communicate about different things than members of print cultures. In a print culture, emphasis is placed on logic, linearity, and exposition. And a speaker's credibility depends on the soundness of the the argument being advanced and his or her reputation for telling the truth.

Unlike print, television operates in the realm of the visual, which evokes emotional responses. Image, not argument, matters most. On television, information is presented free of its context. The evening network news, for instance, is a series of unrelated and unconnected bits of information. Viewers are not told how these bits impact their lives or how (or even if) they are important for social and political decision making. Television is about entertainment; even the news on television is show business.[702] Thus, of all the technological changes since World War II, television has had the most profound impact because it has affected our culture. It has changed how we think and come to understand our social reality. And so, although we continue to have printed artifacts, such as newspapers, magazines, and books, our new televised culture emphasizes emotion, nonlinearity, and entertainment, to the point that even our printed materials take on those characteristics. *USA Today* and *People* magazine are just two examples of how the new format has been adopted by newspapers and magazines.

Because television is a visual medium, the form of our political discourse has changed. On television, the credibility of the speaker depends on viewers' impressions of his or her likeability and attractiveness, not on an established reputation for telling the truth. As Postman wrote, "If on television, credibility replaces reality as the decisive test of truth-telling, political leaders need not trouble themselves very much with reality provided that their performances consistently generate a sense of verisimilitude."[703] Kennedy is said to have won the first debate against Nixon in 1960 not because he gave better answers but because he appeared more presidential and sincere.

Eisenhower was the first president to have at his disposal the use of television. He recognized its importance as a medium to reach the public. He also realized its impact in terms of creating an image. He sought to sell the presidency as one sold a product, and television was the perfect medium through which to do that. The concept of image as opposed to reputation has a visual component to it, and Reagan's advisers took advantage of the visual capabilities of television. They knew the public would perceive Reagan as a strong president if he were shown doing things that fit with the public's perception of a stalwart leader. It was perception, not reality, that mattered.

In addition to form, television has changed the content of our discourse. Political discourse has been reduced to sound bites because television is not a medium that lends itself to exposition. Politicians have no time to develop arguments in support of policies, unless, of course, those arguments can be stated in thirty seconds or less. Nor are politicians permitted the time to reflect on a question and provide a reasoned answer. Discourse is reduced to repetition (interviewees stay on message regardless of the question) and slogans. Calling the estate tax the *death* tax, for example, causes voters to react emotionally to the underlying policy and negates the possibility of any meaningful debate about it so that a reasoned and informed decision can be made. Even abstract words have taken on new meanings. Politicians and others throw about the terms *liberal, conservative,* and *values* with no attempt at defining them. An advertisement put out by a Republican incumbent in a recent governor's race is a case in point. The entire advertisement consisted of different people saying the incumbent's opponent was "too liberal" for the state. Other politicians have described themselves in advertisements as "conservative" and talked about "our values."

How we got to the point where the whole country seems to be polarized into conservatives and liberals can be traced to the segmentation of audiences in the 1950s. Thanks to research coming out of psychology, marketers realized that individuals had different motivations for their buying behavior. At the same time, political scientists saw the relevance of the findings for determining voter behavior. The result was research into motivations to sell both a product and a political candidate. Kennedy was the first presidential hopeful to move away from mass marketing, or appealing to the lowest common denominator, and toward segmentation, or tailoring messages to meet the interests of specific groups of citizens. The effect of segmentation on politics was that presidents no longer had to find and appeal to the common ground among all voters. Eisenhower was the last of the old-style, what's-best-for-the-country centrists. Presidents since Kennedy have increasingly sought to motivate their base rather than trying to establish a shared political agenda because market research suggests the campaign period is too short to change people's attitudes. Market research also indicates that the use of ambiguous terms such as *liberal, conservative,* and *values* with no further context is effective because people assimilate attitudes they consider similar to their own. Thus, when a politician says "I am a conservative," everyone from right-wing conservatives to moderates will think the politician is just like them, which broadens the base.

Republicans have been especially successful in appealing to their base, in part because of the direct mail techniques first used in the 1960s. The strategy is to "stir conservatives to open their checkbooks using sharp attacks, dire warnings, and strong rhetoric"; the goal is to create strong ideological differences to move people to action.[704] Historian Lizabeth Cohen argued that the segmentation of the 1960s in both marketing and politics led consumer-citizens to view the marketplace and government as existing to meet their personal needs and interests. Consequently, government today is judged by the benefits it provides to individual citizens rather than to the public interest, making the United States into a "consumer's republic."[705]

But if citizens are now consumers, then people with consumer expertise are needed to reach them. In other words, marketers are required. The concept of marketing entered presidential politics in the 1950s when Eisenhower talked about selling the presidency like a product. He and the Republican National Committee hired ad agencies to create advertisements and help organize the 1956 national convention. The Democratic National Committee also hired ad agencies in the 1950s but only to create ads. These agencies had no input into strategy, and they tended to come from the nonprofit and government sectors. The RNC, by contrast, went to the corporate world for their ad people. These professionals applied their expertise in selling brands to selling candidates.

Nixon extended the concept of marketing in his presidency when he brought advertising people with him to the White House as advisers. He has been criticized for his heavy-handed tactics against the media. Certainly, Nixon disliked the press, which explained his behavior to some extent. But his advisers were not used to dealing with the media. Advertising people only interact with the media when they want to buy space; for them, media are used to put out a controlled message. Thus, the Nixon White House was imbued with the idea that one could control the president's image by controlling the media. Reagan's advisers were public relations practitioners. They knew they had to build relationships with reporters, which they did. They also knew how to manage the media by keeping the president away from the press and by setting the media's agenda.

Some commentators have criticized the use of corporate people rather than civil servants as political advisers. One of the criticisms is that corporate PR practitioners are expected to serve as advocates for their clients whereas government public information officers are supposed to facilitate information flow to citizens. Such criticism ignores the changed nature of presidential politics. Administrations are in perpetual campaign mode today, as evidenced by the George W. Bush administration. Information flow is not the purpose of government public relations practitioners. Advocacy is, and that has changed the role of the White House press corps.

Traditionally, presidents used the press to get their message to the public. Because they needed the press for that purpose, they tolerated media probes and questions. For their part, the media covered the White House because doing so fulfilled their perception of themselves as watchdogs of the government. They were stand-ins for the public, asking those questions citizens would ask if they could and then reporting the answers. Based on those answers, citizens were able to draw conclusions about the government and its policies.

But with the advent of television and then the Internet, presidents did not have to rely on the press to get their message to the public. They could go directly to the people through televised press conferences, as Kennedy did, or through nonnews shows, as Nixon, Ford, and Clinton did. The Internet expanded the ability of politicians to go directly to the public, as evidenced by the campaign of Howard Dean in the 2000 presidential election. Dean ran an effective grassroots effort via the Internet, until the traditional media brought him down with their coverage of his "primal scream."

While the Bush administration has worked, like the Nixon and Reagan administrations before it, on bypassing the national media and going to the regional press, it has also changed the rules of the traditional White House–press game in dramatic ways. It has significantly stepped up control of the press and even *become* the press on occasion, as in the case of using paid commentators and video news releases. The Bush White House has been able to do these things because the national media have been weakened.

The national media are in a weaker position today due both to cuts in resources and to stepped-up competition. The 2004 *State of the Media* report indicated that newspapers had twenty-two hundred fewer employees than they did in 1990, although when the fact that there were fewer newspapers by 2004 is factored in, the drop was actually about 4 percent. In network television, the number of on-air correspondents was down by more than one-third since 1985. At the same time, the workload had increased by 30 percent, while the nightly news hole had shrunk by 11 percent since 1991 to allow more time for ads and promotions. Cable networks had adopted the Fox News Channel's approach to news gathering to some extent, which entailed relying on anchors and talk shows rather than correspondents. CNN continued to invest in correspondents, however. The consequence of the trend toward a smaller news-gathering staff was a tendency to repackage and disseminate news rather than collecting it.[706]

Part of the reason for the newsroom cuts, of course, is greater competition. The number of news outlets may be growing, but the audience for news is not. In fact, that audience is shrinking. According to the 2004 *State of the Media* report, only 41 percent of people under thirty-five read a newspaper each week, although 55 percent of them obtained news online. The three networks saw a 34 percent decline in viewership since 1994 among all age groups. Cable news viewing had not declined, but it also had not grown since late 2001.[707]

Furthermore, the national media have been weakened by criticisms of liberal bias. Nixon's vice president, Spiro Agnew, started the attack, blasting members of the media for being powerful, liberal elites who were out of touch with the majority of Americans. Agnew charged that the national media were self-appointed watchdogs of the government and asked rhetorically, who watches the watchdog? The media had been caught up in the movements of the sixties: civil rights, antiwar, women's, and consumer. Agnew's attack was meant to rally mainstream Americans who felt their lifestyle was being threatened by these groups challenging the status quo. The media enjoyed a brief heyday after Watergate, but by the time Reagan came to power, allegations of a powerful liberal press out to get the president resurfaced. This time, the media were facing a popular conservative president and a group of advisers who knew how to take advantage of a weakened press. With talk radio and then bloggers jumping onto the liberal-bias bandwagon, the national media have been put solidly on the defensive. Indeed, officials in George W. Bush's administration were able to openly disregard the media without fear of backlash for the first five years of his presidency. That is not to say that solid investigative reporting was not taking place because it still was. The problem was that the majority of Americans did not believe most of the news media, and they saw the watchdog kinds of articles on this administration as nothing more than anti-Bush bashing.

The result was that members of the Bush administration were able to stay on message, repeating exactly the same words regardless of who was speaking. They knew that repetition was the key to persuasion. Repetition increases the likelihood that someone will hear the message, and the more times someone hears a message, the more likely he or she is to remember it and, more important, to come to believe it. If one repeats something often enough, it becomes accepted as fact. For example, a 2006 Harris Poll revealed that 50 percent of Americans still believed Iraq had weapons of mass destruction when the United States invaded. That number was up from 36 percent in February 2005.[708] When Bush's overall approval ratings and public support for the Iraq War plummeted in 2005, however, more politicians (official sources) became willing to express criticism of the administration's policies, which meant the media could be seen as objective in reporting that criticism. In response, Bush changed his media strategy, becoming more willing to give interviews to the major news shows and holding more press conferences.

Ironically, it was the concept of objectivity with its emphasis on official sources and its requirement of a neutral stance, when practiced by docile, passive journalists, that had helped the administration in the repetition of its message and contributed to the shift in power from journalists to their sources. Especially during television interviews, guests who have been trained in dealing with the media and their interviewers do an "orchestrated dance where nobody gets at the truth."[709] Television journalists used to prepare in advance, take the lead during an interview, and ask specific questions. But today, the interviewee is able to wrest control of the interview and dictate its terms. Journalists do not want to appear as though they are browbeating their guests, either because they want the guests to come back at some point or because they are afraid they will appear biased against the interviewees. The power now resides in the guest, and the interview becomes an opportunity to get one's message out or reinforce an existing message.[710] Of course, aggressive, investigative, and objective reporting still is done; stories on the prisoner abuse accounts at the Abu Ghraib prison and Guantanamo Bay are but two examples. But taken as a whole, the media have lost power, and their reliance on some of the conventions of objectivity have allowed the government, corporations, and activist groups to effectively manage the news through public relations efforts.

This is not to say there is anything wrong with persuasion per se. The United States has a long history of persuasive political discourse. The problem occurs when people believe they are receiving independent, objective information but are really receiving one-sided and potentially biased information. Controlling messages limits the amount of information available in a democracy and restricts the parameters of the debate on significant issues. And when members of the public are not actively engaged in critically examining the issues, as many today are not, it becomes even more vital for the news media to ensure that the debate is real.

Walter Lippmann wrote in 1920, "There can be no liberty for a community which lacks the means by which to detect lies."[711] Postman contended that Americans have trouble recognizing contradictions on the part of political leaders because those contradictions only exist in relation to the context.[712] If the context is fragmented, then the audience members will not see the contradictions; moreover, they will not find it particularly interesting if the news media attempt to go back and compare two statements to show a contradiction. It is just old news to repeat what the president said sometime earlier. And therefore, open contradictions can be made with impunity.

The final element that has weakened the power of the national media is the democratization of information. Letters to the editor in newspapers traditionally served as an outlet for citizens to express themselves, but their ability to do so was constrained by the papers' editors because they chose which letters to publish. But then, talk radio emerged as a way for citizens to give their opinions about a wide variety of topics. Although still constrained by the host of the program, since not all callers got on the air, the ability to voice one's opinions was greatly enhanced. Then came the Internet, which has proven to be the ultimate in terms of being able to express an opinion. Web pages, discussion forums, chat rooms, and blogs have all allowed global conversations to take place among people from all over the world. The Internet has empowered public opinion as no other technological medium has. Information now belongs to no one and to everyone.

When people are free to find out information for themselves, they no longer require the services of gatekeepers, and those gatekeepers lose their power. Thus, when the printing press was invented, it brought about a change in religion. Protestant sects developed because people could read the Bible on their own: they no longer needed the pope to interpret God's word for them. Religious leaders did not disappear, but their relationship to their congregations changed. Similarly, with the Internet, people do not need the services of editors to interpret the news for them. The media will not disappear because of blogs and social networking sites, but their relationship to their audience will change.

Meanwhile, the very concept of "news" is changing. The widespread use of digital cameras and camera phones has enabled individuals not just to post their views online but also to capture and post to the Web whatever they consider newsworthy. People are deciding for themselves what they want to know about, what is newsworthy in their world. The traditional media outlets will have to adapt to these changes if they want to stay relevant. CNN has done so by creating a new Web site called CNN Exchange, where users will be able to upload video and audio submissions, or I-reports, directly to the site; these can then be accessed by other users.[713] In a similar vein, the *Washington Post,* the *New York Sun,* and the *Daily Oklahoman* have contracted with a news aggregator to deliver content from hundreds of news and blog sites to their Web sites. When a story appears on the *Post*'s Web site, for example, a box beside it will include the links to articles on the same topic published elsewhere on the Web.[714] The idea is that by providing these links, the three news Web sites will build a relationship with their users and become a trusted resource for them.

Building relationships is, of course, a key focus of the public relations industry. At the same time as the media were suffering from resource cuts and increased competition, public relations was growing in size and sophistication. As of May 2005, there were approximately 235,000 practitioners in the United States, and the *2006 Bureau of Labor Statistics Occupational Outlook Handbook* predicted that the PR industry would grow from 18 to 26 percent between 2004 and 2014.[715] In addition, the industry has become more sophisticated in strategic planning and measurement. Practitioners have also taken advantage of the technological changes to go directly to their clients' publics. Communication vehicles such as Web sites and blogs allow organizations and individuals to interact without an intermediary. But reaching a broad audience through credible sources such as the traditional media is still an important component of public relations planning.

For journalists and PR practitioners alike, fostering trust and credibility is key. The theory of democracy is that people, when informed, can make rational decisions about governance, that they are capable of self-governance. But people cannot make decisions if they do not have information on which to base their decisions. In the past, access to information was the problem. But high literacy rates and technological advances such as cable, the Internet, and satellites have effectively removed the barriers to access. The problem today is with the quality of information available. People do not trust the media, the traditional providers of credible information about the world. They see them as presenting packaged, biased news. And to a great extent, the networks do, although none but Fox would admit it.

At one time, newspapers were openly partisan, but as they became more of a mass medium and needed to reach a broader audience, objectivity developed. Objectivity worked, and it was adopted by radio and television journalists because the news was being disseminated to a geographic audience. The tenets of objectivity—nonpartisanship, fairness, and balance—are required when the audience is diverse and too broad to classify in any meaningful way. But today, the number of news outlets has allowed for fragmentation and segmentation of the audience. Fox News, to cite one example, knew it could not compete directly against the likes of the networks and CNN, so it chose to market itself to a particular audience. Niche marketing, not one-size-fits-all news, is profitable. The citizen, as consumer, wants news that he or she can use and finds interesting. The success of Fox does not suggest a return of the partisan, politically oriented press but rather the development of a market-oriented press. As mass communication scholar Michael Bugeja wrote in *Quill Magazine,* objectivity has lost out to profit and the demands of the market: "Opinion sells better, because it can be aligned with demographics and psychographics of a target audience."[716]

The loss of credibility is the biggest issue facing journalism today. How can journalists continue to claim to be objective, to be providing people with the truth, when persuasion is everywhere in the news? Is an independent, commercially viable press possible? And what happens to democracy in a mediated society when it is difficult to discern credible sources of information? To prevent marginalization, journalists must reevaluate their values and move away from the current conceptualization of objectivity that permits docile, passive reporting. The question is how best to provide people with credible information and a variety of viewpoints while remaining commercially viable.

And public relations needs a strong, credible press, too. PR practitioners have increasingly adopted a marketing mind-set that seeks to control the media rather than build a relationship with reporters to earn coverage. But as Mark Hass of the public relations agency Manning, Selvage and Lee said, journalism and public relations "are in a death grip together. . . . Earned placement has the most credibility. That's what we do. And it's only possible if the Fourth Estate is credible, questioning and relentless in its pursuit of truth."[717]

NOTES

CHAPTER ONE

1. Simon Cottle, ed., *News, Public Relations and Power* (London: Sage Publications, 2003), 3.

2. Melvin L. Sharpe and Betty J. Pritchard, "The Historical Empowerment of Public Opinion and Its Relationship to the Emergence of Public Relations as a Profession," in Donn James Tilson and Emmanuel C. Alozie, eds., *Toward the Common Good: Perspectives in International Public Relations* (Boston: Pearson Education, 2004), 14–36.

3. David T. Z. Mindich, *Just the Facts: How "Objectivity" Came to Define American Journalism* (New York and London: New York University Press, 1998), 11.

4. Maurine H. Beasley, "The Emergence of Modern Media, 1900–1945," in William David Sloan, ed., *The Media in America,* 5th ed. (Northport, Ala.: Vision Press, 2002), 283–302.

5. "Some Effects of Modern Publicity," *Century* 67 (November 1903): 155–56.

6. "The Passing of Corporate Secrecy," *World's Work* 15 (February 1908): 9837.

CHAPTER TWO

7. Roland Marchand, *Creating the Corporate Soul: The Rise of Public Relations and Corporate Imagery in American Big Business* (Berkeley: University of California Press, 1998).

8. Leila A. Sussmann, "The Personnel and Ideology of Public Relations," *Public Opinion Quarterly* 12, no. 4 (Winter 1948–1949): 697–708.

9. Karen S. Miller, "Public Relations, 1900–Present," in William David Sloan and James D. Startt, eds., *The Media in America: A History,* 4th ed. (Northport, Ala.: Vision Press, 1999), 417–34.

10. Karen Miller, *The Voice of Business: Hill & Knowlton and Postwar Public Relations* (Chapel Hill: University of North Carolina Press, 1999).

11. Sussmann, "The Personnel and Ideology," 703. Business leaders were apparently alarmed by the results of a survey done by the Psychological Corporation for General Electric. The survey revealed that Americans were not concerned by the trends toward a socialist state and that arguments in support of free enterprise did not seem to inspire them. Marchand, *Creating the Corporate Soul*.

12. Arthur E. Easterbrook, "Reconversion of Man," *Vital Speeches of the Day* 11, no. 20 (1945): 610–12.

13. Clark Belden, "Wartime Public Relations—A Survey," *Public Opinion Quarterly* 8, no. 1 (Spring 1944): 94–99; William H. Baldwin and Raymond C. Mayer, "On Buying Public Relations," *Public Opinion Quarterly* 8, no. 2 (Summer 1944): 226–31; Marvin M. Black, "The Returning Serviceman's Dilemma," *Public Relations Journal* 1 (November 1945): 32–35.

14. Rex F. Harlow, "Public Relations at the Crossroads," *Public Opinion Quarterly* 8, no. 4 (Winter, 1944–1945): 551–56; Scott M. Cutlip, Allen H. Center, and Glen M. Broom, *Effective Public Relations,* 8th ed. (Upper Saddle River, N.J.: Prentice-Hall, 2000).

15. Belden, "Wartime Public Relations"; Baldwin and Mayer, "On Buying Public Relations."

16. Miller, *The Voice of Business.*

17. Richard O. Lang, "The Economic Outlook for 1952," *Vital Speeches of the Day* 18, no. 10 (March 1952): 293–97.

18. Everett R. Smith, "The Customer Will Be Boss," *Vital Speeches of the Day* 11, no. 22 (September 1945): 693–95.

19. Bradford B. Smith, "Controlled versus Uncontrolled Economy," *Vital Speeches of the Day* 13, no. 2 (November 1946): 48–53; Ralph K. Strassman, "Private Enterprise—Its Social Responsibility," *Vital Speeches of the Day* 12, no. 16 (June 1946): 508–10. President Truman had continued wartime wage and price controls after the war. Gary A. Donaldson, *Abundance and Anxiety: America, 1945–1960* (Westport, Conn.: Praeger, 1997).

20. John T. Flynn, "Insidious Propaganda," *Vital Speeches of the Day* 13, no. 4 (December 1946): 110–14.

NOTES TO CHAPTER TWO

21. Rudolf Flesch, "The Vocabulary of Free Enterprise," *Public Relations Journal* 4, no. 1 (January 1948): 10–12.

22. Strassman, "Private Enterprise"; Charles Luckman, "Big Business Has Lacked Vision," *Vital Speeches of the Day* 13, no. 4 (December 1946): 106–9.

23. James W. Irwin, "Industry's Obligation to the Press," *Public Relations Journal* 4 (December 1948): 25.

24. Baldwin and Mayer, "On Buying Public Relations"; Lee B. Wood, "Public Relations and the Press," *Public Relations Journal* 4 (December 1948): 17–18, 39.

25. George C. Jordan, "Publicity Isn't Free," *Public Relations Journal* 5 (June 1949): 15–16, 32.

26. Irwin, "Industry's Obligation to the Press."

27. James P. Selvage, "Newspapers and Economic Illiteracy," *Public Relations Journal* 5 (April 1949): 4.

28. Dorcas Campbell, "Telling the Press," *Public Relations Journal* 5 (March 1949): 24–25, 30; Ivy Lee Jr., "Facing the Facts . . . From a Public Relations Viewpoint," *Public Relations Journal* 4 (September 1948): 28–33.

29. Campbell, "Telling the Press," 24.

30. Ibid., 30.

31. Sussmann, "The Personnel and Ideology."

32. Black, "The Returning Serviceman's Dilemma."

33. Baldwin and Mayer, "On Buying Public Relations"; Black, "The Returning Serviceman's Dilemma"; Harlow, "Public Relations at the Crossroads." Baldwin and Mayer were concerned that public relations had not developed "effective safeguards against misrepresentations and overselling by irresponsible opportunists" (226).

34. Cutlip, Center, and Broom, *Effective Public Relations.*

35. Alfred McClung Lee, "Trends in Public Relations Training," *Public Opinion Quarterly* 11, no. 1 (Spring 1947): 83–91.

36. Scott M. Cutlip, "History of Public Relations Education in the United States," *Journalism Quarterly* 38, no. 3 (1961): 369.

37. Beasley, "The Emergence of Modern Media, 1900–1945."

38. Francis Cardinal Spellman, "Truth—Watchword of a Free Press," *Vital Speeches of the Day* 18, no. 5 (December 1951): 156–57;

Edwin R. Bayley, *Joe McCarthy and the Press* (Madison: University of Wisconsin Press, 1981).

39. Harry D. Marsh and David R. Davies, "The Media in Transition: 1945–1974," in William David Sloan, ed., *The Media in America: A History*, 5th ed. (Northport, Ala.: Vision Press, 2002), 441–64; Bayley, *Joe McCarthy and the Press.*

40. Arthur Hays Sulzberger, "The Newspaper—Its Making and Its Meaning," *Vital Speeches of the Day* 11, no. 17 (June 1945): 539–43.

41. Marsh and Davies, "The Media in Transition."

42. Ibid.; Bayley, *Joe McCarthy and the Press.*

43. Margaret A. Blanchard, *Revolutionary Sparks: Freedom of Expression in Modern America* (New York: Oxford University Press, 1992).

44. William L. O'Neill, *American High: The Years of Confidence, 1945–1960* (New York: Free Press, 1986).

45. Bayley, *Joe McCarthy and the Press,* 41.

46. Marsh and Davies, "The Media in Transition."

47. Bayley, *Joe McCarthy and the Press,* 41.

48. Ibid., 135.

49. Ibid.

50. Ibid.

51. Richard L. Strout, "Ordeal by Publicity," *Christian Science Monitor,* May 27, 1950, p. WM5.

52. Quoted in Bayley, *Joe McCarthy and the Press,* 149.

53. Marsh and Davies, "The Media in Transition."

54. Bayley, *Joe McCarthy and the Press.*

55. Ibid.

56. Ibid.

57. Ibid.

58. Blanchard, *Revolutionary Sparks.*

59. Bayley, *Joe McCarthy and the Press.*

60. Blanchard, *Revolutionary Sparks,* 261.

61. Ibid.

62. Donaldson, *Abundance and Anxiety,* 77.

63. Craig Allen, *Eisenhower and the Mass Media: Peace, Prosperity, and Prime-Time TV* (Chapel Hill: University of North Carolina Press, 1993).

64. Ibid.

65. Ibid., 13.

66. Ibid.; Mary Ann Watson, *The Expanding Vista: American Television in the Kennedy Years* (New York: Oxford University Press, 1990).

67. Allen, *Eisenhower and the Mass Media,* 13.

68. Ibid., 23.

69. Ibid., 24.

70. Ibid., 26–30.

71. Ibid., 40.

72. Ibid., 21–22.

73. Ibid., 50–51.

74. Ibid., 38.

75. Ibid., 52–53.

76. Ibid., 54–55.

77. Ibid., 60–61.

78. Ibid., 101.

79. Ibid., 112, 206.

80. Ibid., 127.

81. Ibid., 130–32.

82. Ibid., 123.

83. Ibid., 124.

84. Ibid., 171.

85. Vance Packard, *The Hidden Persuaders* (New York: David McKay, 1957; reprint, New York: Pocket Books, 1973), 174.

86. William H. Chafe, *The Unfinished Journey: America since World War II* (New York: Oxford University Press, 2003), 106.

87. Ibid., 111.

88. Ibid.

89. Doug Newsom, Judy VanSlyke Turk, and Dean Kruckeberg, *This Is PR: The Realities of Public Relations,* 7th ed. (Belmont, Calif.: Wadsworth, 2000), 48.

90. Donaldson, *Abundance and Anxiety,* 143.

91. Quoted in O'Neill, *American High,* 38.

92. Irwin Ross, *The Image Merchants* (Garden City, N.Y.: Doubleday, 1959).

93. Karla K. Gower and Margot Opdyke Lamme, "Public Relations and the Railroad/Truckers Brawl," *Journalism History* 29 (Spring 2003):

12–20. At the tenth national conference of PRSA, David Cort found the field undergoing great soul-searching. He noted the Madison Avenue tone was missing to such an extent that the PR practitioners at the conference ignored even the profit motive. He wrote that people talked almost religiously about leading business away from arrogance toward humility. David Cort, "An Angle on Some 'Squares,'" *Nation,* December 7, 1957, 424–26.

94. Ralph B. Wagner, "Don't Neglect Your Relations! Molding the Mass Mind," *Vital Speeches of the Day* 12, no. 6 (January 1946): 179. See also Raymond W. Miller, "Take Time for Human Engineering," *Public Relations Journal* 4 (January 1948): 4–9, 40; Lawrence B. Sizer, "Assignment to Right," *Public Relations Journal* 4 (April 1948): 8–11. Sizer suggested that it was more important to control the human mind than to control the atom.

95. B. F. Skinner, *Walden Two* (Toronto: Macmillan, 1948).

96. Packard, *The Hidden Persuaders.*

97. Ibid., 40. Advertising had become big business in the 1950s, with expenditures going from $58 million in 1949 to more than $1.5 billion by 1959.

98. Ibid., 144–45. Apparently, the use of gimmicks, such as delivering baseballs to newsrooms because "that's the way the ball bounces," was a new development in the fifties. In 1950, the public relations practitioner would have sent a simple news release to a journalist. By 1960, according to one journalist, editors were "besieged by gimmicks." Eleanor Perenyi, "The Overt Persuaders," *Harper's,* September 1960, 20, 22, 24, 26.

99. Solomon Simonson, "The Role of the Mass Media in Communication," *Vital Speeches of the Day* 18, no. 12 (March 1952): 349–51; Harold C. Case, "The Mind's Adventure," *Vital Speeches of the Day* 18, no. 19 (July 1952): 598–600.

100. Henry R. Luce, "Responsibility of the Press in the Cold War," *Vital Speeches of the Day* 19, no. 12 (April 1953): 369.

101. George Gallup, "Mass Information or Mass Entertainment," *Vital Speeches of the Day* 19, no. 15 (May 1953): 473–75.

102. Ibid., 473. Television at first had carried cultural programming such as Broadway plays, but as the number of sets and advertising rev-

enue increased, the programming's resemblance to high culture declined. O'Neill, *American High,* 77.

103. Donaldson, *Abundance and Anxiety,* 133.

104. Ibid.

105. O'Neill, *American High,* 254.

106. Donaldson, *Abundance and Anxiety,* 133.

107. Bayley, *Joe McCarthy and the Press,* 85.

108. The trend toward monopolies of daily newspapers had been ongoing for some time. Between 1936 and 1938, the number of cities with competing daily newspapers fell by 21 percent each year. Alfred Mc-Clung Lee, "Trends Affecting the Daily Newspaper," *Public Opinion Quarterly* 3, no. 3 (July 1939): 497–502. The trend accelerated after World War II.

109. Carl W. Larsen, "Educating the Editors," *Vital Speeches of the Day* 24, no. 19 (July 1958): 606.

110. Clark Mollenhoff, "Freedom of the Press," *Vital Speeches of the Day* 26, no. 8 (February 1960): 249.

111. Mollenhoff said that the term *managing the news* was used by James Reston before the Moss subcommittee in complaining about government information practices. Ibid.

112. Ibid., 251.

113. Ibid., 252.

CHAPTER THREE

114. "John F. Kennedy, Inaugural Address," *Inaugural Addresses of the United States* (Washington, D.C.: U.S. Government Printing Office, 1989), available at http://www.bartleby.com/124/, accessed on October 23, 2006.

115. Chafe, *The Unfinished Journey.*

116. Watson, *The Expanding Vista,* 3.

117. Theodore C. Sorensen, *Kennedy* (New York: Harper and Row, 1965), 85.

118. Ibid., 104. Sorensen suggested that more than three dozen articles carried Kennedy's byline in the period leading up to his run for office.

119. Ibid., 119.

120. Theodore H. White, *The Making of the President, 1960* (New York: Atheneum Publishers, 1961), 51.

121. Sorensen, *Kennedy,* 124.

122. White, *The Making of the President,* 102, 135.

123. Melvyn H. Bloom, *Public Relations and Presidential Campaigns: A Crisis in Democracy* (New York: Thomas Y. Crowell, 1973), 69, 71.

124. White, *The Making of the President,* 64.

125. Ibid., 336.

126. Ibid.

127. Bloom, *Public Relations,* 89; Sorensen, *Kennedy,* 186; White, *The Making of the President,* 337–38.

128. White, *The Making of the President,* 282; Sorensen, *Kennedy,* 195; Bloom, *Public Relations,* 88.

129. White, *The Making of the President,* 281–82. To televise debates, the networks had to get Congress to suspend the equal time rule, which required broadcasters to provide equal time to all candidates for the same office. There were fourteen candidates in all, but obviously, the networks only wanted to provide time for debates between the Democratic and the Republican candidates. Congress suspended the rule for 1960.

130. Watson, *The Expanding Vista,* 9.

131. White, *The Making of the President,* 283.

132. Ibid.

133. Bloom, *Public Relations,* 110.

134. White, *The Making of the President,* 291.

135. Ibid, 292.

136. Watson, *The Expanding Vista,* 12.

137. White, *The Making of the President,* 284–85.

138. Ibid., 287.

139. Ibid., 287–88.

140. John Spanier and Steven W. Hook, *American Foreign Policy since World War II,* 14th ed. (Washington, D.C.: Congressional Quarterly, 1998).

141. Quoted in ibid., 103.

142. Jenkin Lloyd Smith, "Who Is Tampering with the Soul of America? Our Moral Climate," *Vital Speeches of the Day* 28, no. 6 (January 1, 1962): 182; Alan C. McIntosh, "A Challenge to Our American

Press: Carve the Moral Decay from America," *Vital Speeches of the Day* 28, no. 16 (June 1, 1962): 503–8. The two speeches contain exactly the same examples to illustrate the moral decay of the country. One speech was given by the editor of the *Oklahoma Tribune* before the Inland Daily Press Association in Chicago on October 16, 1961. The other was given by the editor and publisher of the *Rock County Star Herald,* in Luverne, Minnesota, before the South Dakota Press Association on April 6, 1962.

143. T. Earle Johnson, "Excellence in Our Lives: We Must Overcome the Cult of Mediocrity," *Vital Speeches of the Day* 28, no. 6 (January 1, 1962): 184.

144. Mark Ethridge, "The Meaning of the News: The Era of Interpretive Writing," *Vital Speeches of the Day* 28, no. 15 (May 15, 1962): 474.

145. Alan Barth, "The Press as Censor of Government: Atrophy of the Editorial Page," *Vital Speeches of the Day* 28, no. 11 (March 15, 1962): 341.

146. Ibid., 342.

147. John F. Kennedy, "The President and the Press," *Vital Speeches of the Day* 27, no. 15 (May 15, 1961): 450–52.

148. Daniel C. Hallin, *The "Uncensored War": The Media and Vietnam* (New York and Oxford: Oxford University Press, 1986), 24.

149. Chafe, *The Unfinished Journey;* Spanier and Hook, *American Foreign Policy.*

150. Chafe, *The Unfinished Journey.*

151. Watson, *The Expanding Vista,* 76.

152. Ibid., 83.

153. Ibid., 76; John W. Hill, *The Making of a Public Relations Man* (New York: David McKay, 1963), 207.

154. Hill, *The Making of a Public Relations Man,* 208.

155. Ibid.

156. Quoted in Watson, *The Expanding Vista,* 76.

157. Ibid., 83–85.

158. Hill, *The Making of a Public Relations Man,* 211.

159. Ibid.

160. Mark Hamilton Lytle, *America's Uncivil Wars: The Sixties Era from Elvis to Richard Nixon* (New York: Oxford University Press, 2006).

161. Ibid.; Chafe, *The Unfinished Journey.*

162. Lytle, *America's Uncivil Wars.*

163. Ibid.

164. Quoted in Chafe, *The Unfinished Journey,* 207.

165. Todd Gitlin, *The Whole World Is Watching: Mass Media in the Making and Unmaking of the New Left* (Berkeley: University of California Press, 1980, 2003, with a new preface by Todd Gitlin), 43.

166. Robert J. Wood with Max Gunther, *Confessions of a PR Man* (New York: North American Library, 1988).

167. Ibid., 81.

168. Ibid. Of course, it may also have been the changing nature of the civil rights protests and not the letter that caused a change in reporting.

169. Ibid.

170. Ibid.

171. Gitlin, *The Whole World;* Hallin, *The "Uncensored War."*

172. Cited in Hallin, *The "Uncensored War,"* 4.

173. Ibid.

174. Ibid., 32.

175. Ibid.

176. Ibid., 125.

177. Ibid.; Watson, *The Expanding Vista.* ABC did not expand its news broadcasts to thirty minutes until January 1967.

178. Quoted in Chafe, *The Unfinished Journey,* 337.

179. Hallin, *The "Uncensored War,"* 34–35.

180. Gitlin, *The Whole World Is Watching.* Gitlin documented the rise and fall of SDS in the media.

181. Bloom, *Public Relations.*

182. Ibid.

183. Ibid.

184. Ibid.

185. Daniel Boorstin, *The Image: A Guide to Pseudo-events in America* (New York: Atheneum, 1972).

186. Bloom, *Public Relations;* Joe McGinniss, *The Selling of the President* (New York: Simon and Schuster, 1968; reprint, New York: Penguin Books, 1988).

187. Bloom, *Public Relations.*

188. Henry Ford II, "Business Ethics in 1961: Management Integrity," *Vital Speeches of the Day* 27, no. 15 (May 15, 1961): 454–57.

189. Harvey C. Jacobs, "The Image of the Image-Makers: The Evolution of Public Relations," *Vital Speeches of the Day* 27, no. 15 (May 15, 1961): 459–62.

190. Richard A. Stimson, "Corporate Recognition of Public Relations," *Public Relations Quarterly* 10, no. 3/4 (Winter 1966): 50–52.

191. Richard L. Harmon, "Job Responsibilities in Public Relations," *Public Relations Quarterly* 10, no. 2 (Summer 1965): 22–24.

192. J. Carroll Bateman, "The Indispensable Man," *Public Relations Quarterly* 12, no. 1 (Spring 1967): 42–46.

193. Philip Lesly, "Real Creativity in Public Relations," *Public Relations Quarterly* 10, no. 3/4 (Winter 1966): 8, 13–16.

CHAPTER FOUR

194. Quoted in Hale Nelson, "The Public Problems of Business," *Vital Speeches of the Day* 38, no. 21 (August 15, 1972): 669.

195. Ibid. Nelson quoted figures from surveys conducted by Social Research, Inc., Opinion Research Corporation, Louis Harris, Inc., and Daniel Yankelovich, Inc.

196. Packard, *The Hidden Persuaders.*

197. John Kenneth Galbraith, *The Affluent Society* (Boston: Houghton Mifflin, 1958).

198. Quoted in Lizabeth Cohen, *A Consumer's Republic: The Politics of Mass Consumption in Postwar America* (New York: Vintage Books, 2003), 345. The theme "We are all consumers" can be found repeatedly in speeches by businesspeople in the 1970s.

199. The first wave came in the Progressive Era, and the second came in the 1930s with the New Deal. Ibid.

200. Priscilla Coit Murphy, *What a Book Can Do: The Publication and Reception of "Silent Spring"* (Amherst and Boston: University of Massachusetts Press, 2005).

201. Quoted in ibid., 99.

202. "More of Rachel," editorial, *Agrichemical West* (October 1962): 24. Quoted in Murphy, *What a Book Can Do,* 98.

203. Quoted in Murphy, *What a Book Can Do,* 98–99.

204. Ibid., 109.

205. Ibid., 102.

206. Ibid., 114.

207. Ibid., 124.

208. Ibid., 117.

209. "Monsanto Chemical Company Published a Rebuttal to Rachel Carson's *Silent Spring*," *PR News* (February 1963), reprinted in David P. Bianco, ed., *PR News Casebook: 1,000 Public Relations Case Studies* (Detroit, Mich.: Gale Research, 1993), 440.

210. Bert C. Goss, "There Oughtn't to Be a Law," *Vital Speeches of the Day* 30, no. 3 (November 15, 1963): 81–84.

211. Murphy, *What a Book Can Do,* 126–27.

212. Ralph Nader, *Unsafe at Any Speed: The Designed-In Dangers of the American Automobile* (New York: Grossman, 1965).

213. Justin Martin, *Nader: Crusader, Spoiler, Icon* (Cambridge, Mass.: Perseus Publishing, 2002), 39.

214. Ibid., 43.

215. Robert L. Bishop and Jane Kilburn, "Penny Whistle or Public's Advocate?" *Public Relations Quarterly* 12, no. 4 (Winter 1968): 27–30.

216. Martin, *Nader,* 44.

217. Ibid., 45.

218. Ibid., 46.

219. Ibid., 47.

220. Ibid., 49. Martin wrote that the two men who were following Nader the day of his testimony started following a *Post* reporter, who looked similar to Nader from the rear, by accident. A security guard thought they looked suspicious and approached the two men. They claimed to be investigating an auto critic for a possible job. The security guard told the *Post* reporter about the men. The *Post* reporter happened to relate the story to his editor in the presence of the reporter Nader had contacted about being followed. Thus, that reporter had independent verification of Nader's story.

221. Ibid., 52–53.

222. Ibid., 59.

223. Ibid.

224. Ibid., 59–60.

225. Ibid., 60–61.

226. Ibid., 72. Charles J. Schreiber, "Public Relations and the Consumer," *Public Relations Quarterly* 11, no. 2 (Summer 1966): 2–3, 39.

227. Martin, *Nader,* 71.

228. Ibid., 90–92.

229. Ibid., 90–93.

230. Ibid., 77, 81.

231. Ibid., 82; Morris B. Rotman, "Consumerism Is Us!" *Vital Speeches of the Day* 38, no. 19 (July 15, 1972): 589–92.

232. Nelson, "The Public Problems of Business," 669.

233. Edward L. Bond Jr. "Developing Responsible Promotion," *Vital Speeches of the Day* 37, no. 5 (December 15, 1970): 124–28.

234. Nelson, "The Public Problems of Business," 669.

235. Howard Frazier, "Consumer Protection," *Vital Speeches of the Day* 36, no. 9 (February 15, 1970): 265–70; Rotman, "Consumerism Is Us!"; Thomas R. Reid, "History's Fourth Turning Point," *Vital Speeches of the Day* 36, no. 12 (April 1, 1970): 369–72. Reid said there were 350 consumer-related bills introduced in the 1969 fall session of Congress.

236. Rotman, "Consumerism Is Us!"

237. Goss, "There Oughtn't to Be a Law."

238. Bond, "Developing Responsible Promotion," 125. Emphasis in original.

239. Schreiber, "Public Relations and the Consumer," 39.

240. Reid, "History's Fourth Turning Point," 371. Emphasis in original.

241. Robert E. Kingsley, "The Function of Controversy," *Public Relations Quarterly* 11, no. 3 (Fall 1966): 7–13; Evelyn Konrad, "Corporate Brinkmanship," *Public Relations Quarterly* 11, no. 3 (Fall 1966): 14–16.

242. Bishop and Kilburn, "Penny Whistle or Public's Advocate?" 30.

243. Jack Bernstein, "Advertising Reporting to Public Relations?—It's Coming," *Public Relations Quarterly* 16, no. 1 (Spring 1971): 5.

244. Ibid., 34; Richard R. Conarroe, "How to Plan and Organize a Public Relations Program," *Public Relations Quarterly* 12, no. 2 (Summer 1967): 24–30.

245. "Past and Future Terms, Myths and Premises," *Public Relations Quarterly* 18, no. 4 (Spring 1974): 10.

246. *Securities and Exchange Commission v. Texas Gulf Sulphur Co.,* 258 F. Supp. 262 (S.D. N.Y. 1966); *Securities and Exchange Commission v. Texas*

Gulf Sulphur Co., 401 F.2d 833 (2d Cir. 1968), *cert. denied,* 394 U.S. 976 (1969). Walt Seifert, "The Outlook for Public Relations: Brighter Than Ever," *Public Relations Quarterly* 18, no. 1 (Summer 1973): 14.

247. Nelson, "The Public Problems of Business," 669.

248. Rotman, "Consumerism Is Us!" 591.

249. Raymond P. Ewing, "A Strategic Approach to Issues Management," in Clarke L. Caywood, ed., *Handbook of Strategic Public Relations and Integrated Communications* (New York: McGraw-Hill, 1997), 173–86; Joseph Nolan, "Protect Your Public Image with Performance," *Harvard Business Review* 53, no. 2 (March-April 1975): 135–42.

250. Quoted in Nolan, "Protect Your Public Image," 140.

251. Nelson, "The Public Problems of Business," 670. Emphasis in original.

252. Ibid.

253. Ewing, "A Strategic Approach."

254. Nelson, "The Public Problems of Business," 669.

255. Cited in ibid., 668.

256. Cited in Arthur R. Taylor, "Business and the Press: Who's Doing What to Whom and Why?" *Vital Speeches of the Day* 42, no. 4 (December 1, 1975): 124.

257. James N. Sites, "The Press, the Economy, and the Nation's Future," *Vital Speeches of the Day* 44, no. 10 (March 1, 1978): 290–94.

258. Quoted in J. T. W. Hubbard, "Business News in Post-Watergate Era," *Journalism Quarterly* 53 (1976): 489.

259. Taylor, "Business and the Press."

260. Sites, "The Press, the Economy."

261. Arthur Ochs Sulzberger, "Business and the Press," *Vital Speeches of the Day* 43, no. 14 (May 1, 1977): 426–28; Lewis H. Young, "Business and the Media," *Vital Speeches of the Day* 45, no. 3 (November 15, 1978): 73–78.

262. Semour Topping, "Business and the News Media," *Vital Speeches of the Day* 45, no. 17 (June 15, 1979): 528–30; Young, "Business and the Media"; James P. Gannon, "Business and the Media," *Vital Speeches of the Day* 46, no. 5 (December 15, 1979): 133–36.

263. Gannon, "Business and the Media."

264. Young, "Business and the Media."

265. Gannon, "Business and the Media."

266. Young, "Business and the Media"; Sites, "The Press, the Economy."

267. Young, "Business and the Media"; Sites, "The Press, the Economy."

268. Robert A. Beck, "Business, the Press, and the Zero-Risk Society," *Vital Speeches of the Day* 44, no. 24 (October 1, 1978): 758–60; Young, "Business and the Media"; Topping, "Business and the News Media"; Gannon, "Business and the Media."

269. Robert J. Wood, "Communication: Top Executive Priority," *Management Review* 68, no. 5 (May 1979): 49–51.

270. Chester Burger, "How to Meet the Press," *Harvard Business Review* 33, no. 4 (July-August 1955): 62–70; Beck, "Business, the Press."

271. Beck, "Business, the Press."

272. J. W. Hull, "The Public Concerns of Private Enterprise," *Vital Speeches of the Day* 37, no. 12 (April 1, 1971): 367–70.

273. Neal W. O'Connor, "The Freedom to Communicate," *Vital Speeches of the Day* 42, no. 6 (January 1, 1976): 181.

274. Ibid.

275. Robert L. Kerr, "Creating the Corporate Citizen: Mobil Oil's Editorial-Advocacy Campaign in *The New York Times* to Advance the Right and Practice of Corporate Political Speech, 1970–80," *American Journalism* 21, no. 4 (Fall 2004): 39–62.

276. Quoted in ibid., 46.

277. Ibid., 50.

278. "Oil Is Not a Cottage Industry," advertisement, *New York Times,* July 1, 1976, sec. 1, p. 29.

279. Kerr, "Creating the Corporate Citizen," 47.

280. "Taking a Stand on the Issues through Advertising," *Association Management* 33, no. 12 (December 1980): 58.

281. John W. Hanley, "Why Ban Reason from the Consumer Safety Debate?" *Vital Speeches of the Day* 43, no. 20 (August 1, 1977): 626–29; John W. Hanley, "Has Emotion Tipped the Scales on Consumer Safety?" *Vital Speeches of the Day* 44, no. 3 (November 15, 1977): 92–95.

282. Robert J. Buckley, "Consumerism and the Economic Dope Habit," *Vital Speeches of the Day* 44, no. 5 (December 15, 1977): 145–50.

283. Chafe, *The Unfinished Journey.*

CHAPTER FIVE

284. Lytle, *America's Uncivil Wars,* 263.

285. Quoted in ibid., 254.

286. Quoted in ibid., 350.

287. Quoted in ibid.

288. Jeb Stuart Magruder, *An American Life: One Man's Road to Watergate* (New York: Atheneum, 1974).

289. William E. Porter, *Assault on the Media: The Nixon Years* (Ann Arbor: University of Michigan Press, 1976).

290. Ibid., 31.

291. Ibid., 34.

292. Joseph McCaffrey, "The Reporter: A Campaign to Intimidate," *Vital Speeches of the Day* 37, no. 15 (May 15, 1971): 478–80; Jeff Blyskal and Marie Blyskal, *PR: How the Public Relations Industry Writes the News* (New York: William Morrow, 1985), 200.

293. Quoted in Lytle, *America's Uncivil Wars,* 350.

294. Quoted in ibid., 350–51.

295. Ibid.

296. Ibid.; Blanchard, *Revolutionary Sparks.*

297. Lytle, *America's Uncivil Wars.*

298. Spiro T. Agnew, "Television News Coverage," *Vital Speeches of the Day* 36, no. 4 (December 1, 1969): 98, 99. The speech reflected Patrick Buchanan's philosophy about the media. He saw the media's role as assisting and supporting the government in its efforts to govern. Thus, the media ought to provide the president with an opportunity to reach the American people with his message without editorial comment or criticism so that the people could make up their own minds about the message. Porter, *Assault on the Media.*

299. Hazel Erskine, "The Polls: Opinion of the News Media," *Public Opinion Quarterly* 34, no. 4 (Winter 1970–1971): 630.

300. Ibid.

301. John Chamberlain, "The American Communications Media," *Vital Speeches of the Day* 40, no. 8 (February 1, 1974): 240–42.

302. White House memorandum, October 17, 1969, quoted in

Joseph C. Spear, *Presidents and the Press: The Nixon Legacy* (Cambridge, Mass.: MIT Press, 1984), 113.

303. Quoted in John Tebbel and Sarah Miles Watts, *The Press and the Presidency* (New York: Oxford University Press, 1985), 507–8.

304. Porter, *Assault on the Media.*

305. See, for example, John W. Macy Jr., "The Critics of Television," *Vital Speeches of the Day* 36, no. 9 (February 15, 1970): 286–88; Reuven Frank, "Freedom of the Broadcast Press," *Vital Speeches of the Day* 36, no. 11 (March 15, 1970): 332–36; Julian Goodman, "U.S. Broadcasting Freedom," *Vital Speeches of the Day* 36, no. 21 (August 15, 1970): 658–59; McCaffrey, "The Reporter"; Reuven Frank, "Broadcasting and the First Amendment," *Vital Speeches of the Day* 38, no. 4 (December 1, 1971): 125–27; Reuven Frank, "The First Amendment: Television News," *Vital Speeches of the Day* 38, no. 20 (August 1, 1972): 629–32.

306. Av Westin, *News-Watch: How TV Decides the News* (New York: Simon and Schuster, 1982), 96. Todd Gitlin said that the media began to move away from showing militancy after the 1968 Democratic Convention in Chicago. They recognized that groups had become more militant partly to gain greater media attention. Gitlin, *The Whole World Is Watching.*

307. Blanchard, *Revolutionary Sparks,* 348.

308. Quoted in Lytle, *America's Uncivil Wars,* 340.

309. William Safire, *Before the Fall: An Inside View of the Pre-Watergate White House* (Garden City, N.Y.: Doubleday, 1975), 341.

310. Blanchard, *Revolutionary Sparks;* Porter, *Assault on the Media.*

311. H. R. Haldeman, action paper, June 15, 1971, quoted in Bruce Oudes, ed., *From: The President—Richard Nixon's Secret Files* (New York: Harper and Row, 1989), 271–72.

312. Blanchard, *Revolutionary Sparks;* Porter, *Assault on the Media.*

313. Blanchard, *Revolutionary Sparks.*

314. Donald M. Gillmor, Jerome A. Barron, Todd F. Simon, and Herbert A. Terry, *Mass Communication Law: Cases and Comment,* 5th ed. (St. Paul, Minn.: West Publishing, 1990): 359.

315. Victoria Cook, *Shield Laws: A Report on Freedom of the Press, Protection of News Sources, and the Obligation to Testify* (Lexington, Ky.: Council of State Governments, 1973), 3.

316. *Branzburg v. Hayes,* 408 U.S. 665 (1972).

317. "Newsmen's Privilege," *Editor & Publisher* 95, no. 7 (July 8, 1972): 6. For a discussion of the trade publications' reaction to the *Branzburg v. Hayes* case, see Karla K. Gower, "Building One's Own Gallows: The Trade Publications' Reaction to a Federal Shield Law, 1972–1974," *Free Speech Yearbook* 35 (1997): 163–74.

318. "Newsmen Urge Passage of Press Immunity Bill," *Editor & Publisher* 95, no. 9 (September 30, 1972): 12.

319. "The No-Confidence Laws," *Editor & Publisher* 95, no. 11 (November 25, 1972): 6.

320. "57% Don't Want Newsmen to Name Their Sources," *Editor & Publisher* 95, no. 12 (December 9, 1972): 13.

321. "Editor's Column," *Quill* 61, no. 1 (January 1973): 5.

322. Mark Feldstein, "The Jailing of a Journalist: Prosecuting the Press for Receiving Stolen Documents," *Communication Law and Policy* 10, no. 2 (Spring 2005): 145.

323. Magruder, *An American Life.*

324. David S. Broder, *Behind the Front Lines* (New York: Simon and Schuster, 1987).

325. Ibid.

326. Magruder, *An American Life,* 218.

327. For a discussion of the use of leaks, see Leon V. Sigal, *Reporters and Officials* (Lexington, Mass.: D. C. Heath, 1973).

328. Magruder, *An American Life.*

329. Ibid., 128.

330. Lytle, *America's Uncivil Wars,* 364.

331. Ibid.

332. Laurence I. Barrett, "Urging Nixon to Quit: The Weekend That Was," *Columbia Journalism Review* 14 (January-February 1974): 66–68. *Time* magazine's editor in chief told Barrett that the magazine did not want to call for Nixon's resignation while Spiro Agnew was vice president. Agnew was forced to resign on October 10, 1973, because he was being investigated for bribery and tax evasion. David Goldman, "Spiro Agnew: How Mr. Law-and-Order Got Busted," *Biography Magazine* 7, no. 11 (November 2003): 26.

333. Chan Ying Kwong and Kenneth Starck, "The *New York Times'*

Stance on Nixon and Public Opinion," *Journalism Quarterly* 53 (1976): 723–27; Robert B. Laing and Robert L. Stevenson, "Public Opinion Trends in the Last Days of the Nixon Administration," *Journalism Quarterly* 53 (1976): 294–302.

334. Broder, *Behind the Front Page;* Ron Nessen, *It Sure Looks Different from the Inside* (Chicago: Playboy Press, 1978). Ford's first chief of staff was Donald Rumsfeld. Partway through his tenure, Ford shook up his cabinet. Rumsfeld was named secretary of defense, and Richard B. "Dick" Cheney was promoted from deputy chief of staff to chief of staff.

335. Mark J. Rozell, *The Press and the Ford Presidency* (Ann Arbor: University of Michigan Press, 1992).

336. Ibid.

337. Ibid.; Hallin, *The "Uncensored War."*

338. William J. Baroody, "The Presidency: How Open?" *Vital Speeches of the Day* 41, no. 20 (August 1, 1975): 625–28.

339. Nessen, *It Sure Looks Different;* Rozell, *The Press and the Ford Presidency.*

340. Rozell, *The Press and the Ford Presidency.*

341. Broder, *Behind the Front Page,* 56. Broder said there is no record of Johnson actually saying that, and Johnson's aides deny it, although there are more scatological versions of the statement around.

342. Ibid.

343. Nessen, *It Sure Looks Different,* 165.

344. Broder, *Behind the Front Page,* 61.

345. Aaron Reincheld, "'Saturday Night Live' and Weekend Update: The Formative Years of Comedy News Dissemination," *Journalism History* 31, no. 4 (Winter 2006): 191; Marianne Partridge, ed., *Rolling Stone Visits "Saturday Night Live"* (Garden City, N.J.: Doubleday, 1979), 9.

346. Reincheld, "'Saturday Night Live.'"

347. Ibid.

348. Ibid.; Nessen, *It Sure Looks Different.*

349. Quoted in Rozell, *The Press and the Ford Presidency,* 186.

350. Jimmy Carter, "Fireside Chat: Unity on U.S. Goals," *Vital Speeches of the Day* 43, no. 9 (February 15, 1977): 261.

351. Rozell, *The Press and the Ford Presidency.*

352. Martin S. Hayden, "Investigative Reporting," *Vital Speeches of*

the Day 42, no. 18 (July 1, 1976): 574; Milton J. Shapp, "The Press Must Remain Free," *Vital Speeches of the Day* 42, no. 20 (August 1, 1976): 617; Howard Simons, "The Press Media," *Vital Speeches of the Day* 43, no. 22 (September 1, 1977): 689–92.

353. Walter B. Wriston, "Liberty, Leadership and License," *Vital Speeches of the Day* 42, no. 14 (May 1, 1976): 424; Simons, "The Press Media."

354. Hayden, "Investigative Reporting."

355. Ibid., 576.

356. Robert L. Gildea, "Doubting Thomas Our Patron Saint?" *Public Relations Quarterly* 22, no. 1 (Spring 1977): 27.

357. Quoted in John B. Oakes, "Freedom of the Press," *Vital Speeches of the Day* 44, no. 19 (July 15, 1978): 588–92.

CHAPTER SIX

358. Broder, *Behind the Front Page,* 141.

359. Gale E. Klappa, "Journalism and the Anti-media Backlash," *Vital Speeches of the Day* 51, no. 12 (April 1, 1985): 376–79; C. M. Kittrell, "There's No Such Thing as a Free Press," *Vital Speeches of the Day* 51, no. 1 (October 15, 1984): 20–22.

360. Klappa, "Journalism and the Anti-media Backlash."

361. Quoted in ibid., 377.

362. Ibid.

363. William S. Paley, "Press Freedom," *Vital Speeches of the Day* 46, no. 21 (August 15, 1980): 670–72.

364. George E. Reedy, "The Press in This Modern World," *Vital Speeches of the Day* 46, no. 7 (January 15, 1980): 221.

365. Ibid.

366. Ibid., 222.

367. Blyskal and Blyskal, *PR,* 12.

368. Ibid.

369. Mark Hertsgaard, *On Bended Knee: The Press and the Reagan Presidency* (New York: Schocken Books, 1989), 218.

370. Ibid.

371. Ibid.

372. "The Case of the People vs. the Press," *Broadcasting* 106, no. 2 (January 9, 1984): 116.

373. Hertsgaard, *On Bended Knee,* 221.

374. Blyskal and Blyskal, *PR.*

375. Ibid.

376. Ibid., 20.

377. Ibid.

378. Ibid.

379. Ibid.

380. Ibid., 24.

381. Hertsgaard, *On Bended Knee,* 6.

382. Cohen, *A Consumer's Republic.*

383. Ibid.

384. David Brooks, "Please Mr. Postman: The Travails of Richard Viguerie," *National Review,* June 20, 1986, 28–32.

385. Cohen, *A Consumer's Republic,* 338.

386. Brooks, "Please Mr. Postman," 28.

387. Cohen, *A Consumer's Republic,* 340.

388. Ibid.

389. Ibid., 342.

390. Ibid.

391. Brooks, "Please Mr. Postman."

392. Cohen, *A Consumer's Republic.*

393. Broder, *Behind the Front Page.*

394. Hertsgaard, *On Bended Knee,* 38.

395. Blyskal and Blyskal, *PR,* 198.

396. Hertsgaard, *On Bended Knee,* 5.

397. Ibid.

398. Quoted in ibid., 33.

399. Ibid., 18.

400. Ibid., 34, emphasis in original.

401. Ibid.

402. "The Case of the People," 116.

403. Ibid.

404. "The Debate and the Spin Doctors," editorial, *New York Times,* October 21, 1984, p. E22.

405. Ibid.

406. William Safire, "Calling Dr. Spin," *New York Times,* August 31, 1986, p. SM8.

407. "The Debate and the Spin Doctors."

408. Hertsgaard, *On Bended Knee.*

409. Broder, *Behind the Front Page,* 180.

410. Hertsgaard, *On Bended Knee,* 48.

411. Quoted in ibid., 25.

412. Broder, *Behind the Front Page,* 178.

413. Alan P. Balutis, "Congress, the President and the Press," *Journalism Quarterly* 53 (Autumn, 1976): 509–15.

414. Hertsgaard, *On Bended Knee.*

415. Ibid.

416. Hallin, *The "Uncensored War."*

417. Hertsgaard, *On Bended Knee,* 74.

418. Ibid.

419. Eric Alterman, *Sound and Fury: The Making of the Punditocracy* (Ithaca, N.Y., and London: Cornell University Press, 1999).

420. Ibid., 72.

421. Ibid., 13.

422. Ibid.

423. Ibid., 97.

424. Quoting Irving Kristol in ibid., 75.

425. Ibid., 87.

426. Ibid.

427. Ibid., 108.

428. Floyd Abrams, "Will the First Amendment Survive the 1980's?" *Vital Speeches of the Day* 51, no. 13 (April 15, 1985): 412.

429. Ibid.

430. Ibid.; "The Case of the People," 116.

431. Broder, *Behind the Front Page,* 183.

432. Ibid.

433. Ibid., 185.

434. Abrams, "Will the First Amendment Survive the 1980's?"; Broder, *Behind the Front Page,* 187.

435. Abrams, "Will the First Amendment Survive the 1980's?"

436. Hertsgaard, *On Bended Knee.*

437. Ibid.

438. Ibid.

439. Ibid., 320.

440. Broder, *Behind the Front Page,* 193.

441. Ibid.

442. Hertsgaard, *On Bended Knee,* 348.

CHAPTER SEVEN

443. Michael D. Murray, "The Contemporary Media: 1974–Present," in William David Sloan, ed., *The Media in America: A History,* 5th ed. (Northport, Ala.: Vision Press, 2002), 459–60.

444. Hertsgaard, *On Bended Knee,* 78.

445. Murray, "The Contemporary Media."

446. Reuven Frank, "Almost Nobody Writes Silence Any More," *Vital Speeches of the Day* 47, no. 10 (March 1, 1981): 293–95.

447. Murray, "The Contemporary Media."

448. Edwin Diamond, *The Tin Kazoo: Television, Politics, and the News* (Cambridge, Mass.: MIT Press, 1975), 65–66.

449. David Shaw, "The Trouble with TV Muckraking," *TV Guide,* October 10, 1981, 7.

450. Ronald E. Rhody, "The Conventional Wisdom Is Wrong," *Vital Speeches of the Day* 49, no. 2 (November 1982): 50–54.

451. Ibid.

452. Murray, "The Contemporary Media," 464.

453. Ibid.

454. James H. Rosenfield, "To Have, To Have Not, or To Have More," *Vital Speeches of the Day* 50, no. 2 (November 1, 1983): 42–45.

455. Murray, "The Contemporary Media," 462.

456. John F. Budd Jr., "Are We 'Smart Enough' for Tomorrow?" *Vital Speeches of the Day* 49, no. 23 (September 15, 1982): 729–31.

457. Fraser P. Seitel, "TV or No TV—That Is the Question," *United States Banker* 98, no. 11 (November 1989): 60–62.

458. Ibid.

459. Murray, "The Contemporary Media," 462.

460. Ibid.; Hertsgaard, *On Bended Knee,* 78.

461. Murray, "The Contemporary Media," 466.

462. Ibid.

463. John J. LaFalce, "The Packaging of Public Policy," *Vital Speeches of the Day* 48, no. 8 (February 1, 1982): 226–35.

464. Hertsgaard, *On Bended Knee,* 79.

465. David H. Weaver and Maxwell E. McCombs, "Journalism and Social Science: A New Relationship?" *Public Opinion Quarterly* 44 (1980): 477–94.

466. Alan Scott and Raymond West, "Personnel Turnover on Small Texas Dailies," *Journalism Quarterly* 32 (1955): 183–89.

467. Harry Marsh, "Correlates of Professionalism and News Performance among Texas Newsmen" (Ph.D. diss., University of Texas, 1974), 51.

468. Broder, *Behind the Front Lines,* 142.

469. Hertsgaard, *On Bended Knee.*

470. Broder, *Behind the Front Lines.*

471. Quoted in LaFalce, "The Packaging of Public Policy," 229.

472. Robert Keith Gray, "Getting the Story and Getting It Right," *Vital Speeches of the Day* 50, no. 24 (October 1, 1984): 764. Emphasis in original.

473. Dan Nimmo and James E. Combs, *Nightly Horrors: Crisis Coverage in Television Network News* (Knoxville: University of Tennessee Press, 1985).

474. Hertsgaard, *On Bended Knee,* 83.

475. Agnew, "Television News Coverage."

476. Wilmar F. Bernthal, "In the Context of Social Change," *Business Forum* 9, no. 2 (Spring 1984): 7–9.

477. Ben Bagdikian, *The Media Monopoly* (Boston: Beacon Press, 1983).

478. Hertsgaard, *On Bended Knee,* 77.

479. Rhody, "The Conventional Wisdom Is Wrong."

480. J. E. Swearingen, "Responsibility in Journalism," *Vital Speeches of the Day* 49, no. 11 (March 15, 1983): 344.

481. Thomas R. Horton, "Business and the Media: An Unholy Alliance?" *Management Review* 77, no. 12 (December 1988): 5.

482. Irvine O. Hockaday Jr., "Journalists and Businessmen Have a Lot in Common," *Vital Speeches of the Day* 51, no. 8 (February 1, 1985): 244–46; Ward Smith, "Business and the Media," *Vital Speeches of the Day* 52, no. 2 (November 1, 1985): 49–51. A speech by noted First Amendment attorney Floyd Abrams four months later, titled "Will the First Amendment Survive the 1980's?" seemed to support Hockaday's contention. Abrams, "Will the First Amendment Survive the 1980's?"

483. Hockaday, "Journalists and Businessmen," 245.

484. Bernthal, "In the Context of Social Change"; "Who Likes the Press and Who Doesn't," *U.S. News & World Report,* January 27, 1986, 78.

485. Bernthal, "In the Context of Social Change," 8.

486. Ibid.; Swearingen, "Responsibility in Journalism."

487. Horton, "Business and the Media," 5.

488. David Finn, "The Public Relations Role in Coping with the Information Crisis," *Public Relations Quarterly* 26, no. 3 (Fall 1981): 5–7.

489. Kittrell, "There's No Such Thing as a Free Press," 21.

490. Lewis H. Young, "The Media's View of Corporate Communications in the 80's," *Public Relations Quarterly* 26, no. 3 (Fall 1981): 9–11.

491. Finn, "The Public Relations Role," 6.

492. "Was Mobil Wise to Blacklist the *Wall Street Journal*?" *Business and Society Review* 85, no. 53 (1984): 38–39.

493. Ibid., 38.

494. "Confront the Press Head-On," *U.S. News & World Report,* May 26, 1986, 62.

495. Ibid.

496. Sandy Graham, "Illinois Power Pans '60 Minutes,'" *Wall Street Journal,* June 27, 1980, p. 24.

497. Quoted in ibid.

498. Quoted in ibid.

499. Quoted in ibid.

500. Ibid.

501. Quoted in ibid.

502. Swearingen, "Responsibility in Journalism."

503. Ibid.

504. Nimmo and Combs, *Nightly Horrors.*

505. Michael R. Greenberg, Peter M. Sandman, David B. Sachsman,

and Kandice L. Salomone, "Network Television News Coverage of Environmental Risks," *Environment* 31, no. 2 (March 1989): 16–44.

506. Joseph E. Reid, "How the Truth Becomes a Lie," *Vital Speeches of the Day* 47, no. 7 (January 15, 1981): 209.

507. Ibid. Although Reid suggested that special interest groups do not use experts, the more common situation was the battling experts, as expressed in a *New York Times* editorial. "The Promise of Fact," *New York Times,* May 1, 1981, p. A30: "In these days of bitter controversy over complex issues of health, safety and environment, every side marshals platoons of experts to present only a version of scientific truth. A confused, often cynical public has learned that there are as many scientific facts as there are sides in a controversy." Gray, "Getting the Story and Getting It Right."

508. Young, "The Media's View of Corporate Communications," 9.

509. Gerald R. Baron, *Now Is Too Late: Survival in an Era of Instant News* (Upper Saddle River, N.J.: FT Prentice-Hall, 2003).

510. Donald R. Stephenson, "Crisis Situations," *Vital Speeches of the Day* 49, no. 10 (March 1, 1983): 315–20.

511. Reid, "How the Truth Becomes a Lie," 209; Philip Lesly, "The Changing Evolution of Public Relations," *Public Relations Quarterly* 27, no. 4 (Winter 1982): 9–15.

512. David Kelley, "Critical Issues for Issue Ads," *Harvard Business Review* 60, no. 4 (July-August 1982): 80–87.

513. LaFalce, "The Packaging of Public Policy," 227; Gray, "Getting the Story and Getting It Right."

514. LaFalce, "The Packaging of Public Policy."

515. Rollo May, *Power and Innocence: A Search for the Sources of Violence* (New York: Norton, 1972). Public relations practitioner Philip Lesly called it the tendency to discommunicate. Lesly, "The Changing Evolution."

516. William F. May, "CEO's and the Public Business," *Vital Speeches of the Day* 46, no. 15 (May 15, 1980): 455.

517. Ira G. Corn Jr., "The Changing Role of Corporations in Political Affairs," *Vital Speeches of the Day* 47, no. 15 (May 15, 1981): 463–68.

518. Ibid.; Kerryn King, "Public Relations and Business Schools," *Vital Speeches of the Day* 48, no. 9 (February 15, 1982): 271–74.

519. May, "CEO's and the Public Business," 456.

520. Ibid., 457; Wes Poriotis, "Corporate Public Relations in a Deregulated Economy," *Vital Speeches of the Day* 47, no. 16 (June 1, 1981): 482–85.

521. Corn, "The Changing Role of Corporations," 465.

522. Poriotis, "Corporate Public Relations."

523. Lesly, "The Changing Evolution"; Philip Lesly, "How the Future Will Shape Public Relations—and Vice Versa," *Public Relations Quarterly* 26, no. 4 (Winter 1981–1982): 4–8.

524. Philip Lesly, "Surviving in the New Two-Tier Society," *Vital Speeches of the Day* 49, no. 17 (June 15, 1983): 534–37.

525. Lesly, "The Changing Evolution"; Lesly, "How the Future Will Shape Public Relations."

526. Lesly, "The Changing Evolution," 10; Lesly, "How the Future Will Shape Public Relations."

527. Richard A. Armstrong, "The Concept and Practice of Issues Management in the United States," *Vital Speeches of the Day* 47, no. 24 (October 1, 1981): 763.

528. Lesly, "Surviving in the New Two-Tier Society."

529. Armstrong, "The Concept and Practice of Issues Management"; Lesly, "Surviving in the New Two-Tier Society."

530. "How a PR Firm Executed the Alar Scare," *Wall Street Journal,* October 3, 1989, p. A22.

531. Ibid.

532. Philip Shabecoff, "Hazard Reported in Apple Chemical," *New York Times,* February 2, 1989, p. A1.

533. "How a PR Firm."

534. Ibid.

535. Ibid. See, for example, "Health Officials Rebuke Schools over Apple Bans," *New York Times,* March 16, 1989, p. B10.

536. Philip Shabecoff, "3 U.S. Agencies, to Allay Public's Fears, Declare Apples Safe," *New York Times,* March 17, 1989, p. A16; "Board Returns Apples to New York Schools," *New York Times,* March 21, 1989, p. B3; Robert A. Hamilton, "'They Have to See the Whole Picture,'" *New York Times,* March 26, 1989, p. CN3; "Fruit Growers Pull Commercials to Protest Report by CBS on Alar," *New York Times,* May 7, 1989, p. 36;

Philip Shabecoff, "Apple Chemical Being Removed in U.S. Market," *New York Times,* June 3, 1989, p. 1; Baron, *Now Is Too Late,* 98.

537. Jarol B. Manheim, *The Death of a Thousand Cuts: Corporate Campaigns and the Attack on the Corporation* (Mahwah, N.J.: Lawrence Erlbaum Associates, 2001), 19.

538. Ibid., 17.

539. Ibid.

540. Ibid.

541. Ibid., 16.

542. Weaver and McCombs, "Journalism and Social Science."

543. John N. Rippey, "Use of Opinion Polls as a Reporting Tool," manuscript, Pennsylvania State University, 1979. Quoted in Weaver and McCombs, "Journalism and Social Science," 490.

544. Ibid.

545. Ibid., 482.

546. Curtis D. MacDougall, *Interpretative Reporting,* 7th ed. (New York: Macmillan, 1977), 12.

547. Neale Copple, *Depth Reporting* (Englewood Cliffs, N.J.: Prentice-Hall, 1964), 19.

548. Philip Meyer, *Precision Journalism: A Reporter's Introduction to Social Science Methods* (Bloomington: Indiana University Press, 1973).

549. Glen M. Broom and David M. Dozier, "An Overview: Evaluation Research in Public Relations," *Public Relations Quarterly* (Fall 1983): 5–8.

550. Harvey K. Jacobson, "Guidelines for Evaluating Public Relations Programs," *Public Relations Quarterly* (Summer 1980): 7.

551. Scott M. Cutlip and Allen H. Center, *Effective Public Relations* (Englewood Cliffs, N.J.: Prentice-Hall, 1952), 5.

552. Albert Walker, "The Evolution of Public Relations According to Cutlip and Center," *Public Relations Quarterly* (Summer 1986): 28–31.

553. Scott M. Cutlip, Allen H. Center, and Glen M. Broom, *Effective Public Relations,* 6th ed. (Englewood Cliffs, N.J.: Prentice-Hall, 1985), 19.

554. Andrew Belz, Albert D. Talbott, and Kenneth Starck, "Using Role Theory to Study Cross Perceptions of Journalists and Public Relations Practitioners," *Public Relations Research Annual 1989,* vol. 1, 125–39.

555. Ibid., 131, 132.

556. Ibid., 132.

557. Ibid., 135.

558. Joel Pomerantz, "The Media and Public Relations: Pride and Prejudice," *Public Relations Quarterly* (Winter 1989–1990): 13.

559. Ibid., 13–16.

560. Ibid., 14.

561. Ibid., 13–16.

562. Chafe, *The Unfinished Journey.*

563. John Naisbitt, *Megatrends: Ten New Directions Transforming Our Lives* (New York: Warner Books, 1982).

564. Cutlip, Center, and Broom, *Effective Public Relations,* 8th ed. Thomas L. Friedman, *The World Is Flat,* 2nd ed. (New York: Farrar, Straus and Giroux, 2006).

CHAPTER EIGHT

565. Martha T. Moore, "Talk Shows Become a Campaign Staple," *USA Today,* September 21, 2000, p. 8A.

566. David Bianculli, "Sax to 'Sock It to Me?'" *Daily News,* October 27, 2004, p. 86.

567. Bill Clinton, *My Life* (New York: Vintage Books, 2005).

568. Thomas Winship, "The President vs. the Press: Cool It," *Editor & Publisher* 127, no. 37 (September 10, 1994): 19.

569. Howard Kurtz, "The Press Bypass," *Washington Post,* January 22, 1993, p. C1.

570. Ibid.

571. Ibid.

572. Clinton, *My Life.*

573. Susan Baer, "President Turns to Campaign Brainstrust to Rekindle Election Success," *Buffalo News,* February 13, 1993, p. 3.

574. Richard Hofstadter, "The Paranoid Style in American Politics," *Harper's,* November 1964, 77.

575. Ibid.

576. Alterman, *Sound and Fury.*

577. Hofstadter, "The Paranoid Style in American Politics."

578. Alexandra Marks, "Are Media Standards Dropping?" *Christian Science Monitor,* January 29, 1998, p. 4.

579. Ibid.

580. Marks, "Are Media Standards Dropping?"

581. Richard Zoglin and Ann Blackman, "The News Wars," *Time,* October 21, 1996, p. 58.

582. Ibid.

583. "Corporate Culture," editorial, *Nation,* June 3, 1996, 3.

584. Zoglin and Blackman, "The News Wars."

585. Moore, "Talk Shows Become a Campaign Staple," p. 8A.

586. Mary Dejevsky, "Bush Reaches 100th Day with Little to Proclaim," *Independent* (London), April 30, 2001, p. 12.

587. Paul West, "Behind Bush's Low-Key Style Is a Blueprint Drafted Well in Advance," *St. Louis Post-Dispatch,* April 25, 2001, p. A8.

588. Ibid.

589. Quoted in "Monitor: The American Press Evaluates the First 100 Days of the Presidency of George Bush," *Independent* (London), May 1, 2001, p. 2.

590. Wilson Lowery, "Media Dependency during a Large-Scale Social Crisis: The Case of September 11th," *Mass Communication Society* 7 (Summer 2004): 339–57; Everett M. Rogers, "Diffusion of News of the September 11 Terrorist Attacks," in A. Michael Noll, ed., *Crisis Communications: Lessons from September 11* (Lanham, Md.: Rowman and Littlefield, 2003), 17–30.

591. "Study Shows TV's Return to 'Soft' News," *PR Week,* June 3, 2002, 3.

592. Jon Pareles, "America Catches Up with Them," *New York Times,* May 21, 2006, pp. S2, 1.

593. Ibid.

594. Ibid.

595. Andrew Buncombe, "US Cartoonists under Pressure," *Independent on Sunday* (London), June 23, 2002, p. 16.

596. Ibid.

597. Gary Younge, "Now Dissent Is 'Immoral,'" *Guardian Leader* (Manchester, UK), June 2, 2003, p. 15.

598. Chris Cobb, "The President's Spin Doctor Brings the News-hounds to Heel," *Ottawa Citizen,* May 24, 2002, p. A18.

599. Ibid.

600. Andrew Gumbel, Andrew Wong, and Ron Edmonds, "How War Coverage Helped Put Murdoch on a Media Roll in Bush's America," *Independent* (London), April 16, 1983, p. 18.

601. Ibid.; Rupert Cornwell, "Don't Believe All the Patriotic Fire on American TV," *Independent* (London), April 23, 2003, p. 17.

602. Cornwell, "Don't Believe All the Patriotic Fire."

603. Ibid.

604. McGinniss, *The Selling of the President.*

605. Peter Huck, "'Someone Gets in My Fact, I Get in Their Face,'" *Guardian* (London), August 29, 2005, p. 10.

606. Ibid.

607. Verne Gay, "What's Hate Got to Do with It?" *Newsday.com,* available at www.newsday.com, accessed on October 18, 2005.

608. Jay Rosen, "Bill O'Reilly and the Paranoid Style of News," *Pressthink,* October 21, 2003, available at journalism.nyu.edu/pubzone /weblogs/pressthink/2003/10/21/oreilly_voice.html, accessed on July 5, 2006.

609. Ibid.

610. "Here's Bill," available at www.billoreilly.com, accessed on July 5, 2006; Bill O'Reilly, *Who's Looking Out for You?* (New York: Broadway Books, 2003).

611. Hofstadter, "The Paranoid Style in American Politics."

612. Rosen, "Bill O'Reilly and the Paranoid Style of News."

613. Institute for Propaganda Analysis, "Announcement," *Propaganda Analysis* 1 (October 1937): 1–2. Emphasis in original.

614. Mike Conway, Maria Elizabeth Grabe, and Kevin Grieves, "Bill O'Reilly's 'No-Spin Zone': Using 1930s Propaganda Techniques and Constructing Villains, Victims, and the Virtuous," paper presented at the annual meeting of the Association for Education in Journalism and Mass Communication, San Francisco, August 2006; Alfred M. Lee and Elizabeth B. Lee, eds., *The Fine Art of Propaganda: A Study of Father Coughlin's Speeches* (New York: Harcourt, Brace, 1939).

615. Ibid.

616. Ibid., 24. Of course, the same propaganda devices could be used to assess speakers on the left as well.

617. Annenberg Public Policy Center, "About One American in Four Considers Rush Limbaugh a Journalist . . . ," available at http://www.annenbergpublicpolicycenter.org, accessed on October 24, 2005.

618. Rosen, "Bill O'Reilly and the Paranoid Style of News."

619. Robert Pear, "U.S. Videos, for TV News, Come under Scrutiny," *New York Times,* March 15, 2004, p. 1.

620. Emil Gallina, "VNRs under Attack," *Communication World* 8, no. 11 (October 1991): 13.

621. Kevin E. Foley, "No Harm, No Foul: Survey Conclusions Overlook TV Media Reality," *PR Tactics* 13, no. 6 (June 2006): 27.

622. John F. Budd Jr. "Corporate Video May Be Hazardous to Credibility," *Vital Speeches of the Day* 47, no. 18 (July 1, 1981): 567–70.

623. Ibid.

624. John F. Budd Jr. "Credibility vs. 'Con,'" *Public Relations Quarterly* 27, no. 1 (Spring 1982): 13.

625. Budd, "Are We 'Smart Enough' for Tomorrow?"

626. Richard Green and Denise Shapiro, "A Video News Release Primer," *Public Relations Quarterly* 32, no. 4 (Winter 1987–1988): 11.

627. Ibid.

628. Adam Shell, "VNRs: In the News," *Public Relations Journal* 48, no. 12 (December 1992): 20.

629. Ibid.

630. Ibid.; Eugene M. Marlow, "Sophisticated 'News' Videos Gain Wide Acceptance," *Public Relations Journal* 50, no. 7 (August–September 1994): 17.

631. John Elsasser, "The Great VNR Debate, Part Two," *PR Tactics* 12, no. 4 (April 2005): 3.

632. Government Accounting Office, *Video News Releases: Unattributed Prepackaged News Stories Violate Publicity or Propaganda Prohibition,* GAO-05-643T.

633. David Barstow and Robin Stein, "Under Bush, a New Age of Prepackaged News," *New York Times,* March 13, 2005, p. 1.

634. Ibid.

635. Ibid.

636. Ibid.

637. Ibid.

638. Ibid.

639. Diane Farsetta, "Fake TV News: Widespread and Undisclosed," *Center for Media and Democracy,* March 16, 2006, available at http://www.prwatch.org, accessed on April 20, 2006.

640. Barstow and Stein, "Under Bush."

641. Joe Mandese, "The Art of Manufacturing News: Forget the White House, PR Firms Take Branded Journalism to a Whole New Level," *Broadcasting and Cable* 135, no. 13 (March 28, 2005): 24.

642. Ibid.

643. Joan Stewart, "More TV Stations Turning to Pay for Play: The Line between Ads and Editorial Continues to Blur," *PR Tactics* 13, no. 6 (June 2006): 26.

644. Edward J. Lordan, "Defining Public Relations and Press Roles in the Twenty-first Century," *Public Relations Quarterly* 50, no. 2 (Summer 2005): 41.

645. Greg Toppo, "White House Paid Journalist to Promote Law," *USA Today,* January 7, 2005, p. 1A.

646. Ibid.

647. Timothy O'Brien, "Spinning Frenzy: P.R.'s Bad Press," *New York Times,* February 13, 2005, p. 1; Noel Griese, "Ketchum, Williams Implicated in New Education Dept. PR Spending Flap," *Crisis Counselor Newsletter,* February 2005, available at http://www.anvilpub.com/crisis_counselor.htm, accessed on February 9, 2005; Ben Silverman, "Public's Perception of PR–Media Relationship Has Blurred," *PR Fuel,* January 12, 2005, available at http://www.prfuel.com/archives/000380.html, accessed on January 27, 2005.

648. Griese, "Ketchum, Williams Implicated."

649. Quoted in ibid.; Maureen Dowd, "For the Right Price, Exceptions Can Be Made," *Tuscaloosa (Ala.) News,* January 31, 2005, p. 7A.

650. Quoted in Douglas Ray, "Decision to Discontinue McManus Is Based on Ethics," *Tuscaloosa (Ala.) News,* February 4, 2005, p. 7A.

651. Griese, "Ketchum, Williams Implicated."

652. Robert Pear, "Buying of News by Bush's Aides Is Ruled Illegal," *New York Times,* October 1, 2005, p. A1.

653. O'Brien, "Spinning Frenzy"; Erica Iacono and Keith O'Brien, "GAO Casts Light on White House Marcomms Outlay," *PR Week,* February 20, 2006, 1. Another report suggests government public relations contracts in 2004 increased by 128 percent over the amount spent by the Clinton administration in 2000, although comparing the last year of a presidency with the first three years is not a fair comparison. Associated Press, "U.S. Transportation Secretary Nominee Let $7.8 Million in PR Contracts as FHWA Head," *International Herald Tribune,* September 20, 2006, available at http://www.iht.com/bin/print_ipub.php?file=/articles/ap/2006/09/20/news/Highway_PR.php, accessed on September 21, 2006. *USA Today* apparently quoted the figure at $250 million. But a GAO report released in 2006 found that the White House had spent $1.6 billion on 343 marketing communications contracts since 2003. Of those, 54 contracts were with public relations firms, for $197 million. Frank Greve, "Journalism in the Age of Pseudoreporting," *Nieman Reports* 59, no. 2 (Summer 2005): 11–13.

654. O'Brien, "Spinning Frenzy."

655. Keith O'Brien, "Lincoln Group Answers Critics with Dixon Hire," *PR Week,* January 30, 2006, 1; Mark Mazzetti and Borzou Daragahi, "The Conflict in Iraq," *Los Angeles Times,* November 30, 2005, pt. A, p. 1; Erica Iacono, "US Military's Placement of Paid Stories Draws Debate," *PR Week,* December 5, 2005, 1.

656. Jonathan Alter, "The Real Price of Propaganda," *Newsweek,* December 12, 2005, 42.

657. Ibid.; Eric Schmitt and David S. Cloud, "Senate Summons Pentagon to Explain Effort to Plant Reports in Iraqi News Media," *New York Times,* December 2, 2005, sec. A, p. 10; Eric Schmitt, "Military Admits Planting News in Iraq," *New York Times,* December 3, 2005, sec. A, p. 13. It was also revealed in 2003 that the military had sent identical letters to newspapers around the country purportedly from soldiers based in Iraq. The letters appeared in at least eleven newspapers and were signed by different soldiers according to their hometowns. The letters talked about the advances being made in Iraq toward reconstruction. Ledyard King,

"Newspapers Print Same Letter Signed by Different Soldiers," *USA Today,* sec. News, p. 7A.

658. Bill Adair, "Corporate Spin Can Come in Disguise," *St. Petersburg Times,* September 10, 2006, available at http://www.sptimes.com /2006/09/10/news_pf/Worldandnation/Corporate_spin_co.shtml, accessed on September 11, 2006.

659. Ibid.

660. Antonio Regalado and Dionne Searcey, "Where Did That Video Spoofing Gore's Film Come From?" *Post-Gazette.com,* available at http://www.post-gazette.com/pg/pp/06215/710851.stm, accessed on August 7, 2006.

661. George Monbiot, "The Denial Industry," *Guardian,* September 19, 2006, available at http://environment.guardian.co.uk/print /0,,3295 79929–121568,00.html, accessed on September 20, 2006.

662. Ibid.

663. Julia Hood, "The PR Industry's Anger over the Williams-DoE Episode Must Now Give Way to Finding Solutions," *PR Week,* January 24, 2005.

664. Ben Silverman, "Public's Perception of PR–Media Relationship Has Blurred," *PR Fuel,* January 12, 2005, available at http://www.prfuel .com/archives/000380.html, accessed on January 27, 2005.

665. Kate Nicholas, "Timesheets Prove a Double-Edged Sword," *PR Week,* April 1, 2005; Anita Chabria, "Sugarman to Plead Guilty at F-H Overbilling Trial," *PR Week,* June 17, 2005.

666. O'Brien, "Spinning Frenzy."

667. Ibid.

668. James G. Hutton, "Integrated Marketing Communications and the Evolution of Marketing Thought," *Journal of Business Research* 37 (1996): 155–62.

669. Quoted in O'Brien, "Spinning Frenzy."

670. "State of the News Media 2004," Project for Excellence in Journalism, 13, available at http://www.stateofthenewsmedia.org/journalist _survey.html, accessed on January 16, 2006.

671. Lori Robertson, "Confronting the Culture," *American Journalism Review* 27, no. 4 (August-September 2005): 35.

672. Ibid.

673. Cynthia L. Kemper, "Living in Spin," *Communication World* 18, no. 3 (April–May 2001): 6.

674. Ibid.

675. Ibid.

676. Quoted in ibid.

677. Bill Kovach, "Watchdog Journalism Is the Only Function of Journalism That Justifies the Freedom That Journalists Enjoy in This Country," *Nieman Reports* 53, no. 3 (Fall 1999): 4.

678. Julia Hood, "When Advertisers Begin to Exert Pressure on Media Outlets, the PR World Feels the Squeeze," *PR Week,* May 30, 2005.

679. "A New Censor?" *Economist,* October 18, 1997, 30.

680. Hood, "When Advertisers."

681. David Carr, "An Obsession with Leaks and Plugs," *New York Times,* September 25, 2006, available at http://www.nytimes.com/2006/09/25/business/media/25carr.htm/, accessed on September 25, 2006.

682. Michael Wolfe, "Panic on 43rd Street," *Vanity Fair,* September 2006, 236–242.

683. Greve, "Journalism in the Age of Pseudoreporting."

684. Ibid., 12.

685. Ibid.

686. Ibid.

687. Ibid., 11.

688. Lyric Wallwork Winik, "Bush's Press Problem," *Parade,* December 11, 2005, 18.

689. Rosen, "Dick Cheney Did Not Make a Mistake"; "Comms Inconsistencies Haunt the White House," editorial, *PR Week,* February 20, 2006, 10.

690. Ibid.

691. Steven Thomma, "Cheney's Missteps Turned Accident into PR Disaster, Experts Say," *Charlotte.com,* February 14, 2006, available at http://www.charlotte.com/mld/charlotte/news/nation/13872002.html, accessed on February 17, 2006.

692. "Comms Inconsistencies Haunt the White House."

693. Rosen, "Dick Cheney Did Not Make a Mistake."

694. Michael Goodwin, "Media Squander Public Trust by Playing Politics," *New York Daily News*, November 3, 2004, sec. Wrap, p. 10; Edward Helmore, "Media: More Spinned against Than Spinners," *Guardian*, September 26, 2004, p. 8; David Greenberg, "In the Free-for-All of Political Spin, Americans May Lose Sight of the Real Issues," *Washington Post*, July 18, 2004, Sec. Book World, p. T04; George Monbiot, "A Televisual Fairyland," *Guardian*, January 18, 2005, p. 19.

695. Dafna Linzer, "CIA Officer Is Fired for Media Leaks," *Washington Post*, April 22, 2006, p. A1; Jane E. Kirtley, "Transparency and Accountability in a Time of Terror: The Bush Administration's Assault on Freedom of Information," *Communication Law & Policy* 11 (2006): 479–500.

696. Suzanne Goldenberg, "Bush Gets Personal with Troublesome US Editors," *Guardian*, January 2, 2006, p. 7.

697. Associated Press, "Bush Calls Disclosure of Program 'Disgraceful,'" *Tuscaloosa (Ala.) News*, June 27, 2006, p. 3A.

698. "Protestors Rally outside New York Times Office, Demanding That the Government Prosecute Daily for Its Treasonous Reporting," *Bulldog Reporter's Daily Dog*, July 12, 2006, available at http://www.bulldogreporter.com/dailydog/issues/1_1/dailydog_media_news/index.html, accessed on July 12, 2006.

699. Carolyn Collins, "Players Seek Cover in Spy Outing," *Weekend Australian*, October 4, 2003, p. T02.

700. "Who Has Your Back?" editorial, *Columbia Journalism Review* 44, no. 4 (September-October 2005): 7.

CHAPTER NINE

701. Neil Postman, *Amusing Ourselves to Death* (New York: Penguin Books, 1986).

702. Ibid.

703. Ibid.

704. William M. Welch and Jim Drinkard, "USA Next Campaign Targets AARP," *USA Today*, February 28, 2005, sec. News, p. 7a.

705. Cohen, *A Consumer's Republic*.

706. "State of the News Media 2004."

707. Ibid.

708. Quoted in Paul Krugman, "Inconvenient Truths Constantly Changing with Propaganda," *Tuscaloosa (Ala.) News,* July 31, 2006, p. 7A.

709. Quoted in Trudy Lieberman, "Answer the &%$#★ Question!" *Columbia Journalism Review* 42, no. 15 (January–February 2004): 40.

710. Ibid.

711. Quoted in Postman, *Amusing Ourselves to Death,* 108.

712. Ibid.

713. "Breakthrough for Citizen Journalists: CNN Plans Major Announcement on Tuesday That It Will Accept Consumer-Generated Audio and Video," *Bulldog Reporter's Daily Dog,* August 1, 2006, available at http://www.bulldogreporter.com/dailydog/issues/1_1/dailydog_media _news/index.html, accessed on August 1, 2006.

714. "Media's Global Village: Using a News Aggregator, Major Dailies Will Now Offer Links to Articles Appearing on Other Outlets' Sites," *Bulldog Reporter's Daily Dog,* August 1, 2006, available at http://www.bulldogreporter.com/dailydog/issues/1_1/dailydog_media _news/index.html, accessed on August 1, 2006.

715. Bureau of Labor Occupational Employment Statistics, available at http://www.bls.gov/oes/home.htm, accessed on January 28, 2007; *2006 Bureau of Labor Statistics Occupational Outlook Handbook,* available at http://www.bls.gov/oco/home.htm, accessed on January 28, 2007.

716. Michael Bugeja, "Journalism's New Bottom Line," *Quill Magazine* 93, no. 8 (October–November 2005): 32.

717. "PR Needs a Credible Press to Thrive: How 9/11 Reportage, Al Jazeera's Slant on Journalism, Al-Qaeda Media Manipulation and the Blogosphere Impact PR," *Bulldog Reporter's Daily Dog,* September 13, 2006, available at http://www.bulldogreporter.com/dailydog/issues /1_1/dailydog_pr_spotlight/5019–1.html, accessed on September 13, 2006.

BIBLIOGRAPHY

BOOKS

Allen, Craig. *Eisenhower and the Mass Media: Peace, Prosperity, and Prime-Time TV.* Chapel Hill: University of North Carolina Press, 1993.

Alterman, Eric. *Sound and Fury: The Making of the Punditocracy.* Ithaca, N.Y., and London: Cornell University Press, 1999.

Bagdikian, Ben. *The Media Monopoly.* Boston: Beacon Press, 1983.

Baron, Gerald R. *Now Is Too Late: Survival in an Era of Instant News.* Upper Saddle River, N.J.: FT Prentice-Hall, 2003.

Bayley, Edwin R. *Joe McCarthy and the Press.* Madison: University of Wisconsin Press, 1981.

Blanchard, Margaret A. *Revolutionary Sparks: Freedom of Expression in Modern America.* New York and Oxford: Oxford University Press, 1992.

Bloom, Melvyn H. *Public Relations and Presidential Campaigns: A Crisis in Democracy.* New York: Thomas Y. Crowell, 1973.

Blyskal, Jeff, and Marie Blyskal. *PR: How the Public Relations Industry Writes the News.* New York: William Morrow, 1985.

Boorstin, Daniel. *The Image; A Guide to Pseudo-events in America.* New York: Atheneum, 1972.

Broder, David S. *Behind the Front Lines.* New York: Simon and Schuster, 1987.

Chafe, William H. *The Unfinished Journey: America since World War II.* New York: Oxford University Press, 2003.

Clinton, Bill. *My Life.* New York: Vintage Books, 2005.

Cohen, Lizabeth. *A Consumer's Republic: The Politics of Mass Consumption in Postwar America.* New York: Vintage Books, 2003.

Cook, Victoria. *Shield Laws: A Report on Freedom of the Press, Protection of News Sources, and the Obligation to Testify.* Lexington, Ky.: Council of State Governments, 1973.

Copple, Neale. *Depth Reporting.* Englewood Cliffs, N.J.: Prentice-Hall, 1964.

Cottle, Simon, ed. *News, Public Relations and Power.* London: Sage Publications, 2003.

Cutlip, Scott M., Allen H. Center, and Glen M. Broom. *Effective Public Relations.* 6th ed. Englewood Cliffs, N.J.: Prentice-Hall, 1985.

———. *Effective Public Relations.* 8th ed. Upper Saddle River, N.J.: Prentice-Hall, 2000.

Diamond, Edwin. *The Tin Kazoo: Television, Politics, and the News.* Cambridge, Mass.: MIT Press, 1975.

Donaldson, Gary A. *Abundance and Anxiety: America, 1945–1960.* Westport, Conn.: Praeger, 1997.

Friedman, Thomas L. *The World Is Flat.* 2nd ed. New York: Farrar, Straus and Giroux, 2006.

Galbraith, John Kenneth. *The Affluent Society.* Boston: Houghton Mifflin, 1958.

Gillmor, Donald M., Jerome A. Barron, Todd F. Simon, and Herbert A. Terry. *Mass Communication Law: Cases and Comment.* 5th ed. St. Paul, Minn.: West Publishing, 1990.

Gitlin, Todd. *The Whole World Is Watching: Mass Media in the Making and Unmaking of the New Left,* with a new preface by Todd Gitlin. Berkeley: University of California Press, 2003.

Hallin, Daniel C. *The "Uncensored War": The Media and Vietnam.* New York and Oxford: Oxford University Press, 1986.

Hertsgaard, Mark. *On Bended Knee: The Press and the Reagan Presidency.* New York: Schocken Books, 1989.

Hill, John W. *The Making of a Public Relations Man.* New York: David McKay, 1963.

Lee, Alfred M., and Elizabeth B. Lee, eds. *The Fine Art of Propaganda: A Study of Father Coughlin's Speeches.* New York: Harcourt, Brace, 1939.

Lytle, Mark Hamilton. *America's Uncivil Wars: The Sixties Era from Elvis to Richard Nixon.* New York: Oxford University Press, 2006.

MacDougall, Curtis D. *Interpretative Reporting.* 7th ed. New York: Macmillan, 1977.

Magruder, Jeb Stuart. *An American Life: One Man's Road to Watergate*. New York: Atheneum, 1974.

Manheim, Jarol B. *The Death of a Thousand Cuts: Corporate Campaigns and the Attack on the Corporation*. Mahwah, N.J.: Lawrence Erlbaum Associates, 2001.

Marchand, Roland. *Creating the Corporate Soul: The Rise of Public Relations and Corporate Imagery in American Big Business*. Berkeley: University of California Press, 1998.

Martin, Justin. *Nader: Crusader, Spoiler, Icon*. Cambridge, Mass.: Perseus Publishing, 2002.

May, Rollo. *Power and Innocence: A Search for the Sources of Violence*. New York: Norton, 1972.

McGinniss, Joe. *The Selling of the President*. New York: Simon and Schuster, 1968; reprint, New York: Penguin Books, 1988.

Meyer, Philip. *Precision Journalism: A Reporter's Introduction to Social Science Methods*. Bloomington: Indiana University Press, 1973.

Miller, Karen. *The Voice of Business: Hill & Knowlton and Postwar Public Relations*. Chapel Hill: University of North Carolina Press, 1999.

Mindich, David T. Z. *Just the Facts: How "Objectivity" Came to Define American Journalism*. New York and London: New York University Press, 1998.

Murphy, Priscilla Coit. *What a Book Can Do: The Publication and Reception of "Silent Spring."* Amherst and Boston: University of Massachusetts Press, 2005.

Nader, Ralph. *Unsafe at Any Speed: The Designed-In Dangers of the American Automobile*. New York: Grossman, 1965.

Naisbitt, John. *Megatrends: Ten New Directions Transforming Our Lives*. New York: Warner Books, 1982.

Nessen, Ron. *It Sure Looks Different from the Inside*. Chicago: Playboy Press, 1978.

Newsom, Doug, Judy VanSlyke Turk, and Dean Kruckeberg. *This Is PR: The Realities of Public Relations*. 7th ed. Belmont, Calif.: Wadsworth, 2000.

Nimmo, Dan, and James E. Combs. *Nightly Horrors: Crisis Coverage in Television Network News*. Knoxville: University of Tennessee Press, 1985.

O'Neill, William L. *American High: The Years of Confidence, 1945–1960*. New York: Free Press, 1986.

O'Reilly, Bill. *Who's Looking Out for You?* New York: Broadway Books, 2003.

Oudes, Bruce, ed. *From: The President—Richard Nixon's Secret Files*. New York: Harper and Row, 1989.

Packard, Vance. *The Hidden Persuaders*. New York: David McKay, 1957; reprint, New York: Pocket Books, 1973.

Partridge, Marianne, ed. *Rolling Stone Visits Saturday Night Live*. Garden City, N.J.: Doubleday, 1979.

Porter, William E. *Assault on the Media: The Nixon Years*. Ann Arbor: University of Michigan Press, 1976.

Postman, Neil. *Amusing Ourselves to Death*. New York: Penguin Books, 1986.

Ross, Irwin. *The Image Merchants*. Garden City, N.Y.: Doubleday, 1959.

Rozell, Mark J. *The Press and the Ford Presidency*. Ann Arbor: University of Michigan Press, 1992.

Safire, William. *Before the Fall: An Inside View of the Pre-Watergate White House*. Garden City, N.Y.: Doubleday, 1975.

Sigal, Leon V. *Reporters and Officials*. Lexington, Mass.: D. C. Heath, 1973.

Skinner, B. F. *Walden Two*. Toronto: Macmillan, 1948.

Sorensen, Theodore C. *Kennedy*. New York: Harper and Row, 1965.

Spanier, John, and Steven W. Hook. *American Foreign Policy since World War II*. 14th ed. Washington, D.C.: Congressional Quarterly, 1998.

Spear, Joseph C. *Presidents and the Press: The Nixon Legacy*. Cambridge, Mass.: MIT Press, 1984.

Tebbel, John, and Sarah Miles Watts. *The Press and the Presidency*. New York: Oxford University Press, 1985.

Watson, Mary Ann. *The Expanding Vista: American Television in the Kennedy Years*. New York: Oxford University Press, 1990.

Westin, Av. *News-Watch: How TV Decides the News*. New York: Simon and Schuster, 1982.

White, Theodore H. *The Making of the President, 1960*. New York: Atheneum Publishers, 1961.

Wood, Robert J., with Max Gunther. *Confessions of a PR Man*. New York: North American Library, 1988.

ARTICLES

Abrams, Floyd. "Will the First Amendment Survive the 1980's?" *Vital Speeches of the Day* 51, no. 13 (April 15, 1985): 412.

Adair, Bill. "Corporate Spin Can Come in Disguise." *St. Petersburg (Fla.) Times,* September 10, 2006. Available at http://www.sptimes.com/2006/09/10/news_pf/Worldandnation/Corporate_spin_co.shtml.

Agnew, Spiro T. "Television News Coverage." *Vital Speeches of the Day* 36, no. 4 (December 1, 1969): 98–101.

Alter, Jonathan. "The Real Price of Propaganda." *Newsweek,* December 12, 2005, 42.

Annenberg Public Policy Center. "About One American in Four Considers Rush Limbaugh a Journalist. . . ." Available at http://www.annenbergpublicpolicycenter.org.

Armstrong, Richard A. "The Concept and Practice of Issues Management in the United States." *Vital Speeches of the Day* 47, no. 24 (October 1, 1981): 763.

Associated Press. "Bush Calls Disclosure of Program 'Disgraceful.'" *Tuscaloosa (Ala.) News,* June 27, 2006, p. 3A.

————. "U.S. Transportation Secretary Nominee Let $7.8 Million in PR Contracts as FHWA Head." *International Herald Tribune,* September 20, 2006. Available at http://www.iht.com/bin/print_ipub.php?file=/articles/ap/2006/09/20/news/Highway_PR.php.

Baer, Susan. "President Turns to Campaign Brainstrust to Rekindle Election Success." *Buffalo (N.Y.) News,* February 13, 1993, p. 3.

Baldwin, William H., and Raymond C. Mayer. "On Buying Public Relations." *Public Opinion Quarterly* 8, no. 2 (Summer 1944): 226–31.

Balutis, Alan P. "Congress, the President and the Press." *Journalism Quarterly* 53 (Autumn 1976): 509–15.

Baroody, William J. "The Presidency: How Open?" *Vital Speeches of the Day* 41, no. 20 (August 1, 1975): 625–28.

Barrett, Laurence I. "Urging Nixon to Quit: The Weekend That Was." *Columbia Journalism Review* 14 (January-February 1974): 66–68.

Barstow, David, and Robin Stein. "Under Bush, a New Age of Prepackaged News." *New York Times,* March 13, 2005, p. 1.

Barth, Alan. "The Press as Censor of Government: Atrophy of the Editorial Page." *Vital Speeches of the Day* 28, no. 11 (March 15, 1962): 341.

Bateman, J. Carroll. "The Indispensable Man." *Public Relations Quarterly* (Spring 1967): 42–46.

Beasley, Maurine H. "The Emergence of Modern Media, 1900–1945." In William David Sloan, ed., *The Media in America.* 5th ed., 283–302. Northport, Ala.: Vision Press, 2002.

Beck, Robert A. "Business, the Press, and the Zero-Risk Society." *Vital Speeches of the Day* 44, no. 24 (October 1, 1978): 758–60.

Belden, Clark. "Wartime Public Relations—A Survey." *Public Opinion Quarterly* 8, no. 1 (Spring 1944): 94–99.

Belz, Andrew, Albert D. Talbott, and Kenneth Starck. "Using Role Theory to Study Cross Perceptions of Journalists and Public Relations Practitioners." *Public Relations Research Annual 1989,* vol. 1, 125–39.

Bernstein, Jack. "Advertising Reporting to Public Relations?—It's Coming." *Public Relations Quarterly* 16, no. 1 (Spring 1971): 5.

Bernthal, Wilmar F. "In the Context of Social Change." *Business Forum* 9, no. 2 (Spring 1984): 7–9.

Bianculli, David. "Sax to 'Sock It to Me?'" *New York Daily News,* October 27, 2004, p. 86.

Bishop, Robert L., and Jane Kilburn. "Penny Whistle or Public's Advocate?" *Public Relations Quarterly* 12, no. 4 (Winter 1968): 27–30.

Black, Marvin M. "The Returning Serviceman's Dilemma." *Public Relations Journal* 1 (November 1945): 32–35.

"Board Returns Apples to New York Schools." *New York Times,* March 21, 1989, p. B3.

Bond, Edward L., Jr. "Developing Responsible Promotion." *Vital Speeches of the Day* 37, no. 5 (December 15, 1970): 124–28.

"Breakthrough for Citizen Journalists: CNN Plans Major Announcement on Tuesday That It Will Accept Consumer-Generated Audio and Video." *Bulldog Reporter's Daily Dog,* August 1, 2006. Available at http://wwwbulldogreporter.com/dailydog/issues/1_1/dailydog_media_news/index.html.

Brooks, David. "Please Mr. Postman: The Travails of Richard Viguerie." *National Review,* June 20, 1986, 28–32.

Broom, Glen M., and David M. Dozier. "An Overview: Evaluation Research in Public Relations." *Public Relations Quarterly* (Fall 1983): 5–8.

Buckley, Robert J. "Consumerism and the Economic Dope Habit." *Vital Speeches of the Day* 44, no. 5 (December 15, 1977): 145–50.

Budd, John F., Jr. "Corporate Video May Be Hazardous to Credibility." *Vital Speeches of the Day* 47, no. 18 (July 1, 1981): 567–70.

———. "Credibility vs. 'Con.'" *Public Relations Quarterly* 57, no. 1 (Spring 1982): 13.

———. "Are We 'Smart Enough' for Tomorrow?" *Vital Speeches of the Day* 49, no. 23 (September 15, 1982): 729–31.

Bugeja, Michael. "Journalism's New Bottom Line." *Quill Magazine* 93, no. 8 (October-November 2005): 32.

Buncombe, Andrew. "US Cartoonists under Pressure." *Independent on Sunday* (London), June 23, 2002, p. 16.

Burger, Chester. "How to Meet the Press." *Harvard Business Review* 33, no. 4 (July-August 1955): 62–70.

Campbell, Dorcas. "Telling the Press." *Public Relations Journal* 5 (March 1949): 24–25, 30.

Carr, David. "An Obsession with Leaks and Plugs." *New York Times,* September 25, 2006. Available at http://www.nytimes.com/2006/09/25/business/media/25carr.htm/.

Carter, Jimmy. "Fireside Chat: Unity on U.S. Goals." *Vital Speeches of the Day* 43, no. 9 (February 15, 1977): 261.

Case, Harold C. "The Mind's Adventure." *Vital Speeches of the Day* 18, no. 19 (July 1952): 598–600.

"The Case of the People vs. the Press," *Broadcasting* 106, no. 2 (January 9, 1984): 116.

Chabria, Anita. "Sugarman to Plead Guilty at F-H Overbilling Trial." *PR Week,* June 17, 2005.

Chamberlain, John. "The American Communications Media." *Vital Speeches of the Day* 40, no. 8 (February 1, 1974): 240–42.

Cobb, Chris. "The President's Spin Doctor Brings the Newshounds to Heel." *Ottawa Citizen,* May 24, 2002, p. A18.

Collins, Carolyn. "Players Seek Cover in Spy Outing." *Weekend Australian,* October 4, 2003, p. T02.

"Comms Inconsistencies Haunt the White House." Editorial, *PR Week,* February 20, 2006, 10.

Conarroe, Richard R. "How to Plan and Organize a Public Relations Program." *Public Relations Quarterly* 12, no. 2 (Summer 1967): 24–30.

"Confront the Press Head-On." *U.S. News & World Report,* May 26, 1986, 62.

Corn, Ira G., Jr. "The Changing Role of Corporations in Political Affairs." *Vital Speeches of the Day* 47, no. 15 (May 15, 1981): 463–68.

Cornwell, Rupert. "Don't Believe All the Patriotic Fire on American TV." *Independent* (London), April 23, 2003, p. 17.

"Corporate Culture." Editorial, *Nation,* June 3, 1996, 3.

Cort, David. "An Angle on Some 'Squares.'" *Nation,* December 7, 1957, 424–26.

Cutlip, Scott M. "History of Public Relations Education in the United States." *Journalism Quarterly* 38, no. 3 (1961): 363–70.

"The Debate and the Spin Doctors." Editorial, *New York Times,* October 21, 1984, p. E22.

Dejevsky, Mary. "Bush Reaches 100th Day with Little to Proclaim." *Independent* (London), April 30, 2001, p. 12.

Dowd, Maureen. "For the Right Price, Exceptions Can Be Made." *Tuscaloosa (Ala.) News,* January 31, 2005, p. 7A.

Easterbrook, Arthur E. "Reconversion of Man." *Vital Speeches of the Day* 11, no. 20 (1945): 610–12.

"Editor's Column." *The Quill* 61, no. 1 (January 1973): 5.

Elsasser, John. "The Great VNR Debate, Part Two." *PR Tactics* 12, no. 4 (April 2005): 3.

Erskine, Hazel. "The Polls: Opinion of the News Media." *Public Opinion Quarterly* 34, no. 4 (Winter 1970–1971): 630–43.

Ethridge, Mark. "The Meaning of the News: The Era of Interpretive Writing." *Vital Speeches of the Day* 28, no. 15 (May 15, 1962): 474.

Ewing, Raymond P. "A Strategic Approach to Issues Management." In Clarke L. Caywood, ed., *Handbook of Strategic Public Relations and Integrated Communications,* 173–86. New York: McGraw-Hill, 1997.

Farsetta, Diane. "Fake TV News: Widespread and Undisclosed." *Center for Media and Democracy,* March 16, 2006. Available at http://www.prwatch.org.

Feldstein, Mark. "The Jailing of a Journalist: Prosecuting the Press for Receiving Stolen Documents." *Communication Law and Policy* 10, no. 2 (Spring 2005): 137–77.

"57% Don't Want Newsmen to Name Their Sources." *Editor & Publisher* 95, no. 12 (December 9, 1972): 13.

Finn, David. "The Public Relations Role in Coping with the Information Crisis." *Public Relations Quarterly* 26, no. 3 (Fall 1981): 5–7.

Flesch, Rudolf. "The Vocabulary of Free Enterprise." *Public Relations Journal* 4, no. 1 (January 1948): 10–12.

Flynn, John T. "Insidious Propaganda." *Vital Speeches of the Day* 13, no. 4 (December 1946): 110–14.

Foley, Kevin E. "No Harm, No Foul: Survey Conclusions Overlook TV Media Reality." *PR Tactics* 13, no. 6 (June 2006): 27.

Ford, Henry, II. "Business Ethics in 1961: Management Integrity." *Vital Speeches of the Day* 27, no. 15 (May 15, 1961): 454–57.

Frank, Reuven. "Freedom of the Broadcast Press." *Vital Speeches of the Day* 36, no. 11 (March 15, 1970): 332–36.

———. "Broadcasting and the First Amendment." *Vital Speeches of the Day* 38, no. 4 (December 1, 1971): 125–27.

———. "The First Amendment: Television News." *Vital Speeches of the Day* 38, no. 20 (August 1, 1972): 629–32.

———. "Almost Nobody Writes Silence Any More." *Vital Speeches of the Day* 47, no. 10 (March 1, 1981): 293–95.

Frazier, Howard. "Consumer Protection." *Vital Speeches of the Day* 36, no. 9 (February 15, 1970): 265–70.

"Fruit Growers Pull Commercials to Protest Report by CBS on Alar." *New York Times,* May 7, 1989, p. 36.

Gallina, Emil. "VNRs under Attack." *Communication World* 8, no. 11 (October 1991): 13.

Gallup, George. "Mass Information or Mass Entertainment." *Vital Speeches of the Day* 19, no. 15 (May 1953): 473–75.

Gannon, James P. "Business and the Media." *Vital Speeches of the Day* 46, no. 5 (December 15, 1979): 133–36.

Gay, Verne. "What's Hate Got to Do with It?" *Newsday.com,* October 18, 2005. Available at http://www.newsday.com.

Gildea, Robert L. "Doubting Thomas Our Patron Saint?" *Public Relations Quarterly* 22, no. 1 (Spring 1977): 25–27.

Goldenberg, Suzanne. "Bush Gets Personal with Troublesome US Editors." *Guardian,* January 2, 2006, p. 7.

Goldman, David. "Spiro Agnew: How Mr. Law-and-Order Got Busted." *Biography Magazine* 7, no. 11 (November 2003): 26.

Goodman, Julian. "U.S. Broadcasting Freedom." *Vital Speeches of the Day* 36, no. 21 (August 15, 1970): 658–59.

Goodwin, Michael. "Media Squander Public Trust by Playing Politics." *New York Daily News,* November 3, 2004, sec. Wrap, p. 10.

Goss, Bert C. "There Oughtn't to Be a Law." *Vital Speeches of the Day* 30, no. 3 (November 15, 1963): 81–84.

Government Accountability Office. *Video News Releases: Unattributed Prepackaged News Stories Violate Publicity or Propaganda Prohibition.* GAO-05-643T.

Gower, Karla K. "Building One's Own Gallows: The Trade Publications' Reaction to a Federal Shield Law, 1972–1974." *Free Speech Yearbook* 35 (1997): 163–74.

Gower, Karla K., and Margot Opdyke Lamme. "Public Relations and the Railroad/Truckers Brawl." *Journalism History* 29 (Spring 2003): 12–20.

Graham, Sandy. "Illinois Power Pans '60 Minutes.'" *Wall Street Journal,* June 27, 1980, p. 24.

Gray, Robert Keith. "Getting the Story and Getting It Right." *Vital Speeches of the Day* 50, no. 24 (October 1, 1984): 764.

Green, Richard, and Denise Shapiro. "A Video News Release Primer." *Public Relations Quarterly* 32, no. 4 (Winter 1987–1988): 11.

Greenberg, David. "In the Free-for-All of Political Spin, Americans May Lose Sight of the Real Issues." *Washington Post,* July 18, 2004, sec. Book World, p. T04.

Greenberg, Michael R., Peter M. Sandman, David B. Sachsman, and Kandice L. Salomone. "Network Television News Coverage of Environmental Risks." *Environment* 31, no. 2 (March 1989): 16–44.

Greve, Frank. "Journalism in the Age of Pseudoreporting." *Nieman Reports* 59, no. 2 (Summer 2005): 11–13.

Griese, Noel. "Ketchum, Williams Implicated in New Education Dept. PR Spending Flap." *Crisis Counselor Newsletter,* February 2005. Available at http://www.anvilpub.com/crisis_counselor.htm.

Gumbel, Andrew, Andrew Wong, and Ron Edmonds. "How War Coverage Helped Put Murdoch on a Media Roll in Bush's America." *Independent* (London), April 16, 1983, p. 18.

Hamilton, Robert A. "'They Have to See the Whole Picture.'" *New York Times,* March 26, 1989, p. CN3.

Hanley, John W. "Why Ban Reason from the Consumer Safety Debate?" *Vital Speeches of the Day* 43, no. 20 (August 1, 1977): 626–29.

———. "Has Emotion Tipped the Scales on Consumer Safety?" *Vital Speeches of the Day* 44, no. 3 (November 15, 1977): 92–95.

Harlow, Rex F. "Public Relations at the Crossroads." *Public Opinion Quarterly* 8, no. 4 (Winter 1944–1945): 551–56.

Harmon, Richard L. "Job Responsibilities in Public Relations." *Public Relations Quarterly* 10, no. 2 (Summer 1965): 22–24.

Hayden, Martin S. "Investigative Reporting." *Vital Speeches of the Day* 42, no. 18 (July 1, 1976): 574–76.

"Health Officials Rebuke Schools over Apple Bans." *New York Times,* March 16, 1989, p. B10.

Helmore, Edward. "Media: More Spinned against than Spinners." *Guardian,* September 26, 2004, p. 8.

"Here's Bill." Billoreilly.com, 2005. Available at http://www.billoreilly.com.

Hockaday, Irvine O., Jr. "Journalists and Businessmen Have a Lot in Common." *Vital Speeches of the Day* 51, no. 8 (February 1, 1985): 244–46.

Hofstadter, Richard. "The Paranoid Style in American Politics." *Harper's,* November 1964, 77.

Hood, Julia. "The PR Industry's Anger over the Williams-DoE Episode Must Now Give Way to Finding Solutions." *PR Week,* January 24, 2005.

———. "When Advertisers Begin to Exert Pressure on Media Outlets, the PR World Feels the Squeeze." *PR Week,* May 30, 2005.

Horton, Thomas R. "Business and the Media: An Unholy Alliance?" *Management Review* 77, no. 12 (December 1988): 5.

"How a PR Firm Executed the Alar Scare." *Wall Street Journal,* October 3, 1989, p. A22.

Hubbard, T. W. "Business News in Post-Watergate Era." *Journalism Quarterly* 53 (1976): 489.

Huck, Peter. "'Someone Gets in My Fact, I Get in Their Face.'" *Guardian* (London), August 29, 2005, p. 10.

Hull, J. W. "The Public Concerns of Private Enterprise." *Vital Speeches of the Day* 37, no. 12 (April 1, 1971): 367–70.

Hutton, James G. "Integrated Marketing Communications and the Evolution of Marketing Thought." *Journal of Business Research* 37 (1996): 155–62.

Iacono, Erica. "US Military's Placement of Paid Stories Draws Debate." *PR Week,* December 5, 2005, 1.

Iacono, Erica, and Keith O'Brien. "GAO Casts Light on White House Marcomms Outlay." *PR Week,* February 20, 2006, 1.

Institute for Propaganda Analysis. "Announcement." *Propaganda Analysis* 1 (October 1937): 1–2.

Irwin, James W. "Industry's Obligation to the Press." *Public Relations Journal* 4 (December 1948): 25.

Jacobs, Harvey C. "The Image of the Image-Makers: The Evolution of Public Relations." *Vital Speeches of the Day* 27, no. 15 (May 15, 1961): 459–62.

Jacobson, Harvey K. "Guidelines for Evaluating Public Relations Programs." *Public Relations Quarterly* (Summer 1980): 7.

"John F. Kennedy, Inaugural Address." *Inaugural Addresses of the United States.* Washington, D.C.: U.S. Government Printing Office, 1989. Available at http://www.bartleby.com/124/.

Johnson, T. Earle. "Excellence in Our Lives: We Must Overcome the Cult of Mediocrity." *Vital Speeches of the Day* 28, no. 6 (January 1, 1962): 184.

Jordan, George C. "Publicity Isn't Free." *Public Relations Journal* 5 (June 1949): 15–16, 32.

Kelley, David. "Critical Issues for Issue Ads." *Harvard Business Review* 60, no. 4 (July-August 1982): 80–87.

Kemper, Cynthia L. "Living in Spin." *Communication World* 18, no. 3 (April-May 2001): 6.

Kennedy, John F. "The President and the Press." *Vital Speeches of the Day* 27, no. 15 (May 15, 1961): 450–52.

Kerr, Robert L. "Creating the Corporate Citizen: Mobil Oil's Editorial-Advocacy Campaign in *The New York Times* to Advance the Right and Practice of Corporate Political Speech, 1970–80." *American Journalism* 21, no. 4 (Fall 2004): 39–62.

King, Kerryn. "Public Relations and Business Schools." *Vital Speeches of the Day* 48, no. 9 (February 15, 1982): 271–74.

King, Ledyard. "Newspapers Print Same Letter Signed by Different Soldiers." *USA Today,* sec. News, p. 7A.

Kingsley, Robert E. "The Function of Controversy." *Public Relations Quarterly* 11, no. 3 (Fall 1966): 7–13.

Kirtley, Jane E. "Transparency and Accountability in a Time of Terror: The Bush Administration's Assault on Freedom of Information." *Communication Law & Policy* 11 (2006): 479–500.

Kittrell, C. M. "There's No Such Thing as a Free Press." *Vital Speeches of the Day* 51, no. 1 (October 15, 1984): 20–22.

Klappa, Gale E. "Journalism and the Anti-media Backlash." *Vital Speeches of the Day* 51, no. 12 (April 1, 1985): 376–79.

Konrad, Evelyn. "Corporate Brinkmanship." *Public Relations Quarterly* 11, no. 3 (Fall 1966): 14–16.

Kovach, Bill. "Watchdog Journalism Is the Only Function of Journalism That Justifies the Freedom That Journalists Enjoy in This Country." *Nieman Reports* 53, no. 3 (Fall 1999): 4.

Krugman, Paul. "Inconvenient Truths Constantly Changing with Propaganda." *Tuscaloosa (Fla.) News,* July 31, 2006, p. 7A.

Kurtz, Howard. "The Press Bypass." *Washington Post,* January 22, 1993, p. C1.

Kwong, Chan Ying, and Kenneth Starck. "'The *New York Times'* Stance on Nixon and Public Opinion." *Journalism Quarterly* 53 (1976): 723–27.

LaFalce, John J. "The Packaging of Public Policy." *Vital Speeches of the Day* 48, no. 8 (February 1, 1982): 226–35.

Laing, Robert B., and Robert L. Stevenson. "Public Opinion Trends in the Last Days of the Nixon Administration." *Journalism Quarterly* 53 (1976): 294–302.

Lang, Richard O. "The Economic Outlook for 1952." *Vital Speeches of the Day* 18, no. 10 (March 1952): 293–97.

Larsen, Carl W. "Educating the Editors." *Vital Speeches of the Day* 24, no. 19 (July 1958): 606.

Lee, Alfred McClung. "Trends Affecting the Daily Newspapers." *Public Opinion Quarterly* 3, no. 3 (July 1939): 497–502.

———. "Trends in Public Relations Training." *Public Opinion Quarterly* 11, no. 1 (Spring 1947): 83–91.

Lee, Ivy, Jr. "Facing the Facts . . . from a Public Relations Viewpoint." *Public Relations Journal* 4 (September 1948): 28–33.

Lesly, Philip. "Real Creativity in Public Relations." *Public Relations Quarterly* 10, no. 3/4 (Winter 1966): 8, 13–16.

———. "How the Future Will Shape Public Relations—and Vice Versa." *Public Relations Quarterly* 26, no. 4 (Winter 1981–1982): 4–8.

———. "The Changing Evolution of Public Relations." *Public Relations Quarterly* 27, no. 4 (Winter 1982): 9–15.

———. "Surviving in the New Two-Tier Society." *Vital Speeches of the Day* 49, no. 17 (June 15, 1983): 534–37.

Lieberman, Trudy. "Answer the &%$#★ Question!" *Columbia Journalism Review* 42, no. 5 (January-February 2004): 40–44.

Linzer, Dafna. "CIA Officer Is Fired for Media Leaks." *Washington Post,* April 22, 2006, p. A1.

Lordan, Edward J. "Defining Public Relations and Press Roles in the Twenty-first Century." *Public Relations Quarterly* 50, no. 2 (Summer 2005): 41.

Lowery, Wilson. "Media Dependency during a Large-Scale Social Crisis: The Case of September 11th." *Mass Communication Society* 7 (Summer 2004): 339–57.

Luce, Henry R. "Responsibility of the Press in the Cold War." *Vital Speeches of the Day* 19, no. 12 (April 1953): 369.

Luckman, Charles. "Big Business Has Lacked Vision." *Vital Speeches of the Day* 13, no. 4 (December 1946): 106–9.

Macy, John W., Jr. "The Critics of Television." *Vital Speeches of the Day* 36, no. 9 (February 15, 1970): 286–88.

Mandese, Joe. "The Art of Manufacturing News: Forget the White House, PR Firms Take Branded Journalism to a Whole New Level." *Broadcasting and Cable* 135, no. 13 (March 28, 2005): 24.

Marks, Alexandra. "Are Media Standards Dropping?" *Christian Science Monitor,* January 29, 1998, p. 4.

Marlow, Eugene M. "Sophisticated 'News' Videos Gain Wide Acceptance." *Public Relations Journal* 50, no. 7 (August–September 1994): 17.

Marsh, Harry D., and David R. Davies. "The Media in Transition: 1945–1974." In William David Sloan, ed., *The Media in America: A History,* 5th ed., 441–64. Northport, Ala.: Vision Press, 2002.

May, William F. "CEO's and the Public Business." *Vital Speeches of the Day* 46, no. 15 (May 15, 1980): 455.

Mazzetti, Mark, and Borzou Daragahi. "The Conflict in Iraq." *Los Angeles Times,* November 30, 2005, pt. A, p. 1.

McCaffrey, Joseph. "The Reporter: A Campaign to Intimidate." *Vital Speeches of the Day* 37, no. 15 (May 15, 1971): 478–80.

McIntosh, Alan C. "A Challenge to Our American Press: Carve the Moral Decay from America." *Vital Speeches of the Day* 28, no. 16 (June 1, 1962): 503–8.

"Media's Global Village: Using a News Aggregator, Major Dailies Will Now Offer Links to Articles Appearing on Other Outlets' Sites." *Bulldog Reporter's Daily Dog,* August 1, 2006. Available at http://www.bulldogreporter.com/dailydog/issues/1_1/dailydog_media_news/index.html.

Miller, Karen S. "Public Relations, 1900–Present." In William David Sloan and James D. Startt, eds., *The Media in America: A History,* 4th ed., 417–34. Northport, Ala.: Vision Press, 1999.

Miller, Raymond W. "Take Time for Human Engineering." *Public Relations Journal* 4 (January 1948): 4–9, 40.

Mollenhoff, Clark. "Freedom of the Press." *Vital Speeches of the Day* 26, no. 8 (February 1960): 248–52.

Monbiot, George. "A Televisual Fairyland." *Guardian,* January 18, 2005, p. 19.

———. "The Denial Industry." *Guardian,* September 19, 2006. Available at http://environment.guardian.co.uk/print/0,,329579929 –121568,00.html.

"Monitor: The American Press Evaluates the First 100 Days of the Presidency of George Bush." *Independent* (London), May 1, 2001, p. 2.

"Monsanto Chemical Company Published a Rebuttal to Rachel Carson's *Silent Spring.*" *PR News* (February 1963). Reprinted in David P. Bianco, ed., *PR News Casebook: 1,000 Public Relations Case Studies,* 440. Detroit, Mich.: Gale Research, 1993.

Moore, Martha T. "Talk Shows Become a Campaign Staple." *USA Today,* September 21, 2000, p. 8A.

"More of Rachel." Editorial, *Agrichemical West* (October 1962): 24.

Murray, Michael D. "The Contemporary Media: 1974–Present." In William David Sloan, ed., *The Media in America: A History,* 5th ed., 459–60. Northport, Ala.: Vision Press, 2002.

Nelson, Hale. "The Public Problems of Business." *Vital Speeches of the Day* 38, no. 21 (August 15, 1972): 668–72.

"A New Censor?" *Economist,* October 18, 1997, p. 30.

"Newsmen Urge Passage of Press Immunity Bill." *Editor & Publisher* 95, no. 9 (September 30, 1972): 12.

"Newsmen's Privilege." *Editor & Publisher* 95, no. 7 (July 8, 1972): 6.

Nicholas, Kate. "Timesheets Prove a Double-Edged Sword." *PR Week,* April 1, 2005.

"The No-Confidence Laws." *Editor & Publisher* 95, no. 11 (November 25, 1972): 6.

Nolan, Joseph. "Protect Your Public Image with Performance," *Harvard Business Review* 53, no. 2 (March–April 1975): 135–42.

Oakes, John B. "Freedom of the Press." *Vital Speeches of the Day* 44, no. 19 (July 15, 1978): 588–92.

O'Brien, Keith. "Lincoln Group Answers Critics with Dixon Hire." *PR Week,* January 30, 2006, 1.

O'Brien, Timothy. "Spinning Frenzy: P.R.'s Bad Press." *New York Times,* February 13, 2005, p. 1.

O'Connor, Neal W. "The Freedom to Communicate." *Vital Speeches of the Day* 42, no. 6 (January 1, 1976): 181.

"Oil Is Not a Cottage Industry." Advertisement, *New York Times,* July 1, 1976, sec. 1, p. 29.

Paley, William S. "Press Freedom." *Vital Speeches of the Day* 46, no. 21 (August 15, 1980): 670–72.

Pareles, Jon. "America Catches Up with Them." *New York Times,* May 21, 2006, pp. S2, 1.

"The Passing of Corporate Secrecy." *World's Work* 15 (February 1908): 9837.

"Past and Future Terms, Myths and Premises." *Public Relations Quarterly* 18, no. 4 (Spring 1974): 10.

Pear, Robert. "U.S. Videos, for TV News, Come under Scrutiny." *New York Times,* March 15, 2004, p. 1.

———. "Buying of News by Bush's Aides Is Ruled Illegal." *New York Times,* October 1, 2005, p. A1.

Perenyi, Eleanor. "The Overt Persuaders." *Harper's,* September 1960, 20, 22, 24, 26.

Pomerantz, Joel. "The Media and Public Relations: Pride and Prejudice." *Public Relations Quarterly* (Winter 1989–1990): 13.

Poriotis, Wes. "Corporate Public Relations in a Deregulated Economy." *Vital Speeches of the Day* 47, no. 16 (June 1, 1981): 482–85.

"PR Needs a Credible Press to Thrive: How 9/11 Reportage, Al Jazeera's Slant on Journalism, Al-Qaeda Media Manipulation and the Blogosphere Impact PR." *Bulldog Reporter's Daily Dog,* September 13, 2006. Available at http://www.bulldogreporter.com/dailydog/issues/1_1/dailydog_pr_spotlight/5019–1.html.

"The Promise of Fact." Editorial, *New York Times,* May 1, 1981, p. A30.

"Protestors Rally outside New York Times Office, Demanding That the Government Prosecute Daily for Its Treasonous Reporting." *Bulldog Reporter's Daily Dog,* July 12, 2006. Available at http://www.bulldogreporter.com/dailydog/issues/1_1/dailydog_media_news/index.html.

Ray, Douglas. "Decision to Discontinue McManus Is Based on Ethics." *Tuscaloosa (Ala.) News,* February 4, 2005, p. 7A.

Reedy, George E. "The Press in This Modern World." *Vital Speeches of the Day* 46, no. 7 (January 15, 1980): 221.

Regalado, Antonio, and Dionne Searcey. "Where Did That Video Spoofing Gore's Film Come From?" *Post-Gazette.com,* August 7, 2006. Available at http://www.post-gazette.com/pg/pp/06215 /710851.stm.

Reid, Joseph E. "How the Truth Becomes a Lie." *Vital Speeches of the Day* 47, no. 7 (January 15, 1981): 209.

Reid, Thomas R. "History's Fourth Turning Point." *Vital Speeches of the Day* 36, no. 12 (April 1, 1970): 369–72.

Reincheld, Aaron. "'Saturday Night Live' and Weekend Update: The Formative Years of Comedy News Dissemination." *Journalism History* 31, no. 4 (Winter 2006): 190–97.

Rhody, Ronald E. "The Conventional Wisdom Is Wrong." *Vital Speeches of the Day* 49, no. 2 (November 1982): 50–54.

Robertson, Lori. "Confronting the Culture." *American Journalism Review* 27, no. 4 (August–September 2005): 34–41.

Rogers, Everett M. "Diffusion of News of the September 11 Terrorist Attacks." In A. Michael Noll, ed., *Crisis Communications: Lessons from September 11,* 17–30. Lanham, Md.: Rowman and Littlefield, 2003.

Rosen, Jay. "Bill O'Reilly and the Paranoid Style of News." *Pressthink,* October 21, 2003. Available at http://journalism.nyu .edu/ pubzone/weblogs/pressthink/2003/10/21/oreilly_voice.html.

Rosenfield, James H. "To Have, To Have Not, or To Have More." *Vital Speeches of the Day* 50, no. 2 (November 1, 1983): 42–45.

Rotman, Morris B. "Consumerism Is Us!" *Vital Speeches of the Day* 38, no. 19 (July 15, 1972): 589–92.

Safire, William. "Calling Dr. Spin." *New York Times,* August 31, 1986, p. SM8.

Schmitt, Eric. "Military Admits Planting News in Iraq." *New York Times,* December 3, 2005, sec. A, p. 13.

Schmitt, Eric, and David S. Cloud. "Senate Summons Pentagon to Explain Effort to Plant Reports in Iraqi News Media." *New York Times,* December 2, 2005, sec. A, p. 10.

Schreiber, Charles J. "Public Relations and the Consumer." *Public Relations Quarterly* 11, no. 2 (Summer 1966): 2–3, 39.

Scott, Alan, and Raymond West. "Personnel Turnover on Small Texas Dailies." *Journalism Quarterly* 32 (1955): 183–89.

Seifert, Walt. "The Outlook for Public Relations: Brighter Than Ever." *Public Relations Quarterly* 18, no. 1 (Summer 1973): 14.

Seitel, Fraser P. "TV or No TV—That Is the Question." *United States Banker* 98, no. 11 (November 1989): 60–62.

Selvage, James P. "Newspapers and Economic Illiteracy." *Public Relations Journal* 5 (April 1949): 4.

Shabecoff, Philip. "Hazard Reported in Apple Chemical." *New York Times.* February 2, 1989, p. A1.

———. "3 U.S. Agencies, to Allay Public's Fears, Declare Apples Safe." *New York Times,* March 17, 1989, p. A16.

———. "Apple Chemical Being Removed in U.S. Market." *New York Times,* June 3, 1989, p. 1.

Shapp, Milton J. "The Press Must Remain Free." *Vital Speeches of the Day* 42, no. 20 (August 1, 1976): 616–18.

Sharpe, Melvin L., and Betty J. Pritchard. "The Historical Empowerment of Public Opinion and Its Relationship to the Emergence of Public Relations as a Profession." In Donn James Tilson and Emmanuel C. Alozie, eds., *Toward the Common Good: Perspectives in International Public Relations,* 14–36. Boston: Pearson Education, 2004.

Shaw, David. "The Trouble with TV Muckraking." *TV Guide,* October 10, 1981, 7.

Shell, Adam. "VNRs: In the News." *Public Relations Journal* 48, no. 12 (December 1992): 20.

Silverman, Ben. "Public's Perception of PR-Media Relationship Has Blurred." *PR Fuel,* January 12, 2005. Available at http://www. prfuel.com/archives/000380.html.

Simons, Howard. "The Press Media." *Vital Speeches of the Day* 43, no. 22 (September 1, 1977): 689–92.

Simonson, Solomon. "The Role of the Mass Media in Communication." *Vital Speeches of the Day* 18, no. 12 (March 1952): 349–51.

Sites, James N. "The Press, the Economy, and the Nation's Future." *Vital Speeches of the Day* 44, no. 10 (March 1, 1978): 290–94.

Sizer, Lawrence B. "Assignment to Right." *Public Relations Journal* 4 (April 1948): 8–11.

Smith, Bradford B. "Controlled versus Uncontrolled Economy." *Vital Speeches of the Day* 13, no. 2 (November 1946): 48–53.

Smith, Everett R. "The Customer Will Be Boss." *Vital Speeches of the Day* 11, no. 22 (September 1945): 693–95.

Smith, Jenkin Lloyd. "Who Is Tampering with the Soul of America? Our Moral Climate." *Vital Speeches of the Day* 28, no. 6 (January 1, 1962): 182.

Smith, Ward. "Business and the Media." *Vital Speeches of the Day* 52, no. 2 (November 1, 1985): 49–51.

"Some Effects of Modern Publicity." *Century* 67 (November 1903): 155–56.

Spellman, Francis Cardinal. "Truth—Watchword of a Free Press." *Vital Speeches of the Day* 18, no. 5 (December 1951): 156–57.

"State of the News Media 2004." Project for Excellence in Journalism. Available at http://www.stateofthenewsmedia.org/journalist _survey.html.

Stephenson, Donald R. "Crisis Situations." *Vital Speeches of the Day* 49, no. 10 (March 1, 1983): 315–20.

Stewart, Joan. "More TV Stations Turning to Pay for Play: The Lines between Ads and Editorial Continues to Blur." *PR Tactics* 13, no. 6 (June 2006): 26.

Stimson, Richard A. "Corporate Recognition of Public Relations." *Public Relations Quarterly* 10, no. 3/4 (Winter 1966): 50–52.

Strassman, Ralph K. "Private Enterprise—Its Social Responsibility." *Vital Speeches of the Day* 12, no. 16 (June 1946): 508–10.

Strout, Richard L. "Ordeal by Publicity." *Christian Science Monitor,* May 27, 1950, p. WM5.

"Study Shows TV's Return to 'Soft' News." *PR Week,* June 3, 2002, 3.

Sulzberger, Arthur Hays. "The Newspaper—Its Making and Its Meaning." *Vital Speeches of the Day* 11, no. 17 (June 1945): 539–43.

Sulzberger, Arthur Ochs. "Business and the Press." *Vital Speeches of the Day* 43, no. 14 (May 1, 1977): 426–28.

Sussmann, Leila A. "The Personnel and Ideology of Public Relations." *Public Opinion Quarterly* 12, no. 4 (Winter 1948–1949): 697–708.

Swearingen, J. E. "Responsibility in Journalism." *Vital Speeches of the Day* 49, no. 11 (March 15, 1983): 344.

"Taking a Stand on the Issues through Advertising." *Association Management* 33, no. 12 (December 1980): 58.

Taylor, Arthur R. "Business and the Press: Who's Doing What to Whom and Why?" *Vital Speeches of the Day* 42, no. 4 (December 1, 1975): 123–25.

Thomma, Steven. "Cheney's Missteps Turned Accident into PR Disaster, Experts Say." *Charlotte.com,* February 14, 2006. Available at http://www.charlotte.com/mld/charlotte/news/nation/13872002.html.

Topping, Semour. "Business and the News Media." *Vital Speeches of the Day* 45, no. 17 (June 15, 1979): 528–30.

Toppo, Greg. "White House Paid Journalist to Promote Law." *USA Today,* January 7, 2005, p. 1A.

Wagner, Ralph B. "Don't Neglect Your Relations! Molding the Mass Mind." *Vital Speeches of the Day* 12, no. 6 (January 1946): 179.

Walker, Albert. "The Evolution of Public Relations According to Cutlip and Center." *Public Relations Quarterly* (Summer 1986): 28–31.

"Was Mobil Wise to Blacklist the *Wall Street Journal*?" *Business and Society Review* 85, no. 53 (1984): 38–39.

Weaver, David H., and Maxwell E. McCombs. "Journalism and Social Science: A New Relationship?" *Public Opinion Quarterly* 44 (1980): 477–94.

Welch, William M., and Jim Drinkard. "USA Next Campaign Targets AARP." *USA Today,* February 28, 2005, sec. News, p. 7a.

West, Paul. "Behind Bush's Low-Key Style Is a Blueprint Drafted Well in Advance." *St. Louis Post-Dispatch,* April 25, 2001, p. A8.

"Who Has Your Back?" Editorial, *Columbia Journalism Review* 44, no. 3 (September–October 2005): 7.

"Who Likes the Press and Who Doesn't." *U.S. News & World Report,* January 27, 1986, 78.

Winik, Lyric Wallwork. "Bush's Press Problem." *Parade,* December 11, 2005, 18.

Winship, Thomas. "The President vs. the Press: Cool It." *Editor & Publisher* 127, no. 37 (September 10, 1994): 19.

Wolfe, Michael. "Panic on 43rd Street." *Vanity Fair,* September 2006, 236–42.

Wood, Lee B. "Public Relations and the Press." *Public Relations Journal* 4 (December 1948): 17–18, 39.

Wood, Robert J. "Communication: Top Executive Priority." *Management Review* 68, no. 5 (May 1979): 49–51.

Wriston, Walter B. "Liberty, Leadership and License." *Vital Speeches of the Day* 42, no. 14 (May 1, 1976): 422–25.

Young, Lewis H. "Business and the Media." *Vital Speeches of the Day* 45, no. 3 (November 15, 1978): 73–78.

———. "The Media's View of Corporate Communications in the 80's." *Public Relations Quarterly* 26, no. 3 (Fall 1981): 9–11.

Younge, Gary. "Now Dissent Is 'Immoral.'" *Guardian Leader,* June 2, 2003, p. 15.

Zoglin, Richard, and Ann Blackman. "The News Wars." *Time,* October 21, 1996, 58.

DISSERTATIONS AND UNPUBLISHED MANUSCRIPTS

Conway, Mike, Maria Elizabeth Grabe, and Kevin Grieves. "Bill O'Reilly's 'No-Spin Zone': Using 1930s Propaganda Techniques and Constructing Villains, Victims, and the Virtuous." Paper presented at the annual meeting of the Association for Education in Journalism and Mass Communication, San Francisco, August 2006.

Marsh, Harry. "Correlates of Professionalism and News Performance among Texas Newsmen." Ph.D. diss., University of Texas, 1974.

Rippey, John N. "Use of Opinion Polls as a Reporting Tool." Manuscript, Pennsylvania State University, 1979.

LEGAL DECISIONS

Branzburg v. Hayes, 408 U.S. 665 (1972).

Securities and Exchange Commission v. Texas Gulf Sulphur Co., 258 F. Supp. 262 (S.D. N.Y. 1966).

Securities and Exchange Commission v. Texas Gulf Sulphur Co., 401 F.2d 833 (2d Cir. 1968), *cert. denied*, 394 U.S. 976 (1969).

GOVERNMENT DOCUMENTS

Bureau of Labor. "Occupational Employment Statistics." Available at http://www.bls.gov/oes/home.htm.

————. *2006 Bureau of Labor Statistics Occupational Outlook Handbook.* Available at http://www.bls.gov/oco/home.htm.

INDEX

105; 1952 election, 62, 63; 1956 election, 62; and press conferences, 28, 51; and promotion, 24; and public relations, 26; and television, 24, 26, 29, 41, 210; and U2 spy plane, 48

Eisenhower, Milton, 26; and journalists, 24; and Roosevelt, 24, 25

elections: and advertising agencies, 63; 1956, 29–30; 1960, 41, 45; 1964, 62–63; and television, 45

Ellsberg, Daniel, 103, 105

entertainment, 36

Entertainment Tonight, 148

Environmental Protection Agency, 163, 198

environmentalism, 68, 72, 160, 162

Espionage Act, 104

Evans, Rowland, 62

ExxonMobil, 197

"fake news," xvii, 190–191

FBI. *See* Federal Bureau of Investigation

FCC. *See* Federal Communication Commission

FDA. *See* Food and Drug Administration

Federal Bureau of Investigation (FBI), 119

Federal Communication Commission (FCC), 37, 45, 80, 102, 189

Federal Trade Commission (FTC), 79, 81

Fenton, David, 162–164

Fenton Communications, 162, 164

Fichenberg, Robert, 108

Financial News Network, 149

First Amendment, 101, 102, 103, 108, 143, 153, 247n

Fitzwater, Marlin, 205–206

Fleeson, Doris, 30

Fleishman-Hillard, 198

Food and Drug Administration (FDA), 81

Ford, Gerald R., 113, 152, 173, 241n; and image, 116–118, 132; and media, 114–116, 214

Ford Motor Company, 76, 82

Fortune, 35, 53, 65

Fox News, 179, 182, 184, 185, 204, 205, 215, 220, 221

framing, 135, 142, 144, 181, 182

Franken, Al, 117

Freedom of Information Act, 142

freedom rides, 55, 56

front groups, 33, 198

FTC. *See* Federal Trade Commission

Furness, Betty, 65

Galbraith, John Kenneth, 67

Gallagher, Maggie, 195

Gallup, George: and television, 36

Gallup poll, 101, 109, 153

GAO. *See* Government Accountability Office

General Electric Corporation (GE), 65, 224n

General Motors (GM), 74, 84, 197; and Nader, 75–78, 80; and public relations, 75

Gergen, David, 118, 143, 144, 145, 175; and media relations, 133, 135; and news management, 134

Gerstner, William, 156–157

Gillmor, Donald, 106

Gitlin, Todd, 56, 239n

Goldwater, Barry, 62, 63, 129, 130, 176

Karla K. Gower is an associate professor of advertising and public relations at the University of Alabama and author of *Liberty and Authority in Free Expression Law: The United States and Canada* and *Legal and Ethical Restraints on Public Relations.*

Kurt Andersen is the host of the Peabody Award–winning program *Studio 360* on public radio, the former editor in chief of *New York* magazine, the cofounder of *Spy* magazine, and author of the novels *Turn of the Century* and *Heyday.*